EARLY CHILDHOOD EDUCATION: POLICY ISSUES FOR THE 1990s

Social and Policy Issues in Education: The University
of Cincinnati Series

Kathryn M. Borman, *Series Editor*

Contemporary Issues in U.S. Education, *edited by Kathryn M. Borman,*
Piyush Swami, and Lonnie D. Wagstaff

Early Childhood Education: Policy Issue for the 1990s, *edited by Dolores*
Stegelin

Effective Schooling for Disadvantaged Students: School-based Strategies for
Diverse Student Populations, *edited by Howard Johnston and*
Kathryn M. Borman

Home Schooling: Political, Historical, and Pedagogical Perspectives, *edited*
by Jane Van Galen and Mary Anne Pitman

in preparation
Assessment Testing and Evaluation in Teacher Education, *edited by*
Suzanne W. Soled

Children Who Challenge the System, *edited by Anne M. Bauer and Ellen*
M. Lynch

Explaining the School Performance of Minority Students: Anthropological
Perspectives, *edited by Evelyn Jacob and Cathie Jordan*

Early Childhood Education:
Policy Issues for the 1990s

edited by

Dolores A. Stegelin

University of Cincinnati

ABLEX PUBLISHING CORPORATION
NORWOOD, NJ

Copyright © 1992 by Ablex Publishing Corporation

Printed in the United States of America.

Library of Congress Cataloging-in-Publication Data

Early childhood education : policy issues for the 1990s / edited by
Dolores A. Stegelin.
    p. cm.—(Social and policy issues in education)
    Includes bibliographical references (p.) and index.
    ISBN 0-89391-797-4
    1. Early childhood education—United States. 2. Education and
state—United States. 3. Child care services—Government policy—
United States. I. Stegelin, Dolores. II. Series.
LB1139.25.E265 1992
372.21′0973—dc20   92-3171
                                                                          CIP

Ablex Publishing Corporation
355 Chestnut Street
Norwood, New Jersey 07648

TO MY FAMILY AND ALL EARLY CHILDHOOD ADVOCATES

Contents

Preface

Issues related to the well-being of young children and their famiiies have never been greater. The 100th Congress debated over 100 bills related to children and families, an unprecedented number in our country's history. This dramatic emergence of legislation at both the state and federal levels indicates a definitive trend in policy development and signals a need for greater understanding about the issues related to policy making for young children. Bipartisan sponsorship of several key pieces of legislation related to child care and parent support also reflects a universal acceptance of child-related issues on the part of policy makers at local, state, and national levels.

My own professional experience has led me to the conclusion that, for too long, child-related policy making has been segregated from the practitioners who know best what is appropriate and good for young children. Both because early childhood policy is new and because practitioners have typically isolated themselves from the complexities of policy making, prior decisions related to child policy have been made in isolation from appropriate developmental practice. This book is written with the hope that policy making on behalf of young children can begin to be a reflection of shared and mutual understandings of what is best for children.

With prior professional experiences in primarily academic settings, I learned first hand about the realities and complexities of policy making while serving in my first policy position as director of the Office of Child Development for the Commonwealth of Kentucky. As part of the educational reform movement in that state, a state-level office was established and I was privileged to be asked to serve as the first director. From this new vantage point I was able to ascertain the traditional separation between practice related to young children and their families and the decision-making process of the legislature. I am deeply indebted to the early childhood advocates who struggled with me to begin to influence policy for young children in a state where poverty is too common and educational reform too difficult. The lessons I learned in that policy capacity forever shaped my views of young children and led to my determination to write this book.

This policy text is designed to serve as a tool for many groups: students in child development and early childhood education; early childhood advocates; legislators; and those who are involved in the shaping of policy for young children, such as state and national agencies. The authors of this text are the leading child proponents in the United States. If one traces the history of early childhood research and policy development over the past decade, the names of these authors will surface in a very visible way. Perhaps the greatest strengths of this book are the comprehensiveness of the issues addressed and the unequivocal quality of the authorship. Indeed, if one were to revisit the field of early childhood education in another decade, these individuals would be among the greatest contributors to the field of child policy.

Finally, I am hopeful that the book will serve as a catalyst and a source of inspiration for those individuals who are becoming actively involved in the advocacy efforts for young children. Never before have so many different individuals, child populations, interest groups, and agencies been involved in the early childhood movement. The best policy making is informed policy making. There is a wide window of opportunity for parents, teachers, school officials and administrators, curriculum specialists, and state education officials to impact directly the policy process on behalf of young children. When practitioner and parental hands are linked with informed decision makers, then the results can be exciting and forward-thinking. Each of us needs to find our own place in the arena of early childhood advocacy and then begin to make a difference. This text is written with that goal in mind.

I would like to thank the authors who so willingly contributed to this policy textbook. Governor Clinton's enthusiasm for participation in this process was a source of inspiration for other authors and myself. Writing a chapter for a book is a new assignment for a governor, as well as for the agency administrators who contributed to the book. Their roles are so diverse and time consuming that finding precious time to focus on a coherent policy piece is a monumental task. Nonetheless, I wanted this book to reflect contributions of individuals who are at the forefront in current early childhood policy making, thus the contributions of these individuals were essential. All of the authors showed commitment to the book and timeliness in their writing. The quality of the initial drafts was exceptional, thus facilitating the overall editing process. It is my hope that this book will make a significant contribution to policy development and will serve as a helpful tool for students who are learning about policy formation. It certainly is a historian's delight, as these authors are the giants of the field of early childhood policy and they promise to make significant contributions in the 1990s.

Dee Stegelin

Chapter 1
Early Childhood Policy: An Introduction

Dolores A. Stegelin
University of Cincinnati

RATIONALE

Early childhood education policy has evolved with growing momentum during this century. Recent developments in policy related to children and families at both the state and federal levels point to the field of early childhood education as one that is growing in both substance and visibility in the United States (Kagan, 1989; Weikart, 1989). Significant pieces of legislation have evolved in state houses and at the federal level, especially since the early 1980s, all of which document the rapidity with which early childhood education is surfacing as a public policy issue. At the same time, the information available to decision makers regarding issues that are directly impacting young children remains limited (Hetrick & Van Horn, 1988; Schweinhart, Koshel, & Bridgman, 1987).

Considerable research documentation exists establishing a clear relationship between early childhood development and later adult competence and success (Schweinhart & Weikart, 1986; Schweinhart, Weikart, & Larner, 1986; Barnett, 1985; Brown, 1985; Lazar, Darlington, Murray, Royce, & Snipper, 1982). However, the need clearly exists for easily assimilated, research-based information that can be utilized by legislators, policy analysts, child advocates, university and college professionals, school administrators, and others involved in the

1

teaching and implementation of public policy related to young children
and their families (Weikart, 1989; Hetrick & Van Horn, 1988).

Defining the Policy Issues

The sociocultural context for early childhood policy continues to
change. The 1980s brought emerging forces together so that the concept of early childhood education and development now includes broader social and family dimensions. Today, public opinion and policy for
young children revolve around such issues as: (a) developmental and
educational programs for infants, toddlers, preschoolers, and early
elementary age children; (b) delivery systems for young children, such
as home-based, center-based, nonprofit, and proprietary systems; (c)
funding mechanisms such as parent fees, employer assistance, tax
credits, public vouchers, or purchase of services; and (d) standards of
accountability such as state licensing, local regulations, parental monitoring, professional accreditation, and assessment (Weikart, 1989;
Lombardi, 1986).

By examining these issues, decision makers may become more sensitive to the needs of parents, the complex lifestyles of today's American families, and the available policy options to support these needs.
Brown (1985) documents the critical impact of research in changing
Head Start policy and the critical need for research-based information,
presented in a practical way, to continue the link between research
and policy decision making. Hetrick and Van Horn (1988) state the
need for brokers of information related to policy decision making.

Traditionally, individuals in the field of early childhood education
have advocated for change by reacting to the suggestions and solutions
made by people inside the political structure, rather than by assuming
a proactive role in the making of public policy (Lombardi, 1986). In the
past, public policy makers have not been adequately informed on
issues related to young children. Kilmer (1980) calls for more active
involvement on the part of child advocates in the role of policy making
and states, "rather than being disdainful about the decision making
process, (early childhood specialists) need to appreciate the skills of
politicos and to work in tandem with them to understand how to affect
the system" (p. 250).

Schweinhart, Koshel, and Bridgman (1987) indicate that those who
are responsible for directing the debate and shaping the programs
related to young children must have continuing access to pertinent
information from research and experience. Key early childhood policy
questions identified by Schweinhart, Koshel, and Bridgman are these:

1. Which children should be served?
2. For what part of the day should early childhood programs operate?
3. How much money should be invested in these programs?
4. Through what structures should the money be channeled? (p. 525).

The Need for a Policy Text

The need for a concise, up-to-date source on the mosaic of early childhood issues for the coming decade is unprecedented. Hetrick and Van Horn (1988) indicate that policy makers are desperate for information that will help them answer the difficult questions they face. In a recent survey of the education policy community in 15 states, Hetrick and Van Horn found that the available information does not satisfy the needs of policy makers (Hetrick & Van Horn, 1988).

The primary purpose of this edited book on early childhood policy is to make available to decision makers, policy analysts, governmental leaders, early childhood development educators, administrators and specialists, and early childhood advocates a source of accurate, relevant information, written by researchers and leaders who are directly involved in the development, implementation, and evaluation of policy and programs for young children and their families.

Early Childhood Policy: A Historical Perspective

An examination of the history of public policy related to young children reveals that child care issues have been most salient. Child care began in the 1800s as a charitable function for women who worked outside of the home only out of economic necessity, usually as a widow or the wife of an incapacitated husband (Farnum, 1987). Family members provided support for child care; the use of external resources for child care functions was almost nonexistent. However, as society has evolved during this century, families have become more urbanized and mobile. Relatives and extended family networks are not as available and female employment has risen dramatically so that family-based child care supports are no longer available. According to Farnum (1987), "Grandma and Aunt Mary are at work, too" (p. 19).

Early childhood policy has evolved primarily through the outcomes of wars and national crises. During these times, families have had to rely on extraordinary means to meet the demands of child care and family support. Men have traditionally become involved in military efforts and, as a result, more disabled fathers have existed at these times, also.

One of the first real national crises that resulted in expanded child needs was the Civil War. According to Farnum (1987), in the aftermath of the Civil War, churches and communities in some Eastern cities developed children's charities that cared for children while their mothers worked. While these early child care centers were more like orphanages than the more developmentally oriented child care settings of today, they were the first vestiges of systematic child care in the American culture

Psychology and the Study of Children

The advent of psychology in the university settings of the United States during the 1920s also propelled children to the forefront (Irwin & Bushnell, 1980). University laboratory schools were established across the country in the mid-1920s, primarily as a means of studying young children (Irwin & Bushnell, 1980) and observing and recording their normal development. These children were exceptions, however, and enjoyed early childhood programs that were atypical from most child care settings in the public sector. Still, the advent of child psychology, the establishment of laboratory schools, and the enhanced study of children all contributed to the increased visibility of children and to the evolution of early childhood development policy, which came into fruition nearly 50 years later.

The Depression brought about a few child care centers that provided meals, play, and parent education. However, it was World War II that brought government into the child care business in a major way. Large centers were developed in areas where numbers of women were employed in munitions plants, shipyards, and other war-related industries (Farnum, 1987). California, a leader in the nation's efforts to develop programs for young children, established these child care programs through federal monies provided through the Lanham Act.

The Early State Leadership Role

California was one of the leading states in the provision of comprehensive programs for young children and has influenced other states to take more active policy roles on behalf of young children. These programs are characterized by monitored supervision, quality nutrition, health services such as immunizations and minor medical care, and they also serve as a support for families. Today, over half of the states have implemented child development programs, primarily since the mid-1980s (Schweinhart, 1989; Schweinhart, Koshel, & Bridgman, 1987).

Even though child care programs expanded rapidly after World War II, they were still viewed primarily as charitable functions. Only a few states, such as California, elected to continue many of these centers that were abandoned by federal funding after the war. Many wives of veterans chose to continue to use these centers as they worked to put their husbands through school with veteran benefits and support.

Post-World War II: An Era of Transition

The post-World War II era was a period of transition for American families. Child care was moving from its charitable image but still was not regarded as a necessity for families with young children. The persistent efforts of such states as California were responsible for the maintenance of the momentum toward national child care concern and public policy.

The research focus of the 1960s, along with the emphasis on the Great Society, brought together powerful forces that would eventually vault early childhood policy into its present visibility. The advent of early childhood programs for disadvantaged and at-risk youngsters, the valuable research conducted during these initial efforts, and the accountability issues that were raised, all contributed to the evolution of early childhood development as a powerful public policy issue. The 1960s saw a renaissance of interest in early childhood education as a means of addressing child and family poverty (Schweinhart & Weikart, 1986). A clear link was established between the positive outcomes of early childhood programs for children from low-income families and longitudinal research findings. The early intervention efforts of the 1960s resulted in early childhood issues being couched within a deficit model. Early childhood education was equated with early intervention for special needs or at-risk children. As a result, federal and state funds began to be used for programs for young children before they entered public school. Kindergarten programs expanded and Head Start and other early childhood programs became popular, too. The 1960s marked a significant passage for early childhood education. The field began to be defined as more than day care and in its place came the concept of early childhood education being a comprehensive, developmental focus on young children, ages birth to eight years, with special attention to special-needs youngsters.

The 1970s saw an expansion and refinement of research methodologies related to child development, parent–child relationships, and specific developmental outcomes directly related to early childhood experiences. The 1970s also saw tremendous growth in the teacher training programs for teachers of young children. The federally sponsored Child Development Associate Program was born in the mid-1970s in an effort to make available competency-based training programs for individuals desiring to work with young children. Universities and colleges began to expand their curricular offerings in programs that were termed "child development" or "early childhood education."

Research proliferated in child development and early childhood education. Interdisciplinary research emerged as education, psychology, sociology, medicine, and related fields collaborated in their research efforts. Children came to be seen as complex, evolving individuals who have very special developmental needs in four distinct areas: social, cognitive, emotional, and psychomotor.

The Young Child in the 1990s: Toward Innovative Policy

In America, the young child of the 1990s is growing up amid a world of changing priorities. Social and economic forces that influenced their parents are now eroded and in their place are even more complex social forces. Toffler (1981), writing in *The Third Wave*, stated: "A powerful tide is surging across much of the world today creating a new, often bizarre, environment in which to work, play, marry, raise children or retire" (p. 1). Today's world seems strangely adult-focused. Children often feel like helpless recipients in the tides of change (Wortham, 1987). Children and their parents are pioneers in a world where there are no precedents for such simultaneous trends as high mobility, dual-earner parents, minimal extended-family support, single-headed households, and early academic expectations, all converging on the American family, regardless of its particular form or makeup.

When reviewing the types of programs available today, it appears that three out of every ten U.S. children under the age of 5 are enrolled in day care homes, day care centers, or nursery schools. Most of these children (62%) are in programs that are publicly sponsored, licensed, or registered (Schweinhart, 1989).

The 1980s marked an escalation in policy efforts for young children. As examples, the National Governors' Association focused on children's issues and hosted a national conference and final report entitled *The First Sixty Months* (National Governors' Association, 1987). Former Governor Riley of South Carolina urges governors to continue playing expanding roles in the development of legislation to support early childhood education (Riley, 1986). Over 26 states have adopted new legislation that expands programs for young children (Schwein-hart & Weikart, 1986). McCormick (1986) reports on the New York City Commission's prekindergarten programs for all 100,000 local four-year-olds.

The 100th Congress introduced more than 100 child- and family-related bills, many of them with bipartisan sponsorship (Kagan, 1989). In 1988, the National Association of State Boards of Education re-leased a comprehensive Task Force Report entitled *Right from the Start*, advocating a proactive and responsible role for public schools in the development of futuristic early childhood programs (National Association of State Boards of Education, 1988). State Departments of Education are initiating innovative early childhood programs, partic-ularly for disadvantaged preschoolers (Kristensen & Billman, 1987; White, 1987; Schweinhart, Koshel, & Bridgman, 1987: Meyerhoff & White, 1986; Morado, 1986). Pool (1986) reports that the National Association of Elementary School Principals (NAESP) began a recent thrust toward expansion of quality early childhood programs in the schools, with a significant emphasis on *quality*.

Finally, corporate America is awakening to the critical needs of working parents and young children in a variety of ways. Weikart (1989) indicates that corporate America is acutely aware of the grow-ing movement of women into the paid work force and that as the number of young persons (18 to 24 years of age) dwindles, the quality of the workers available for entry-level positions becomes increasingly important. Brad Butler, former CEO of Procter & Gamble Corporation, inspired and encouraged the Committee for Economic Development to address the long-term needs and benefits of early childhood education as an assurance of a better-prepared and more literate work force for America (Committee for Economic Development, 1985).

Innovative business-school-community partnerships also indicate a new emphasis on quality early childhood programs. The Cincinnati Youth Collaborative serves as an example of this kind of partnership (Stegelin, 1988). Supported by community involvement and business leadership and funding, the Cincinnati Public Schools joined hands with the community to establish pilot preschool programs for disad-vantaged African-American and Appalachian 3-year-olds in public elementary school settings. Still in its infancy, this pilot program represents new funding and collaborative efforts and may signal the expansion of such programs across the United States.

THE STATUS OF EARLY CHILDHOOD POLICY

In spite of the accelerating impetus on issues directly related to children and families during the past two decades, the late 1980s found early childhood policy mired in a complex set of forces (Kagan, 1989). Kagan, associate director of the Bush Center in Child Development and Social Policy at Yale University and a leading authority on early childhood policy, states:

> By traditional standards, the task should have been comparatively simple. Armed with approved mandates and appropriated dollars, an unprecedented number of cities and states set off to implement high-quality early childhood programs in the late 1980s. The time seemed ripe: well-publicized research extolled the benefits of early intervention; demographics reflecting the massive movement of women into the paid labor force fortified the need for additional services for young children; and a consensus about definitions of good early childhood pedagogy and practice, not prevalent 20 years before, had emerged. (p. 434)

Kagan goes on to declare that fundamental shifts in the way we view children and families must be matched also by equally dramatic shifts in the way policies are crafted for young children and their families.

The Changing Definition of the Child

The evolution of early childhood policy mirrors a changing definition of the child in our culture. As the 1990s emerge, the way in which Americans view the young child reflects deeply rooted changes in the fabric of our society. The deficit model associated with early intervention of the 1960s has given way to a more comprehensive and integrated view of the young child as a part of a functioning, vital family constellation. The term *early childhood education* now has collective meanings, primarily those of child care, early intervention, preschool, kindergarten, and family support programs.

Establishment of quality early childhood education programs is seen as an economic investment in America's future. Thus the need to develop and launch a rationale and debate for early education has lessened and in its place has emerged a critical need to forge innovative state and federal policies that, in some way, combine the forces at hand so that integrated, well-conceptualized programs emerge in a collaborative way for young children and their families (Kagan, 1989).

The Growing Need for Policy Awareness in Early Childhood

Early childhood education and development has evolved from a simplistic, charitable notion into a complex field that embraces the needs of young children and their parents in a quickly changing society that is often adult-oriented rather than child-oriented. The forces that are at work to produce this complexity are identified in the following:

1. New family forms and parenting styles that include rapidly increasing rates of maternal employment and parental desires for more flexibility and support in the work/family arena (Kagan, 1989; Weikart, 1989; McCormick, 1986; Schweinhart & Weikart, 1986).
2. Business and corporate involvement in child care and family and parent support roles and the realization by big business that subsequent hiring of competent, capable adults in their work forces means intervention with at-risk and disadvantaged preschoolers today (Committee for Economic Development, 1985).
3. New federal and state legislation that addresses the needs of young children. An example is federal law P.L. 99–457 which extends services for developmentally delayed and handicapped youngsters by school districts to the 3–5-year-old population (Peterson, 1987). Several pieces of legislation at the federal level during the 1988 year propelled issues such as child care and early start programs to the forefront.
4. The awareness of politicians that early childhood issues impact all of America's families. The presidential debates and the campaign of 1988 focused on the American family, the complexity of lifestyles, and the need for child and family support programs (Kagan, 1989).
5. A growing awareness of multicultural influences and sensitivity to a world that seems to be growing smaller, psychologically, on a daily basis. Minority children and their families are now deemed to be in need of consideration for special programs and enhanced support programs. The feeling deepens that what happens in other parts of the world directly impacts us as Americans.
6. Expansion of early childhood development programs and enrollments across the United States points to the growing need for these services. Enrollments in nursery schools, child care programs, and other early education programs continue to escalate rapidly (Weikart, 1989). These increases are the result of several combined forces: (a) maternal employment, (b) increased focus on

academic readiness or developmental needs, (c) emphasis on serving young children who are impoverished or at-risk, and (d) sensitivity to the need for early intervention for special needs children.

7. Professionalism as a focus in the field of early childhood education. Advocacy groups and organizations have sprung up across the country in an effort to constructively influence the policy process. Standards for excellence are being established by national organizations (National Association for the Education of Young Children, 1986). Teacher training requirements are being regulated and evaluated. The issue of wages and salaries for child care personnel and early childhood professionals in general remains a critical concern. Standards for developmentally appropriate child care settings are being established and monitored by the states. Sensitivity to special-needs preschoolers has increased the need for integrated early childhood settings and for early childhood professionals to work together for advocacy.

The Role of the Individual in Policy Development

As stated earlier, many early childhood specialists have not felt comfortable in the public policy arena in the past (Kilmer, 1980). According to Lombardi (1986), some of the common barriers to individual participation include the following:

1. Feelings of powerlessness to change anything
2. Lack of knowledge regarding government regulations
3. Fear of the political process
4. Lack of confidence in their own expertise
5. Lack of time (p. 65).

Due to the rapid escalation of early childhood as a policy issue, many teacher training institutions have elected to expand their curricular offerings to include coursework on advocacy and public policy development. Roper (1987) states that early childhood education professionals are resisting the harsher voices of educational reform better than most other teacher training fields. Early childhood specialists continue to be assertive and advocate the need for creative, developmentally appropriate learning settings; they seem to be resisting the trends toward mass testing, structured learning, and accountability based primarily on testing measures.

Early childhood development students and specialists are graduating with more sophisticated levels of understanding of the political process. The idea that academic settings must of necessity be separate from the political process is diminishing. Indeed, with the causes for young children becoming so complex and pervasive in our society, the need for policy training seems inherent for early childhood development students who will become the future teachers, administrators, legislators, and leaders of our nation.

National efforts like the passage of the Head Start legislation, the subsequent pieces of legislation related to Head Start, and the veto of the Child Development Act are examples of why early childhood advocacy is essential (Lombardi, 1986; Brown, 1985). Fiscal restraints at both the federal and state levels often force difficult decisions related to cutbacks in programs. Individuals must be able to combine forces to present a unified, informed, and persuasive stance on behalf of the preservation of programs for young children. Often the early childhood advocate simply has not had the training or experience to carry out advocacy efforts in a forceful and persistent way. The need for expanded training in early childhood advocacy and the policy process seems unprecedented.

SALIENT EARLY CHILDHOOD ISSUES
FOR THE 1990s

The field of early childhood education and development is growing rapidly and many different interest groups exist within the field. From a review of the literature and a study of current pieces of legislation at the federal and state levels, the following policy issues are at the forefront:

1. *Child Care.* Child care at all age levels from infancy through school age. These policy questions focus on provision of developmentally suitable programs, availability to all parents, licensing and regulation, involvement of public schools, and development of new funding avenues. The need for quality, accessible child care continues to rise dramatically in this country, especially for infants and toddlers.

Seligson (1986) reports that the majority of America's schoolchildren reside in homes where both parents (or the only parent) work outside the home. Some states have already enacted legislation in support of before-and-after school care; others are still considering this issue. Federal monies are now available for the establishment of after-school programs through Dependent Care Grants. Day (1986) and others advocate for child care in the public school setting in order to provide more continuity and less fragmentation in provision of developmental programs for the birth to age eight population.

2. *Delivery Systems: Federal, State, and Community*. There is a need to address delivery systems for quality programs for young children, such as home-based, center-based, nonprofit, for-profit, school-based, and community-based sites. Along with the expansion of these delivery systems comes the need to study carefully the outcomes of these various settings on the development of young children. The need for integrated collaborative efforts has never been greater. Fragmentation of the child and the family must be addressed (Kagan, 1989).

3. *Funding Mechanisms and Wage Equity*. Funding mechanisms to support the development of programs for young children are critical to their success. These include the following funding avenues: (a) parent fees, (b) family support and social welfare programs, (c) employer-sponsored benefit packages, (d) tax credits, (e) public vouchers, (f) purchase of services, (g) federally funded or subsidized programs, (h) state-funded or subsidized programs, and (i) open enrollment programs with sliding scale fees available for all parents, regardless of socioeconomic status.

Projecting into the future, Schweinhart (1989) forecasts that the major funding avenues will be for programs in these three areas: (a) publicly subsidized private early childhood programs; (b) federal programs like Head Start, and (c) state-funded public school programs. Paramount in the funding issue is upgrading salaries and wages for child care personnel who currently are paid less than all other social professions (Weikart, 1989).

4. *Accountability and Standards*. As legislation is developed and passed that support programs for young children, the issue of accountability for the public dollar is paramount. What outcomes should be expected and how should they be measured? Who should be responsible for establishing licensing standards and how should they be monitored? How can state and federal officials work together to help standardize program regulations for federally and state-sponsored early childhood programs? Also at question are issues related to developmentally appropriate means of testing and assessing young children (National Association for the Education of Young Children, 1986).

5. *Early Childhood Programs for Impoverished and Special Needs Children*. National sensitivity to the long-term negative impacts of

poverty on children is growing (Peterson, 1987). Also, there is an awareness that all children are developmentally more alike than different, thus the need for expanded, integrated early childhood programs that include special-needs children in regular settings is also growing. The long-term benefits of quality early childhood programs for disadvantaged children is well-documented in the literature. These benefits include major positive consequences for society-at-large, such as decreased dropout rates, decreased teenage pregnancy rates, increased rates of employment, and increased rates of post-secondary educational efforts (Schweinhart & Weikart, 1986).

6. *Public School Early Childhood Programs.* A recent effort by a national task force resulted in clear recommendations being made regarding early childhood programs in the public school sector. The National Association of State Boards of Education released its report, *Right from the Start*, in November, 1988, and strongly recommends a developmental approach to these programs and the creation of early childhood administrative units in the public school setting (NASBE, 1988; Morado, 1986).

7. *Developmentally Appropriate Curriculum and Related Research.* The National Association for the Education of Young Children (NAEYC) proposes standards for developmentally appropriate methods of teaching young children and for assessing and measuring developmental variables of this population (NAEYC, 1986). Hatch and Freeman (1988) report that young children in kindergarten are victims of the push for academics primarily because of pressure exerted on teachers by parents, the changes in children due to early exposure to television, a proliferation of published teaching materials and curriculum, and expectations of society.

The use of standardized tests with preschool children remains an area of controversy and one in need of further research. Weikart (1989) declares that a primary research need in early childhood development includes continued justification and documentation of the effects of early childhood programs, particularly child care for very young children, on the development of these children.

8. *Family Support Systems.* With social patterns now focusing on the family unit as an interactive group of individuals with support needs, the concept of family support programs has grown. Such researchers as Galinsky and Hooks (1977) and Kagan (1989) advocate for expanded programs for children and families that help alleviate the stressors caused by working mothers, complex transportation arrangements, a general fragmentation of child care services, and other family stressors.

SCOPE AND AUTHORSHIP OF THE TEXT

This text on early childhood education policy focuses on the salient concerns related to the following specific policy issues: (a) infant/toddler child care, (b) federal and state child care policy, (c) corporate involvement in family support systems and programs, (d) integration of early childhood programs at the state level, (e) state policy related to disadvantaged and at-risk children, (f) preschool programs in the public schools, (g) program needs related to handicapped and developmentally delayed preschoolers, and (h) the need for collaboration in service delivery to young children and their families.

The authors of this edited text are all individuals who are recognized at the national level as being at the forefront of early childhood policy. A brief biography of each author is now presented. Specifically, Dr. Eleanor Stokes Szanton is with the National Center for Clinical Infant Programs and is instrumental in raising the most critical issues related to research needs and program practices in infant and toddler child care. Dr. Szanton addresses the important concern of parents today as they seek quality, dependable care for their very young children. Infant/toddler child care remains a pressing issue in America and Dr. Szanton makes policy recommendations related to this topic.

Ellen Galinsky, former president of the National Association for the Education of Young Children (NAEYC), discusses the growing need for family support programs and identifies policy areas related to this emerging concept. Ms. Galinsky is a well-known and widely acclaimed researcher and author and is a co-director of the Families and Work Institute of New York. She brings a comprehensive perspective from the vantage point of a researcher, writer, educator, national advocate, and a working parent.

Dr. David Weikart and Dr. Lawrence Schweinhart focus on the need for policy makers to address social problem solving rather than program development per se. From their well-known research at High/Scope, they propose that early childhood policy should be driven by the need to alleviate crime, illiteracy, and poverty, three of the most serious national problems today. Schweinhart and Weikart, co-investigators of the Perry Preschool Project, are responsible for much of the research-based rationale that has inspired policy makers to address early childhood education at both the state and federal levels.

Robert A. Cervantes, associate superintendent of the California State Department of Education, makes a strong argument for the integration of comprehensive early childhood programs. As director of all early childhood development programs implemented through the California State Department of Education, Mr. Cervantes brings tremendous perspective to the need for coordination and collaboration of early childhood programs. California, long recognized as a leader in state-initiated programs for young children, expends millions of dollars each year on child care and developmental preschool programs. Mr. Cervantes' thoughtful recommendations for statewide policy and practice, particularly in the area of child care, are helpful to policy analysts and program administrators in other states.

The Children's Defense Fund has been cited as playing a critical role in federal policy making for children and families. Helen Blank, director of Child Care at the Children's Defense Fund, works to expand support for child care/child development. Ms. Blank was instrumental in organizing the Alliance for Better Care and developing the Act for Better Child Care (the ABC) Bill. She writes about emerging child care issues to address in forging federal and state policies.

Bill Clinton, Governor of Arkansas and nationally recognized child advocate, is chairman of the National Governors' Association Committee on Children. Governor Clinton focuses his writing on policy issues related to developing welfare and educational programs for disadvantaged and at-risk preschool children. Governor Bill Clinton, who is popular across the country as a spokesman for children and families, brings a special sensitivity and commitment to the plight of the disadvantaged child and his or her family.

Dr. Thomas Schultz, executive director of the National Association of State Boards of Education, brings national perspective to the expanding role of the public schools in the arena of early childhood education. Dr. Schultz has studied the complex forces at work in the public school sector and makes practical recommendations for forging developmentally appropriate practice for young children. The recent NASBE Report, *Right from the Start* (NASBE, 1988), is summarized along with specific suggestions for school district policy related to early childhood education.

Dr. Sharon Lynn Kagan is Senior Research Associate at the Bush Center in Child Development and Policy at Yale University. In this capacity, Dr. Kagan addresses the critical issues related to early childhood education and development at the national level. Dr. Kagan served as the first director of the New York City Office for Early Childhood Education and maintains close ties to this innovative program for 4-year-olds. The author of numerous scholarly articles and the editor of several books, Dr. Kagan shares her views on the need for preschool collaboration at the national level.

Dr. Stacie Goffin is involved in teacher training, research and writing, and early childhood policy development and has focused much of her work on the role of the public school in the implementation of developmentally appropriate practice. Working in the Kansas City area, Dr. Goffin has been highly successful in creating imaginative and effective linkages between the university, the public school sector, the community at large, and the parent population. She brings insight into weaving effective partnerships that lead to developmentally appropriate classrooms for young children in public school settings.

Drs. Karen and Pat Gallagher are researchers in the area of educational administration and early childhood special education, respectively. Both have written extensively in the area of policy development, particulary related to public school administrators and the ecology of special education programs. Associated with the University of Cincinnati, these researchers provide an overview of the history of special education and the evolving ecology of early childhood special education. They present policy implications useful for school administrators and others involved in the successful implementation of new state and federal legislation related to early childhood special education.

Dr. Peg Elgas is a researcher in the area of play and is interested in developing more effective play environments for young children in all settings. She provides insight into the final analysis of this book and provides food for thought as she synthesizes the policy content of the authors. Dr. Elgas is with the University of Cincinnati and is interested in promoting integrated teacher education programs that encourage diversity and multicultural opportunities for future early childhood teachers.

Dr. Dolores (Dee) Stegelin is currently associate professor of early childhood education at the University of Cincinnati. Dr. Stegelin served as the first director of the Office of Early Childhood Education and Development in the Commonwealth of Kentucky, where she drafted the state's first *Five Year Plan for Early Childhood Education*. Dr. Stegelin's research interests include public school involvement in early childhood education, policy issues, and collaboration among early childhood providers. Dr. Stegelin opens this text with an introductory chapter on early childhood policy and, with Dr. Elgas, concludes the book with a summary of the policy issues discussed by the authors.

REFERENCES

Barnett, W. (1985). *The Perry Preschool Program and its long-term effects: A benefit-cost analysis* (High/Scope Early Childhood Policy Papers, No. 2). Ypsilanti, MI: High/Scope Press.

Brown, B. (1985). Head Start: How research changed public policy. *Young Children, 41*, 9–13.

Committee for Economic Development (CED). (1985). Investing in our children: Business and the public schools. *Committee for economic development*. New York: Committee for Economic Development.

Day, B. (1986). On early education: A conversation with Barbara Day. *Educational Leadership, 44,* 28–30.

Farnum, L. (1987). Child care and early education: A partnership with elementary education. *Thrust, 6,* 19–20.

Galinsky, E., & Hooks, W. (1977). *The new extended family day care that works.* Boston: Houghton Mifflin.

Hatch, J., & Freeman, E. (1988). Who's pushing whom? Stress and kindergarten. *Phi Delta Kappan, 70,* 145–147.

Hetrick, B., & Van Horn, C. (1988). Educational research information: Meeting the needs of state policy makers. *Theory Into Practice, 27,* 106–110.

Irwin, D., & Bushnell, M. (1980). *Observational strategies for child study.* New York: Holt, Rinehart and Winston.

Kagan, S. (1989). Early care and education: Tackling the tough issues. *Phi Delta Kappan, 70,* 433–439.

Kilmer, S. (1980). Early childhood specialists as policy makers. *Education and Urban Society, 12,* 241–251.

Kristensen, N., & Billman, J. (1987). Supporting parents and young children: Minnesota early childhood family education program. *Childhood Education, 63,* 276–282.

Lazar, I., Darlington, R., Murray, H., Royce, J., & Snipper, A. (1982). Lasting effects of early education. *Monographs of the Society for Research in Child Development, 47* (1–2 Serial No. 194).

Lombardi, J. (1986). Training for public policy and advocacy. *Young Children, 42,* 65–69.

McCormick, K. (1986). If early education isn't on your agenda now, it could be—and soon. *The American School Board Journal, 41,* 30–34.

Meyerhoff, M., & White, B. (1986). New parents as teachers. *Educational Leadership, 44,* 42–46.

Morado, C. (1986). Prekindergarten programs for 4-year olds: State involvement in preschool education. *Young Children, 42,* 69–71.

National Association for the Education of Young Children (NAEYC). (1986). Position statement on developmentally appropriate practice in early childhood programs serving children from birth through age 8. *Young Children, 42,* 4–19.

National Association for the Education of Young Children (NAEYC). (1986). Position statement on developmentally appropriate practice on programs for 4- and 5-year olds. *Young Children, 42,* 20–29.

National Association of State Boards of Education (NASBE). (1988). *Right from the start.* Alexandria, VA: National Association of State Boards of Education.

National Governors' Association and Center for Policy Research. (1987). *The first sixty months: A handbook of promising prevention programs for children 0–5 years of age.* Washington, DC: NGA.

Peterson, N. (1987). *Early intervention for handicapped and at-risk children.* Denver: Love Publishing Co.

Pool, C. (1986). Here come the four-year-olds. *Principal, 65,* 4.

Riley, R. (1986). Can we reduce the risk of failure? *Phi Delta Kappan, 68,* 214–219.

Roper, S. (1987). Secondary school specialist says ECE people are resisting the harsher voices of "reform" better than their colleagues who teach older children. *Young Children, 43,* 12–13.

Schweinhart, L. (1989). Early childhood programs in the U. S. today. *High/Scope Resource, 8,* 9–13.

Schweinhart, L., Koshel, J., & Bridgman, A. (1987). Policy options for preschool programs. *Phi Delta Kappan, 68,* 524–529.

Schweinhart, L., & Weikart, D. (1986). Early childhood development programs: A public investment opportunity. *Educational Leadership, 68,* 4–12.

Schweinhart, L., Weikart, D., & Larner, M. (1986). Consequences of three preschool curriculum models through age 15. *Early Childhood Research Quarterly, 1,* 15–45.

Seligson, M. (1986). Child care for the school-age child. *Phi Delta Kappan, 67,* 637–640.

Stegelin, D.A. (1988). *The Cincinnati Youth Collaborative: A community partnership for disadvantaged preschoolers.* Presentation to the Kentucky Association on Children Under Six, Ft. Mitchell, KY.

Toffler, A. (1981). *The third wave.* New York: Bantam Books.

Weikart, D. (1989). Hard choices in early childhood care and education: A view to the future. *Young Children, 45,* 25–30.

White, B. (1987). Education begins at birth. *Principal, 66,* 15–18.

Wortham, S. (1987). Balancing priorities. *Childhood Education, 63,* 322–323.

Part I

Early Childhood Policy Development at the State and National Levels

Chapter 2

State Policy Related to Disadvantaged and At-Risk Preschoolers

Governor Bill Clinton
State Capitol, Little Rock, AR

For as long as I can remember, Americans have found it very difficult to talk about family policy as a political issue. I think that is largely because we are a country that has (as one of its foremost values) the importance of individualism, the importance of individual families, and the idea that the government ought not to reach into individual or family life any more than is absolutely necessary. Furthermore, I think that whenever we talk about family policy as a political issue, we can't help bringing to bear our own experiences and our own understandings. Sometimes, that can be very painful, and it is always very personal.

In order to make that connection, I suppose I should begin by making some measure of disclosure about my own past. I was raised until I was four by my grandparents. My grandmother was a working woman, a nurse. My mother was also a nurse who worked outside the home throughout my childhood.

I have also been deeply influenced by the activities of my wife. She is the chairman of the board of the Children's Defense Fund, a member of the board of the Child Care Action Campaign, headed by Eleanor Guggenheimer, who has been working on the child care issue for nearly 60 years. My wife was also a member of the board of The

National Commission on Education and the Economy, and she helped to found the Arkansas Advocates for Children and Families.

In 1987, I announced after a great deal of soul searching that I would not enter the Democratic presidential primaries, in large measure because my wife and I are parents of an only child who at that time was seven years old. I concluded the only chance we would have to win would be for both of us to be gone six or seven days a week for a year and a half. It seemed to me if you do that, particularly to an only child at that age, the risk of some permanent psychological damage to the child is considerable. I couldn't see going through the rest of my life making speeches about something so important to me that would be blatantly hypocritical.

THREE PRIMARY CHALLENGES TO THE FAMILY

The challenges to our families and to our country are many. But we could all agree that there are three great challenges to the strength and success of families.

Poverty

The first is poverty. One in four children under the age of five in the United States today is living below the poverty line. That is an astonishing statistic when measured against the background of what is often called the longest peacetime economic expansion in our history. The birth rate is growing among poor families, so the percentage of poor children under the age of five will increase if we don't do something about it. These children are far more likely to be born with low birth weights and, therefore, far more likely to have avoidable mental and physical disabilities that will stay with them the rest of their lives. These handicaps may lead to failure in school, failure as citizens, increased rates of hospitalization, welfare dependency, and incarceration. We are paying for these families now on the back end rather than the front end. They are likely to be ill-prepared for the lives they have to live today, and they are almost certainly ill-prepared for the world we are moving toward.

Work

The second great challenge to families is one not confined to just poor people. It is work. By 1995, two thirds of all preschool children will have mothers in the work force. Many of them wish to work, and many have to work either because they are the sole support of their children or because their husbands earn so little. Two-thirds of all married women in the work force have husbands with incomes under $15,000. So, they, too, are there not only because they may wish to work but because they must.

There are important economic reasons the rest of us should not discourage too many of these women from working. By 1995, according to the United States Department of Labor, we will have a labor shortage in this country if present trends continue. Nonetheless, it is deeply disturbing to me to see how the work patterns of so many American families discourage child bearing among some of those who would be the best and the strongest parents.

My wife chairs a committee of the American Bar Association that looks into the practices of law firms in this country: how they treat their women associates, how they treat their women partners, how women are hired as compared with men, and how they progress through the law firms. There are some shocking findings in this research indicating, among other things, that young women lawyers get very clear signals from a lot of major law firms that if they ever want to become partners they shouldn't entertain the thought of having children.

Practices like that are not confined to law firms. The parental leave practices of many of our larger employers discourage working women from having children. Many of those who could be the most successful parents, therefore, are passing up opportunities they would dearly love to have. We have to resolve this conflict. Life's most important job is still parenthood.

Family Structure

The third great challenge is the changes in the structure of the American family itself. Lenore Weizman in her book, *The Divorce Revolution* (Weizman, 1987), points out that not only has the divorce rate continued to increase in our country but women, who are usually left with dependent children, are on the average 42 percent worse off in terms of their income within three years after the divorce. Our inability to enforce child support laws adequately has resulted in a precipitous decline in the incomes of American women and, therefore, of their children. This is compounded by high rates of teen pregnancy and other out-of-wedlock births. Our teen pregnancy rate is still more than twice as high as that of any of the major countries with which we compete.

THE NEED FOR FAMILY CONNECTIONS

If you were to visit me, you would see the office of an exceedingly sentimental person. I have a lot of things there made by artists and craftsmen from my home state: two tables, a Bowie knife, paintings, and old pictures of my family. There is a picture of my grandmother and her brother and sister in 1916 by a little rural school in Southwest Arkansas; a picture of my grandfather taken in 1923, standing by a great old saw mill furnace into which he is shoveling wood chips; and a picture of me in 1952 at the age of six lying on my back in a hospital bed with a broken leg and holding my great-grandfather's hand. While we didn't have much money, we were a great strong family in which everyone felt loved, a part of something bigger than himself or herself, a family in which the adversities of death, divorce, and other problems could be dealt with and reconciled.

One of the biggest problems we have in this country today is that there are so few children who could ever have their pictures taken holding their great-grandfathers' hands, or who would ever have a picture of a grandmother as a school child to look at on the mantel or mantelpiece. They will never have these kinds of connections that have sustained so many of us throughout our lives. Unfortunately, these trends of poverty, family changes, and work tend to reinforce each other among the most vulnerable of our people.

THE GOVERNMENT AS A CATALYST

What are we to do about it? What is the role of government? As someone who has spent the better part of his adult life unashamedly as a politician, I can tell you that there are very few government programs which operate to save people. The government is not a savior. Yet the government cannot be a spectator either. What we have tried to do in my state, what I believe the federal government should move to do, and what people in both parties are beginning to grapple with is to construct a role for government not as savior, not as spectator, but as catalyst and partner.

Health Initiatives

Our first goal should be to help the parents succeed, and when they fail, to save as many children as we can. We should commit ourselves to bringing healthy babies into this world and to keeping them as healthy as we can. It's the most inexpensive thing we can do to strengthen the American family. Even against the background of the budget cuts of the last few years, federal legislation was passed in 1986 to allow states to provide Medicaid coverage to pregnant women whose income is up to 100 percent of the federal poverty line and their children up through age five; and later Congress gave states the option for coverage for health benefits to those with incomes up to 185 percent of the federal poverty line.

The kind of maternal and child care delivery system we have is important. States must make sure that they have good preventive health care networks in place. Then even in the poorest places in America we can bring down the infant mortality rate, bring down the low birthweight rate, and deal with low birthweight babies in a more effective way. A nurse midwife program in eastern Arkansas, a very poor area, has produced an infant mortality rate 30 percent below the national average.

Beginning with the newborn baby and continuing throughout adolescence, we need to maintain a good network of primary health care. In our state more than 80 percent of the immunizations are being done by our state Department of Health. The cost to the state of giving a child a full series of immunizations has risen from $21.34 in 1985 to $63.92 in 1988. This has not been easy on the budget of this already financially strapped agency; but Dr. Joycelyn Elders, Director of the Department, has made it a policy that all children in the state will have an opportunity to start out on the right foot. Another initiative the Health Department has undertaken, albeit a controversial one, is to implement 13 clinics (with expanded health services) in schools across the state. Services ranging from routine check-ups to counseling to birth control advice and distribution (in two schools) are available to 13,377 students across the state.

Those are the kinds of things we have to do through public health networks, working with private providers to deal with the health needs of the family. A sick child or a permanently disabled child will less likely be able to work, will be less likely to have a successful family, and will be an economic burden rather than a boon to society. For example, it was recently reported that nearly $100 million is spent in Arkansas yearly by social service agencies on problems generated by teen pregnancies. It is extremely important that policy makers and politicians realize the importance of prevention initiatives which may cost more now but which can save millions later.

One fairly simple initiative the Arkansas Department of Health has recently undertaken is to promote comprehensive vision and hearing screening for all preschool children. Obviously, early intervention for children with vision and hearing problems will prevent development of more extensive problems in the future and will allow children to avoid school performance problems. The preschool program is designed to train child care staff in early childhood programs to screen children in their care. Training sessions were held throughout the state by Health Department consultants during 1989–1990. Day care programs with trained staff will be loaned machines for the screening procedure. The Health Department hopes to have all children in child care screened by the end of 1990. It is important to note that before this program was undertaken these types of screens hardly ever were performed before a child was in school. This will help us not only to find the problems sooner, but to correct them sooner so the child can have a good start in school.

Child Care Needs

Secondly, we must change the fact that we are the last advanced economy in this world to acquire an adequate system of child care. We can't expect the federal government to solve all the problems, since we have had several years of cutbacks in federal subsidies for child care. Many states, including poor states like mine with limited revenues, are trying to make up the difference by putting up state funds for child care. In addition, states have particular responsibilities to make sure that the child care centers are good ones with high standards and well-trained people. There are countless American parents who go to work every day worried sick that their children are in a child care center without adequate education, without any kind of training, without any kind of stimulation—just stuck in front of a television all day without learning anything. They can't afford to give any more of their income to child care. It's up to the states, at least under the present system, to make sure that those child care workers are trained and that every center has a strong educational component. The child care tax credit at the federal and state levels can be a real aid in allowing working parents to send their children to more expensive, quality child care centers. It needs to be revamped and concentrated on the people who need it most—the middle-income level people. I think that if this is done, we can have less revenue loss and more benefit to the people who are most in need. But we need direct federal investment, too, for those whose incomes permit no benefits from tax credit.

Here are two examples of how Arkansas has served as a catalyst in developing solutions to the child care dilemma: (a) Act 202 of 1989 created the Arkansas Child Facilities Guarantee Loan Fund to support the development and expansion of child care facilities. Oversight and administrative authority for the fund was given to the Arkansas Early Childhood Commission, which is housed in the Governor's Office. Certain considerations must be included in granting loan guarantees: geographic distribution, community need, the median family income of a community, proof of viable administrative and financial management on the part of the guarantee applicant, intended licensure of the facility, and attainment of the goal that 25 percent of the potential market for the facility be comprised of families at or below the median income for the state. The Fund is designed to create increased access to existing lending sources in Arkansas for those persons interested in developing child care programs. (b) Arkansas will introduce the first information and referral system for the public at large early in 1990. This service, provided by the Arkansas Child Care Resource Center, will give parents across the state help in gaining information about child care facilities in their area and about characteristics of quality programs. The Center will have computerized listings of all licensed and registered child care facilities in the state and will provide parents with information through a toll-free number. Parents may request information on the type of child care available, ages of children served in these facilities, and geographic location. Educational materials on how to choose quality child care will also be made available to parents upon request. The service will also be available to corporations by contract as an employee benefit program and can be individualized to serve employees of a particular company.

It is important to note that the child care issue has been on the front burner for the nation's governors for the past several years. We were successful in making child care a prominent piece of the Family Support Act of 1988 and have continued to work with the federal government on other landmark legislation in this important area.

This leads to my final point. We need to develop greater partnerships with businesses. Very few businesses have business-based child care centers. Those that do are very proud of them, and most of them are very, very successful. Smaller businesses may not be able to have child care centers, but there are all kinds of other options available. States need to be catalysts in working with businesses to help them make those options available to their employees. We cannot afford to continue to live with the prospect of having most children born to very poor mothers, because working parents fear that they can't afford to have kids or they do not know who is going to take care of them, or they don't have the support systems they need.

You may argue that we ought to go back to a former time when every mother stayed home with a child until the age of two or three.

Given the economic problems and social disorder of the present day, it seems to me that this is just pie-in-the-sky rhetoric. It costs the average family, for example, three times the percentage of its income to live in a home than it did a generation ago.

Parent Support Initiatives

The work requirements of most two-parent families bring us back to the parental-leave issue. Maybe there is no comprehensive legislative policy that solves the problem, but it is wrong for us to say to the working people, "We don't want you to have kids; and if you do, you will lose your job." We have to work out a system of parental leave for people not only when they have babies, but also when their children are sick. People need to be able to leave work when their children are in trouble at school or if there is an event at school where the parents need to be.

Have you ever gone to a school meeting when the parents are introduced, and looked at the expressions on the faces of the kids who don't have anybody there? It's like a body blow. If the private sector cannot afford to accommodate good strong parenting policies, there is something wrong with the free enterprise system. Every company that has accommodated child care needs, every company that has accommodated the desire of parents to be good parents, the most fundamental emotional drive people have, has improved employee morale, improved productivity, and increased profits on the bottom line. Nobody is losing money by doing right on these issues. We just need more people to believe they can do it.

Early Education Programs

In the area of education we have to face the fact that too many children are being born into families where they will not get the kind of preparation they need unless the government steps in. Only about 18 percent of the eligible kids in this country are now covered by the Head Start Program, a proven success. We should cover them all and, in addition, we should develop specific strategies to bring the parents of poor children into the process of preparing their children for school.

Our state has 4,000 children and parents involved in a project we borrowed from Israel, called "HIPPY"—Home Instruction Program for Preschool Youngsters. Israel developed this project 20 years ago to work with immigrants coming in from poorer societies, Jewish families that were not as well educated as the native Israelis, or those who had come as immigrants from Europe. The aim was to find a way to get those kids up to par with the others by the time they started school. The program basically involves using a set of simple notebooks to teach parents, no matter how illiterate they might be, to teach the children to prepare for kindergarten. Basic concepts such as the differences between big and small, open and shut, bright and dark, as well as basic colors, shapes, numbers, and basic reasoning skills are taught. When my wife found out about this program in 1985 almost by accident, we called the founder, Dr. Avima Lombard, in Israel, and asked her to come to Arkansas to see if her program could work in our state. There are now HIPPY projects in five other countries besides Israel and in seven U.S. states. Arkansas has the only statewide program, the largest in the world outside of Israel. Currently, Arkansas children and parents participate in 19 sites covering 27 counties. Parents, usually mothers, of four-year-old children are required to work with their children 15 minutes a day, 5 days a week, 30 weeks a year, for 2 years, the second year while the child is in kindergarten. The mother is instructed through role playing, so that even parents with very limited reading skills can still participate. She is trained by a paraprofessional who also has a four-year-old child and who comes from the same community. Twice a month, the aide visits the parent in the home and works with her on the weekly lessons. On alternating weeks, the mothers gather for group meetings where they not only will work with their aide to learn the next week's instruction, but also will have an opportunity to visit with other mothers, share their experiences, talk about their problems, and have an enrichment program. HIPPY is structured to ensure not only the success of the child but also the success of the parent. The program has been highly successful, and test scores have shown significant increases after children and parents have been through the program.

This is the kind of thing our country has to do. Why does it work? Because it puts the family first and gives parents a chance to succeed. It's not true that all poor people are lazy or dumb or want to do wrong. Most of them are good people who want to do right, who feel just as trapped in their circumstances as we know they are. They know something is wrong, they just don't know what to do about it. The most successful family policies will be those that enable parents to succeed. We should always work on that first.

There will be those who fail or those who need help. One of the things we have done in our state is to require every elementary school to have a counselor. It's expensive and most states don't do it. When you hire all those counselors, that's money you could be putting into other teachers' pay, which we know needs to be raised everywhere. But there are so many kids who come into those schools without any kind of role models at all, with no one to turn to, and the counselors can make a difference.

There has to be a role in all of this for individuals and for communities, and I believe we can look to Sweden for a good example. In that country, one that we normally think of as having a highly centralized socialistic bureaucracy, all social programs are community-based, organized, and run with a lot of flexibility to meet the different demands of each community. Why is that important to us? Because if you look at these children, most of them are not going to be reached by the President, the Congress, the governor, or the state legislature. Most of them cannot be helped by money alone. If they come from a family in trouble, no program will work that doesn't have the life and energy of a committed human being behind it.

We must work to make sure parents can impart their dreams to their children. We must see that those children can then carry those dreams into old age. If we do it, the economic future of America will be insured. People will pursue their self-interest, and they will triumph the way we have for 200 years. But, if we continue to neglect the basic human needs of our people, our families will show the strain, and our country will begin to sink. The choice is ours. I think the choice is clear.

REFERENCE

Weizman, L. (1987). *The divorce revolution.* New York: The Free Press.

Chapter 3

Birthing Collaborations in Early Care and Education: A Polemic of Pain and Promise

Sharon Lynn Kagan
Yale University, New Haven, CT

Not only should day care program activities at the Federal level be better coordinated: the Federal government has a major responsibility to encourage and assist more effective coordination of child care services at the state and local levels. (Keyserling, 1972)

We recommend . . . that a small portion of all federal funds for child care, and pre-school educational and related programs and services be earmarked by appropriate legislative or administrative action for allocation to those states, urban counties, and cities that establish in their governmental structures an Office of Child Development, or its equivalents, as an intragovernmental mechanism for the coordination of the full range of child care and development, early education and related health and family service programs. (National Academy of Sciences, 1972)

Reflecting concern about growing fragmentation and discontinuity that characterized the early care and education field, the above prestigious and thoughtful groups bellowed these faintly heard calls for collaboration nearly two decades ago. Then and now, despite widespread recognition of the need for collaboration, it remains an understudied, underimplemented concept. This chapter explores the rationale for, and history of, collaboration, and realistically assesses its utility and potential in early childhood.

Recognized as today's "buzzword" (Benard, 1989), collaborations are burgeoning in profit, nonprofit, and voluntary sectors in our country and abroad. They have captured the attention of researchers, academics, and practitioners in fields as diverse as education, health, psychology, mental health, social work, business, industry, and the arts. Nearly ubiquitous, collaborations know no geographic or disciplinary boundaries. Whether termed partnerships, linkages, coordinating councils, or round tables, the existence of so many collaborative efforts demonstrates that America is at the brink of a practical renaissance regarding how it delivers goods and services.

Nowhere is the press more strongly felt than in the human service field. Fueled by desires to improve the quality and distribution of services, the need for services to be maximally cost-efficient and family-responsive, and the recognition that today's complex needs often transcend traditionally rigid bureaucratic lines, collaborations are emerging with different forms and purposes. In spite of differences, most collaborations are vehicles for joint problem solving and developing the trust and mutual respect that enhance the possibility of successfully addressing increasingly complex issues (Lieberman, 1986). Such widespread interest in collaboration is matched only by widespread differences in attitudes about their potential. Some see collaboration among agencies or organizations as the natural response to a changing zeitgeist, an unavoidable strategy to address the inadequacies of an increasingly bureaucratic and technologically sophisticated social order. Others see collaboration as a potential solution, an inventive and long-absent strategy that minimally addresses, and maximally solves, intractable social service delivery problems. Many whose attitudes fall between are skeptical about collaboration, hoping it fulfills its potential, yet wary of the complex challenges inherent in implementing effective collaborations.

This enigmatic melange of past and present calls for collaboration coupled with healthy skepticism provides significant justification for reflection upon why collaboration recurrently emerges as a social panacea despite its "Pandora's Box" quality. What is the rationale for such broad-based endorsement and what are the implications for early care and education?

THE MANY RATIONALES FOR COLLABORATION

Over 25 years ago, major thinkers recognized the inadequacies of the then-prevailing bureaucratic system and wrote about a new social system they envisioned for the future. They predicted that organizational survival in the post-industrial world would depend less upon competition and more upon the recognition and realization of organizational interdependence (Bennis, 1966). Such dramatic changes were the nearly inevitable responses to emerging organizational and value changes, demographic shifts, and dissatisfaction with extant bureaucracies. In retrospect, their predictions were fairly accurate. The press for collaboration represents a pervasive response to a shifting sociocultural ethos, one hallmarked by changes in the nature of organizations, workers, theoretical perspectives, and social problems and services.

The Changing Nature of Organizations

As Bennis predicted, organizations in today's post-industrial society face a markedly different environment than their predecessors in the preindustrial and industrial periods. Characterized by a slow rate of change, the preindustrial and industrial organizational order was comparatively stable (Appley & Winder, 1977; Bennis, 1966). Such stability supported a hierarchical structure of bureaucracy and enabled managers to focus attention primarily on the internal workings of the organization. Dubbed a "closed system" (Gamm, 1983), this orientation fostered organizational independence where each organization acted in isolation. Organizations competed fiercely among themselves following a value system that incorporated free market competition and Darwin's survival of the fittest theory. Competition was considered healthy because when resources or clients were in short supply, companies were forced to produce better goods and services. Thus, despite comparative societal stability, organizations competed and had no incentive or perceived need to collaborate.

In contrast, turbulence, complexity, and uncertainty characterized the postindustrial society (Appley & Winder, 1977; Bennis, 1966; Emery & Trist, 1973; Trist, 1977). As science and technology advanced, work became more technical and management more complicated. In addition, the increasingly unstable economy of the 1970s, compounded by stricter environmental policies, deregulation, and a dramatic rise in foreign competition demanded new approaches to business. The previously functional closed system became dysfunctional, giving rise to a more open system (Gamm, 1983). Managers recognized the need to anticipate and incorporate external and internal forces in order to be effective. New management techniques required organizations to function inclusively, soliciting collaborative input from all "team" workers. Thus, a realignment of intra- and interorganizational perspectives fostered a new corporate collaborative ethos.

The Changing Nature of Workers

In addition to the external pressures of an increasingly complex and uncertain world, organizations faced internal pressures due to the changing nature of the American worker. The legacy of the civil rights movement not only raised the American consciousness regarding fairness and equity and helped empower the disenfranchised, but it fostered the desire for individual self-worth, involvement, and validation. Interestingly, the values of individual fulfillment, autonomy, cooperation, and participation in decisions (Carew, 1976; Kanter, 1983; Kraus, 1980; Slater, 1970; Trist, 1976) espoused by the civil rights movement were consistent with those supporting collaborative relationships within and among organizations.

Such changes in attitudes are not unrelated to unprecedented increases in worker education (Kanter, 1983). Education instilled confidence and technical expertise in workers so that the new work force began to demand management styles focusing on interactive problem solving and integrative work. Workers had opinions and wanted them recognized. Gradually, research emerged that documented the importance of the interrelationship between the individual and the organization (Brewer & deLeon, 1983; Greenfield, 1973). In fact, the most successful organizations were those where the corporate value system was compatible with employees' personal value systems (Kraus, 1980). In short, motivated by the knowledge that workers wanted to be more involved and by the documented benefits of such involvement, particularly as evidenced in the Japanese work setting, corporate America turned to collaboration, at least in principle.

Changing Theoretical Perspectives

In addition to practical motivations, theoretical advances enhanced commitment to collaboration. Often referred to as the ecological perspective, espoused most ardently by Urie Bronfenbrenner (1979), emphasis solely on the individual gave way to a holistic orientation that stressed the interrelatedness of the individual, the family, and the community. Historically discrete entities (e.g., the worlds of home and work; children's programs and families) became intertwined. Corporate America recognized the need to be concerned about its workers and their families; the child and family replaced the child alone as the unit of intervention in preschool programs. Individuals and businesses focused on interdependence rather than independence.

For those in the human services, the ecological orientation took on special meaning. For some, it became the scapegoat for the intractability of social problems, the rationale for a quagmired system. After all, it was easier to concentrate on one aspect of a problem rather than the whole, to address problems of the individual rather than addressing broad societal problems. For other social scientists and human service deliverers, the ecological orientation unleashed an alternate framework—a systems perspective—for addressing service delivery problems. Understanding that fragmentation, duplication of services, and inequity for clients were the undesirable but inevitable results of the current delivery system, the systems approach called for an integrative strategy that underscored the need for collaboration.

Changing Dimensions of Social Problems and Social Services

Early in the 20th century, stability hallmarked the American Zeitgeist—stability in relationships, occupations, and place of residence. But with increasing technological sophistication, urbanization, and the strengthening of the women's movement, America became more transient. Not only did women seek greater economic independence, but economic recessions and underemployment reduced the ability of families to survive on only one income. The median annual earnings of the head of a family under age 30 with children declined by 39 percent between 1973 and 1986. Despite women's efforts to compensate for the reduced earnings of their spouses, real family income remained below the 1973 levels for over a decade (Rosewater, 1989). Increased divorce rates, escalating numbers of single-parent families, and the feminization of poverty characterized the new demographics. Increased family stress manifested itself in growing annual percentages of child and spousal abuse (National Committee for the Prevention of Child Abuse, 1988; U.S. Bureau of Justice Statistics, 1986) and in increased alcohol and drug abuse (National Institute on Drug Abuse, 1987). Poverty took on dimensions never before evidenced (Ellwood, 1988; Wilson, 1987).

As the magnitude of social problems escalated, so did their complexity. Social problems could not be neatly categorized by bureaucratic agency; they transcended organizational structure. Unable to keep pace with responsibilities assigned them, much less collaborate to address burgeoning social problems, health, welfare, and education systems suffered an onslaught of criticism. A sense of crisis permeated the human service delivery system (Gage, 1976), accompanied by specific accusations of fragmentation, duplication of services, and wasted resources (Gamm, 1983). Reconciling increased costs with decreased performance was a bitter pill an increasingly conservative public would not swallow. Bureaucratic requests for additional funds often fell on the deaf ears of disenchanted and fiscally constrained policy makers.

Faced with a crisis of confidence, critical human and technological resource shortages, and escalating public demands, human service agencies began to think more creatively and turned to collaboration as one means of coping with escalating challenges. For example, schools began collaborating with business and industry so that by 1986, over 40,000 school–business partnerships existed in the nation (Otterbourg & Timpane, 1986). Health and education institutions also formed collaboratives. In nearly every corner of the human service sector, recognition of the limitations of the extant delivery structure and its legacy of inadequate services propelled collaboration forward as a potential antidote to a highly dysfunctional system.

THE IMPETUS TO COLLABORATE IN EARLY CARE AND EDUCATION

Early care and education was at the forefront of the press for collaboration. Though driven by many of the same social, demographic, and political forces, the impetus for collaboration in early childhood is more intense for several reasons. First, social policy has left a legacy of particularly deep-seated fragmentation in this field. Second, the growing attention accorded early care and education in the late 1980s brought the issue front and center: As programs expanded, so did competition for available resources. Third, the field began to realize a collective pedagogical commitment, thereby reducing destructive mistrust. And fourth, new mandates, requiring interagency councils and planning teams, hastened the collaborative ethos of the late 1980s.

A Legacy of Fragmentation

To those close to the field of early care and education and to students of American child and family policy, the fragmentation that characterizes services to our nation's youngest citizens is well known and documented (Kagan, 1989; Scarr & Weinberg, 1986). Such fragmentation is the unfortunate legacy of a policy vision most notably characterized by no cohesive mission or undergirding plan (Steiner, 1981). Lacking political will and an integrated vision, early childhood programs emerged at different times with different purposes. Some, like child care, were designed to meet the needs of working parents. Others, particularly private nursery schools, were established to socialize young children to societal values. Still other programs were initiated in response to crises. The Lanham Act established a comprehensive system of child care so that Rosie the riveter could do her part to assist the World War II effort. Head Start—a mid-1960s response to the nation's war on poverty—was launched with the twin goals of empowering and employing low-income parents, and providing enriched services to their youngsters.

Efforts with such distinct missions naturally generated distinct program guidelines and operational cultures, with the operational result that programs serving children of the same age and family income can and do differ on every nonpedagogical variable: how much funding they receive, who regulates them and to what extent, and to whom and to what degree they are accountable. It is a little-recognized fact that within most communities a given four-year-old from a low-income family could end up in a program (a) that either requires all lead teachers to hold BAs and to be certified in early childhood or requires only high school diplomas of lead teachers; (b) where either the physical setting requires stringent regulation or is exempt from all regulation; (c) where either considerable resources are devoted to staff training and advancement or none are earmarked for this purpose; (d) that is either accountable to an education system or to a welfare department; or (e) that either requires extensive pre-entry health screening or none for program eligibility. These differences have yielded inequitable services for children, families, and programs—particularly in the areas of staffing, regulation, and access.

Staffing. There is no agreement about what level of training or experiential proficiency is necessary to work as a lead teacher or teacher assistant with preschool-aged children. Certification requirements vary not only by state but by program auspices. The National Association for the Education of Young Children (NAEYC), the professional association of the field, is currently working on a model of professional development that should alleviate part of the dilemma, but only part. No matter how clearly roles are specified or certification requirements delineated, until the compensation dilemma is corrected, staffing will remain the critical challenge. Today, the field is nearly paralyzed by a 41 percent annual turnover rate (Whitebook, Howes, & Phillips, 1989). With high salaries, better benefits, and more prestigious positions awaiting workers in other fields, early care and education is left bereft of staff. Staff who do stay in the field are often lured to other programs, often those in schools where salaries and benefits are more favorable, thus exacerbating within-field turnover and fragmentation. Further, because there are no cross-system incentives or comprehensive career ladders that apply in all early care and education settings, staff discontinuity persists, threatening program quality for children.

Regulation. In addition to compelling staffing quandaries, early care and education's different roots and traditions have led to widely varying program guidelines and regulatory inconsistencies (Grubb, 1983; Morgan, 1986; Nelson, 1982). In many states, schools and/or churches are exempt from child care regulation, making it considerably easier and less costly for them to launch new programs. Ironically, it is easier for unregulated programs to open even though data clearly indicate that higher quality is related to higher regulation (Kagan & Newton, 1989; Whitebook, Howes, & Phillips, 1989). Such regulatory inconsistencies do not safeguard quality or assure equal protections, even for all children within one community. They legitimize differences, fuel fragmentation, and beg for a collaborative approach to redress inequity.

Access. The legacy of fragmentation has resulted in unequal access to services for children and to segregation once children are enrolled in programs. Without comprehensive planning, grave inequities exist regarding which children have access to care. Fewer poor children receive early care and education services because there are an insufficient number of subsidized slots to meet need. Particularly oppressive, inequitable access negates research that indicates that low-income children benefit most from early intervention programs. Sadly, those who need services most get them least. Further, once children are enrolled in services, they are segregated by income because program eligibility criteria specify adherence to economic guidelines. And in many communities this income segregation translates into racial segregation. Such inequities compromise program quality for all children and provide an additional impetus for collaboration.

An Intensified Sense of Systemic Pain

While the legacy of fragmentation has always been apparent in the field of early care and education, program expansion in the mid- to late 1980s dramatically intensified competition and acrimony. With the proliferation of support for young children, current and potential providers scrambled for new dollars. And because no scientific knowledge indicates that any single structural entity or program is best suited to administer programs for young children and their families (Sugarman, 1987), the administrative authority for potential new dollars was debated as well. Determined at state and local levels, such decisions led policy makers to face Solomon's quandary: They needed to select between agencies—typically education and human services—with neither being ideal. Such choices of consequence generated anxiety for providers and policy makers, accelerating tensions in the field.

Once a policy decision regarding agency aegis for new programs was made, problems festered at the practice level. Goodman and Brady's (1988) analysis of Head Start and state-funded preschool programs poignantly documents that 44 percent of the reported programs competed for children, 59 percent for staff, 52 percent for space, and 37 percent for all three. When Head Start was the primary program offering services to low-income children, competition, though extant, was less prevalent. However, with state-level pre-kindergarten expansions, most of which are also targeted to low-income youngsters, limited access to space and resources has accelerated competition.

As programs continue to expand in various sectors, these troublesome conditions become increasingly pervasive and difficult to tolerate. The advent of the Family Support Act of 1988, with its provisions for enhanced child care services for low-income parents enrolled in training or employment, poses serious space, staff, and supply problems for the entire field. Gradually, the field is coming to realize that no program is immune. Like an amoeba, the child care and early education community reforms itself with each new piece of legislation. Yet, in the 1990s, there is a growing sense that no single program will be able to solve the challenges independently. So pervasive, they affect all providers and beckon collaborative solutions.

Growing Commonality Within the Field

Though badly fragmented from policy and regulatory perspectives, early care and education is coming together pedagogically. After decades of debate, the field has reached consensus on what constitutes quality and has codified its practices in a widely read volume, *Developmentally Appropriate Practices* (DAP) (Bredekamp, 1987). Quality criteria for early childhood programs, irrespective of sponsorship or auspices, have been amassed and translated into a voluntary certification program, the Center Accreditation Project (CAP). Head Start, school-based, and profit and nonprofit programs have all participated in this credentialing program. Serving as catalysts for programs to acknowledge their similarities, DAP and CAP are revolutionizing the field. No longer biased by preconceived judgments or program stereotypes, early childhood professionals are beginning to speak the same pedagogical language and to value their common core. Such steps bode well and provide additional incentives for collaboration.

Mandate

Recognizing that systemic problems plague the field, some federal and state legislation has required the establishment of collaborative mechanisms in the form of interagency councils and committees. For example, P.L. 99-457 calls for state-level interagency councils. In some states, these groups have been augmented by local-level coordinating bodies. In Florida, the Department of Health and Rehabilitative Services has funded several projects to promote local interagency councils that hasten the delivery of special education services to very young children.

Mandates have been beneficial for several reasons. First, they have helped to legitimize collaboration as a worthwhile and important endeavor. Second, when mandates are accompanied by a funding appropriation to expend staff time and resources on building cross-agency bridges, the functional efficacy of the collaboration is enhanced. From preliminary analysis, mandates seem to be most successful when an ethos for collaboration predates the formal mandate and when resources are allocated to support it (Kagan, Lonow, & Levin, 1989). Learning from these experiences, much pending legislation calls for cross-agency collaboration, with some specifying the precise form (interagency agreement, interagency councils) and others leaving such strategic decisions to states and/or municipalities. Whether given life primarily because of need, desire, or mandate, collaborations in early care and eduction are gaining currency. Just what are they doing and what are they accomplishing?

EARLY CARE AND EDUCATION COLLABORATIONS IN ACTION

Though still fragile, early care and education collaborations take the form of community councils, advisory groups, task forces, commissions, and resource and referral centers. While they vary dramatically on most operational characteristics (size, resources, staff, longevity, real and perceived power within the community), typically they aim to accomplish one or more of the following goals: (a) to increase the quantity and quality of available services, (b) to ensure more equitable distribution of services, (c) to minimize expenses and service duplication, (d) to address staff and space shortages, (e) to equalize regulations across early childhood programs, (f) to improve training opportunities, and (g) to build public support and advocacy for early care and education.

To meet these goals, collaborations may sponsor or seed a variety of activities: Some sponsor joint training for Head Start, child care, and school staff; some jointly buy materials and supplies; some develop community-wide data collection mechanisms; some garner private support to fund resource and referral systems; some develop short- and long-term planning procedures and advocacy strategies; and some address regulatory inconsistencies. In short, collaborations tend to tailor their activities to meet specific goals, usually addressing service needs or attuning the service delivery system's capacity to function more cohesively and efficiently.

As idiosyncratic as their activities appear, collaborations do share certain characteristics. Like children, all collaborations seem to pass through predictable developmental stages. For collaborations, these include formation, conceptualization, development, implementation, evaluation, and termination/reformation. But, like children, collaborations pass through the stages at different rates. Their normal development, like children's, is affected by hosts of mediating variables. For children, the variables that mediate development include intelligence, family income, birth order, and family stability, to mention a few. For collaborations, mediating variables include goals, resources, and the distribution of power and authority. To better understand collaborations in action, a description of their common developmental stages and the mediating variables that affect their implementation is presented.

Developmental Stages

While authors use different nomenclature to classify the stages through which collaborations pass, when codified, six stages seem to best delineate the process. Four stages—formation, conceptualization, development, and implementation—have been labeled by Flynn and Harbin (1987); two additional stages—evaluation and termination—described by Brewer and deLeon (1983) round out the process. While progression through the stages is typically linear, a change in mission or direction, or a review of the collaborative structure may necessitate a transition back to a previous stage (Flynn & Harbin, 1987). Further, while these stages appear discrete, in reality there is considerable overlap between them.

Formation. During the formative stage, the idea for collaboration is born and its general domain identified. Also, the collaboration explores the viability of its vision, in part by determining if the collaboration will threaten organizational "turf" (Lippitt & Van Til, 1981). Membership is determined.

Conceptualization. The conceptualization phase is reached when the collaboration's participants adopt a formal policy statement of goals and objectives. Theorists agree that strong collaborations typically develop clear definitions of member and team roles at this point (Flynn & Harbin, 1987; Lippitt & Van Til, 1981; O'Connell, 1985).

Development. The third stage involves translating the vision, goals, and objectives into concrete strategies. Completing the initial planning cycle, this phase focuses on developing the concrete strategies that convert philosophy to practice. Groups create structures, identify work tasks, and determine responsible parties and timelines for work accomplishment.

Implementation. Having successfully passed through the first three stages, the collaboration puts its plans into action at administrative and service delivery levels.

Evaluation. The evaluation process compares performance levels to expectations; it assesses the relationship between goals and results. Typically such evaluation needs to consider the adequacy of the efforts, to determine if sufficient resources were delivered to solve the problem and if the results achieved warranted the expenditure (Brewer & deLeon, 1983).

Termination/Reformation. Termination means that the collaboration as it has come to exist is ended, either as the result of successful resolution of the initial problem or failure of the collaboration to achieve benefits that outweigh the costs. In the termination phase, plans are made to end the collaboration or to reconstitute it with fresh missions and objectives.

Mediating Variables

While such developmental stages are helpful as predictors for those who are engaged in collaborative work or as descriptors for analysts studying collaboration, neither group would suggest that developmental stages alone account for the complexity of collaborations in action. As suggested earlier, collaborations' passage through these stages is dramatically affected by a set of variables that mediate the pace and effectiveness of the natural developmental trajectory. And it is this intersection of the developmental stages with important mediating variables (goals, resources, and power and authority) that helps account for the rich variation evidenced in active collaborations.

Goals. Agreeing on common goals is the most important single step a collaboration takes. Although goals typically emanate from a mutually identified need, not all parties (particularly if the collaboration has diverse representation) will agree. Reaching satisfactory consensus is critical from the process and product perspectives. Before intense work can successfully proceed, agreement on a common product is necessary. And because discussions of goals are often held in the early collaborative stages, the process used can set the tone for ongoing collaborative interactions. Goal setting, while laborious, must be deliberative and handled with sensitivity.

Resources. Broadly defined, resources are categorized as fiscal, physical, or human. Clearly, collaborations vary dramatically in the amount of resources in each category. While it would be quite natural to assume that the more plentiful the resources, the more effective the collaboration, in fact there is little agreement in the literature to support this hypothesis (Kraus, 1980). Experience does suggest that some resources are necessary to sustain the collaboration and that ideally all parties should contribute to the collaboration. Such contributions fortify the commitment to the collaborative enterprise, as well as provide enhanced means to carry out the mission. Not only the resources themselves, but the pooling of resources is considered to have profound influence on the collaborative process (Dunkle & Nash, 1989; Flynn & Harbin, 1987).

Power and Authority. A critical variable that mediates the trajectory of the collaboration is the distribution of power and authority among the members of the collaboration, and the collective power of the collaboration when compared with other collectives (agencies, task forces, etc.). One important source of power is access to or control over resources. Organizations lacking resources are more likely to seek out collaborative relationships than those who are resource-rich. Beyond resources, expertise, information, and access are potent sources of power within the collaborative relationship. An organization may possess recognized expertise about the issue at hand, may control part of the public policy process by virtue of previous connections, or may be in a position to oppose the project (Gray & Hay, 1986). Being an initiator of the collaboration is a further source of power.

Theorists believe that in an ideal collaboration, the goal is egalitarian sharing of power and authority among the group members. This power sharing may be achieved in several ways: task division, information sharing, trust building, and involving implementors in the decision-making processes. But by far the most important dimension of power and authority is the role of the leader. Collaborations seem to thrive when leadership is facilitative and when it is shared or even rotated among members. How collaborations deal with issues of power and authority, resources, and mandates directly influences the pace and direction of their work.

EARLY CARE AND EDUCATION COLLABORATIONS: NEXT STEPS

Amplify Knowledge of the Collaborative Process

Although collaborations are gaining currency in practice, we are far from fully understanding their processes and evaluating their potential for the field. Several important steps must be taken if we are to move in that direction. First, frameworks for analysis of models, like the one suggested above that integrates developmental stages and mediating variables, must be created and applied so that information is systematically garnered and evaluated. To do this, greater financial support for studying collaborations in early care and education must be obtained.

Second, we need to build on the repertoire of past knowledge. The Child Care Coordinating Councils and Project Developmental Continuity, now largely defunct in their original form, focused on cross-agency collaboration and yielded important, though underpopularized, lessons. In addition to retrieving and reassessing this information, we must understand current collaborations within their own context and incorporate the growing body of new knowledge from the field of organizational development.

Moreover, specific information about the current functioning of early care and education collaborations is necessary: How do they function, what influences their functioning, and what is the relationship between how they function and their impact? We need to understand what types of collaborations work under what conditions. We need to better understand what motivates groups to collaborate: Is it "systemic pain"—the inability to carry out responsibilities—or is it the lure of "building the better mousetrap?" Until such investigations are conducted in early care and education, newly emerging collaborations will have difficulty building upon past collaborative experiences.

Reach Consensus on Definition

Great ambiguity surrounds the definition of collaboration. Most often confounded with its kindred terms, cooperation and coordination, some writers and/or groups use the terms interchangeably (e.g., The American Psychological Association, 1988, and the United States Department of Education, 1986, classify collaboration as a synonym "used for" cooperation). Others suggest that differences are characterized by spheres of influence. For example, Elder and Magrab (1980) define coordination as cooperative efforts within an agency, and collaboration as coordinated efforts across agencies.

The most prevalent view is that cooperation, coordination, and collaboration constitute a hierarchy or ladder (Black & Kase, 1963; Elder & Magrab, 1980; Hord, 1986; Morgan, 1985; Stafford, Rog, & Vander Meer, 1984). Definitional clarity is most pristine at the base of the hierarchy where, it is generally agreed, *cooperation* involves informal personal relationships that exist without clearly defined structures and without the pooling of resources or power (Hord, 1986). Confusion surrounding the distinction between the next two hierarchical levels— *coordination* and *collaboration*—revolves around differences in (a) intensity of joint planning, with collaborations involving more, and (b) differences in attitudes about shared power, with some defining collaboration as a "cooperative venture based on shared power and authority" (Kraus, 1980).

In any domain, definitional ambiguity must be clarified before advances can be made. This is particularly true in the collaborative domain because so many disciplines, each with their own views and languages, are involved.

Develop a True Policy Commitment

The quotations that opened this chapter demonstrate that the press for federal commitments to collaboration was evident nearly two decades ago. Little has happened in the ensuing years to counter those recommendations. In fact, as this chapter has shown, much has happened to underscore their veracity and import.

But a true policy commitment must go deeper than earmarking a "small portion" of federal dollars for this purpose. Providing modest support for coordination alone will doom these efforts. One has only to look at the history of 4-C to recognize that the paltry allocation of $9,000 per site coupled with insufficient technical support was never adequate incentive, let alone funding, to mount the herculean tasks assigned these sites. Reflecting these sentiments, the National Academy of Sciences Report (1972) declared, "It is a great tribute to the social-mindedness and dedication of large numbers of local people that, despite lack of federal support, so much 4-C leadership and useful activity materialized as did" (p. 39).

Yes, a portion of all federal and state dollars must be spent on collaboration, but the portion must be adequate to the task. Collaborative support must be garnered to initiate and sustain collaborations and to provide incentives to address the infrastructural ills that precipitate the need for collaboration in the first place.

Beyond dollars, there is a tremendous need for a new policy ethos that accords respect and autonomy to local and state collaborative processes. Currently, regulatory provisions are so inflexible that efforts to redress systemic inconsistencies flounder. Arcane program regulations prohibit programs from expanding to full-day services despite collaborative assessments that document such need. To create collaborations and then deprive them of the right to implement their work mocks the process and the product, ensuring their eventual demise. Simply sanctioning collaboration without fully supporting it guarantees that 20 years from now we will still be reading obscure quotes. The old adage, "The more things change, the more they stay the same" will still be true. Our charge is immediate. We must collectively acknowledge that, though filled with pain and promise, collaboration is the necessary birthright of an equitable system of early care and education.

REFERENCES

American Psychological Association. (1988). *Thesaurus of psychological index terms* (5th ed.). Washington, DC: Author.

Appley, D. G., & Winder, A. E. (1977, July-August-September). Introduction [Special issue]. *Journal of Applied Behavioral Science, 13*(3), 264–267.

Benard, B. (1989, October). Working together: Principles of effective collaboration. *Prevention Forum, 10*(1), 4–9.

Bennis, W. G. (1966). *Changing organizations: Essays on the development and evolution of human organization.* New York: McGraw-Hill.

Black, B. J., & Kase, H. M. (1963, March). Interagency cooperation in rehabilitation and mental health. *Social Service Review, 37*(1), 26–32.

Bredekamp, S. (Ed.). (1987). *Developmentally appropriate practices in early childhood programs serving children from birth through age 8.* Washington, DC: National Association for the Education of Young Children.

Brewer, G. D., & deLeon, P. (1983). *The foundations of policy analysis.* Chicago: The Dorsey Press.

Bronfenbrenner, U. (1979). *The ecology of human development: Experiments by nature and design.* Cambridge MA: Harvard University Press.

Carew, D. K. (1976). *Some necessary values: Toward collaborative organizations.* Unpublished manuscript. University of Massachusetts.

Dunkle, M., & Nash, M. (1989, March 15). Creating effective interagency collaboratives. *Education Week, 8*(25), 44.

Elder, J. O., & Magrab, P. R. (1980). *Coordinating services to handicapped children: A handbook for interagency collaboration.* Baltimore: Paul H. Brookes.

Ellwood, D. T. (1988). *Poor support: Poverty in the American family.* New York: Basic Books.

Emery, F. E., & Trist, E. L. (1973). *Towards a social ecology.* New York: Plenum Press.

Flynn, C. C., & Harbin, G. L. (1987). Evaluating interagency coordination efforts using a multidimensional interactional, developmental paradigm. *RASE, 8*(3), 35–44.

Gage, R. W. (1976, Winter). Integration of human services delivery systems. *Public Welfare, 34*(1), 27–32.

Gamm, L. D. (1983, October). Interorganizational relations and the management of voluntary health organizations. In M. S. Moyer (Ed.), *Managing voluntary organizations: Proceedings of a conference held at York University* (pp. 25–43). Toronto, Canada.

Goodman, I. F., & Brady, J. P. (1988). *The challenge of coordination.* Newton, MA: Education Development Center, Inc.

Gray, B., & Hay, T. (1986). Political limits to interorganizational consensus and change. *The Journal of Applied Behavioral Sciences, 22*(2), 95–112.

Greenfield, T. B. (1973). Organizations as social inventions: Rethinking assumptions about change. *Journal of Applied Behavioral Sciences, 9*(5), 551–573.

Grubb, E. B. (1983). Day-care regulation: Legal and policy issues. *Santa Clara Law Review, 25,* 303–374.

Hord, S. M. (1986). A synthesis of research on organizational collaboration. *Educational Leadership, 43*(5), 22–26.

Kagan, S. L. (1989). Early care and education: Tackling the tough issues. *Phi Delta Kappan, 70*(6), 433–439.

Kagan, S. L., Lonow, D., & Levin, J. (1989). *An overview of collaboration in three states.* Unpublished manuscript.

Kagan, S. L., & Newton, J. (1989). For-profit and nonprofit child care: Similarities and differences. *Young Children, 45*(1), 4–10.

Kanter, R. M. (1983). *The change masters.* New York: Simon & Schuster.

Keyserling, M. D. (1972). *Windows on day care* (A report on findings of the National Council of Jewish Women). New York: National Council of Jewish Women.

Kraus, W. A. (1980). *Collaborations in organizations.* New York: Human Sciences Press.

Lieberman, A. (1986, February). Collaborative work. *Educational Leadership.* pp. 4–6.

Lippitt, R., & Van Til, J. (1981, July-December). Can we achieve a collaborative community? Issues, imperatives, potentials. *Journal of Voluntary Action Research* [Special issue: Interagency Collaboration], *10*(3–4), 7–17.

Morgan, G. (1986). *The national state of child care regulation 1986.* Watertown, MA: Work/Family Directions.

Morgan, J. (1985, April). *Putting the pieces together: Making interagency collaboration work. Preschool interagency council: A model.* Tallahassee: Florida State Department of Education. (ERIC Document Reproduction Service No. ED 296 507).

National Committee for the Prevention of Child Abuse. (1988, April). *Newsletter.* Author.

National Academy of Sciences. (1972). *Report of the panel on the assessment of the community coordinated child care program.* Washington, DC: National Academy of Sciences, National Research Council, Division of Behavioral Sciences.

National Institute on Drug Abuse. (1987). *National trends in drug use and related factors among American high school students and young adults.* Washington, DC: U.S. Government Printing Office.

Nelson, J. R., Jr. (1982). The federal interagency day care requirements. In C. D. Hayes (Ed.), *Making policies for children: A study of the federal process* (pp. 151–205). Washington, DC: National Academy Press.

O'Connell, C. (1985). *How to start a school/business partnership.* Bloomington, IN: Phi Delta Kappa Educational Foundation.

Otterbourg, S. D., & Timpane, M. (1986). Partnerships and schools. In P. Davis (Ed.), *Public-private partnerships: Improving urban life* (pp. 60–73). New York: Academy of Political Science.

Rosewater, A. (1989). Child and family trends: Beyond the numbers. In F. J. Macchiarola & A. Gartner (Eds.), *Caring for America's children* (pp. 4–19). New York: Academy of Political Science.

Scarr, S., & Weinberg, R. A. (1986, October). The early childhood enterprise: Care and education of the young. *American Psychologist, 41*(10), 1140–1146.

Slater, P. (1970). *The pursuit of loneliness: American culture at the breaking point.* Boston: Beacon Press.

Stafford, B. G., Rog, D., & Vander Meer, P. (1984, June). *A review of literature on coordination, an annotated bibliography and a survey of other collaborative efforts.* Nashville: Tennessee Children's Services Commission. (ERIC Document Reproduction Service No. ED 251 235).

Steiner, G. Y. (1981). *The futility of family policy.* Washington, DC: The Brookings Institute.

Sugarman, J. M. (1987). *Institutionalizing child development activities* (Draft concept paper for Department of Social and Health Services). Olympia, WA.

Trist, E. (1977, July-August-September). Collaboration in work settings: A personal perspective [Special issue]. *Journal of Applied Behavioral Science, 13*(3), 268–278.

Trist, E. (1976). Toward a postindustrial culture. In M. Dunnetter (Ed.), *Handbook of industrial and organizational psychology* (pp. 1011–1033). Chicago: Rand-McNally.

U.S. Bureau of Justice Statistics. (1986, August). *Preventing domestic violence against women* (Special Report). Washington, DC: Author.

U.S. Department of Education. (1986). *Thesaurus of ERIC descriptors* (10th ed.). Phoenix, AZ: Oryx Press.

Whitebook, M., Howes, C., & Phillips, D. (1989). *Who cares? Child care teachers and the quality of care in America* (Executive Summary, National Child Care Staffing Study). Oakland, CA: Child Care Employee Project.

Wilson, W. J. (1987). *The truly disadvantaged: The inner city, the underclass and public policy.* Chicago: University of Chicago Press.

Chapter 4
Beyond the Sandbox: State Issues In Early Childhood Education*

Robert A. Cervantes
Assistant Superintendent, Child Development Division, California
State Department of Education, Sacramento, CA

INTRODUCTION

Child care and child development issues—once relegated to the back-waters of the social, economic, and educational discussions—are now part of the public policy agenda. Driven principally by social and economic forces such as birthrates, dual and single working parents, and school and welfare reform, child care has generated a great deal of local and national attention. Increasingly the public is questioning their state's role in providing child care and child development programs. Extensive media coverage, state and federal public policy debate regarding the purposes, needs, types, and funding for early childhood education, and child care programs increasingly occupy our attention. Various federal government proposals promise to keep the debate lively. The decade of the 1980s represents the recognition that effective child development programs can ameliorate the many difficulties faced by young children. The decade of the 1990s will determine if states can put into practice this recognition.

* The views expressed are solely those of the author and do not necessarily represent those of the California State Department of Education.

The purpose of this chapter is to contribute to the dialogue, and hopefully, provide clarity on child care as a state policy issue. A brief synthesis of early childhood education programs in California is presented first and is followed by a brief discussion of imperatives for child care and development, review of some significant research, and discussion of delivery systems policy issues. I begin with the California experience because of its history and comprehensive system of child care and development programs. However, this is not so much a reiteration of California's programs as it is a challenge to other states to profit by our experience as they visualize and work to meet their child care and child development needs.

HISTORY OF CALIFORNIA CHILD DEVELOPMENT PROGRAMS

California history of providing child care services formally began with the Parent Participation Preschool Program established in 1929. This was followed by the enactment of the Child Care Center Program for the care of children of working mothers during World War II, which was funded by the federal Lanham Act of 1943 and was also administered by the State Department of Education. After World War II the Child Care Center Program was continued through state funding.

The 1962 amendments to the Social Security Act (Title IV-A) provided new federal funding for the expansion of child care services in California. A decade later, the California Legislature passed the Child Development Act providing significant new state funding for expansion of child care and development programs. This bill also formally established the State Department of Education as the single State agency responsible for the administration of child care and development programs throughout the State of California. Under its jurisdiction the Department consolidated several programs administered by other state agencies. Subsequently, in 1981, the State Legislature "bought out" the Federal Title XX (formerly Title IV-A) funds and replaced it entirely with State general funds. California now has the largest child care and child development system in the nation. Program funding currently amounts to approximately $342 million for direct child care and development services.

California's programs resulted from progressive legislative action spanning some 60 years. The demand for child care and development programs will nevertheless continue to grow because of the increasing need of children and families and increasing evidence of research demonstrating the effectiveness of these programs. The recognized value becomes more apparent when one considers the social, economic, and educational benefits of early intervention. Children who receive high-quality age-appropriate social, cognitive, physical, and intellectual skills development in their preschool years will generally achieve higher levels of educational attainment than nonparticipants. Concurrently, preschool child care and development programs allow low-income families, and in particular single heads of household, to either work or enroll in a job training program, thus enabling them to become economic contributors rather than economic dependents. Indeed we have found that access to state subsidized child care and development is the key difference between working and being on welfare. Most important, the programs promote family stability by providing a safe and nurturing environment not otherwise available for children of low-income parents.

We have learned over the years that it is critical to understand two significant points when discussing child care development programs. First, program quality, which consists of a trained, committed staff, appropriate developmental and sequential instruction, appropriate ratios, a safe and nurturing environment, health and nutrition components, parental support services, and strong management and fiscal accountability, is critical to success. Second, an early investment in child development pays significant social and economic benefits in addition to educational dividends. A summary of California's Child Care and Development programs is presented in Table 4.1.

Eligibility for services for the typical family, a single mother with two preschool children, consists of an income means test of 84 percent of the State median income, or in this case an income of just under $24,000 annually. Parent fees on a sliding scale are also assessed generating another $4 million that in turn is used to provide additional services to children. Some programs provide services regardless of income such as for teen parents (the School-Age Parenting and Infant program), and protective services for abused and neglected children. The Resource and Referral program services are available to the entire public at no cost. Public entities such as school districts, city and county governments, and private nonprofit agencies provide children's services under an annual contract. Currently some 414 public agency contractors serve 60 percent of the children while some 651 private nonprofit providers serve 40 percent of the children. A strong mix of agencies, I believe, is a major strength of the California model, albeit the incidence of oversight is greater for private nonprofit agencies.

Table 4.1.   Summary of Major Programs

Program	Focus	Funding (in millions)	Children Served
General Child Care (Schools)	Center-based child development	$145.3	37,620
General Child Care (Private Agencies)	Center-based child development	65.4	13,640
State Preschool	Part-day child development	36.7	21,240
Alternative Payment	Vendor-voucher program for day care home or center-based care	28.2	5,880
Latchkey	Before & after school care	15.5	15,000
Campus	On-campus care	11.1	3,760
School-Age Parenting	Counseling, parenting education, and child care for teen parents	7.3	3,200
Family Child Care Homes	Child care in family day care homes	7.3	1,200
Company Welfare Departments	Vendor program care in family day care or center	6.5	2,700
State Migrant	Child care for settled migrants	7.8	2,330
Federal Migrant	Child care for current migrants	2.1	788
Protective Services	Voucher program for actual or potentially abused, neglected, or exploited children	1.1	2,307
Resource & Referral	Child Care Information and Referral	7.8	NA
Total:		$342.0M	109,665

SPECTRUM OF CHILDREN'S SERVICES

Children's services programs are known by many names: child care, child development, State Preschool, and Head Start are often heard. In reality the names are more often representative of program intent and funding source rather than specific developmental content. They contain great similarities and differences. The State Preschool program in California is a half-day educational program primarily for 4-year children and is quite similar to the Federal Head Start program. Child development center-based programs are also characterized as educational programs. These are full-day programs of about 9 hours composed of varied social-emotional, cognitive, and physical developmental activities. Child care programs are similar to child development but often characterized as less rigorous in curriculum and staff qualifications requirements. One representation of these programs is presented in Figure 4.1.

As evidenced by this representation there are great variations in program thrust and characteristics. Custodial care, it is generally agreed, is the least desirable. It consists both of informal and formal (ongoing) care of a child without emphasis on developmental activities though provided in a safe environment. Custodial care all too often consists of self-play or television-watching. Formal child care is characterized by a state license and structured developmental activities— which vary in quality and content—and staff with varied formal training. Child development programs by contrast usually have high staff-to-children ratios, strong emphasis on an educational program that is age and developmentally appropriate, and they are directed at fostering a child's social-emotional, cognitive, and gross and fine motor coordination. Key staff such as teachers and site directors hold teaching credentials. These types of programs are most often wholly supported by State funds.

Again, it is important to stress that there is overlap between child care and child development programs. A high-quality child care program often resembles a child development program. The key criterion

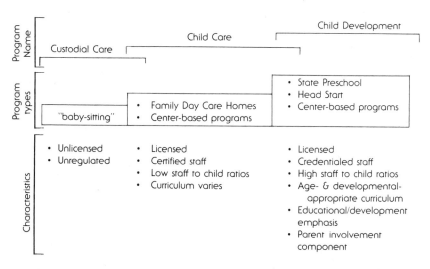

Figure 4.1. Child Care and Development Program Representation

and determinate of a program regardless of name is the sustained presence of quality indicators such as:

1. A safe and nurturing environment.
2. Formally trained, committed, and motivated staff.
3. Use of age and developmentally appropriate activities to enhance a child's social-emotional, cognitive, language, and fine and gross motor skills.
4. Family support and involvement such as parent education and support services referral.
5. Strong fiscal and program management.

IMPERATIVES FOR EARLY CHILDHOOD EDUCATION

Increasingly, the public is demanding to know what states are doing to meet the child care needs. With rare exception, state efforts in developing policies and programs are modest if they exist at all. In large part, the demand for an articulate state role appears largely attributed to the changing condition of children and families. While children have opportunities that were unthinkable several decades ago, they also face an array of new social and economic problems. There is an increasing number of children who are experiencing poverty, and who come from families with drug and alcohol problems and single-parent households. Conversely, the majority of America's children are healthier and more affluent, and they complete more years of schooling. The fact of the matter is that in this nation there is a bipolar group of children: advantaged and disadvantaged. These conditions are often traceable to the economic status and educational opportunities and achievement of children's parents. In California, for example, despite general economic affluence, an increasing number of children live in poverty. The poverty rate has doubled from 1969 to 1987 (Kirst, 1988). Among Hispanic children the poverty rate is five times that of white children (California State Department of Education, 1987). A recent comprehensive report on the condition of children in California (Kirst, 1988) found that:

- 15 percent of babies born in public hospitals are drug- or alcohol-addicted.
- 50 percent of all children will live in a single parent household before their 18th birthday.
- 25 percent of children are born to an unmarried mother. (The rate is 50 percent for black children.)

- 37 percent of mothers with children under 6 years old work; 54 percent of mothers with children 6 to 14 years also work.

These problems, of course, have dire economic, social, and educational consequences. States responsive to these problems have generally utilized a variety of social welfare services. Educational institutions are increasingly called upon to carry a major responsibility through a multiplicity of nutrition and categorical programs.

Responding to child care and development needs is a difficult task for government. The issue begs the question of the juxtaposition of individual needs with government interest. In effect, should the government provide such services, and, if so, in what manner and form? State and local governments provide for the safety and welfare of their citizens in any number of ways as evidenced through fire and police protection, planning and environmental ordinances, public education, and a variety of social service programs. States have standards for licensing of homes for the elderly, for hospitals, and child care in centers and homes. Given that the welfare and safety or "public trust" function is provided for, should government become involved in the direct funding and support of child care and development services? The question is indeed real and important, but the answer is largely academic. In my view a public trust function goes beyond providing and protecting the "public good," but also enhances the quality of life. Put another way, poverty, welfare, and undereducation are expensive in two ways: (a) The public foots the bill for social services, criminal justice costs, and a variety of remedial programs; (b) the victims of poverty do not contribute economically. Recent research provides telling evidence that poverty and its effects dollar-wise and in human cost is indeed dire. The extent to which government seeks to go beyond protecting the public to include support of services such as child care and development programs is to enhance life opportunities and the quality of life. Viewed from this perspective "child care" is a family-maintenance, social, educational, and economic issue that government cannot afford to ignore.

POLICY PERSPECTIVES ON CHILD CARE AND DEVELOPMENT

Of major significance to policy makers is understanding the consequences of a social-welfare versus educational development perspective. The matter is of critical importance in that a social-welfare perspective will invariably drive the establishment of a certain type of children's services—primarily custodial-type child care. By contrast an educational and developmental perspective will generally lead to early intervention and enrichment programs via child development. Child development programs have proven effective in enhancing the social, educational, and economic opportunities of poor children in overcoming problems that often result in school failure. While child care programs provide a valuable service and have their place, publicly supported programs must be comprehensive and incorporate quality child development to prevent further erosion of protection, service, and opportunity to children who otherwise are without voice. Without question states will face this issue. An investment in child development will provide a return on that investment, and is most certainly worth doing right with quality standards even at the risk of having smaller programs. An investment in a quality, developmental- and age-appropriate curriculum is a worthy investment.

ECONOMICS OF EARLY INTERVENTION

There is strong evidence that early intervention beginning in preschool is a good economic investment. In brief: Intervention is cost-effective as compared to remediation. The difference is literally in the millions of dollars and hundreds of thousands in life opportunities.

The acclaimed Perry Preschool Program study (Clements, Schweinhart, et al., 1984) is a classic example of the documented economic benefits of early intervention. In this study, some 100 poor minority children took part. Few of the children's parents had completed high school, over half came from homes with a single parent, and all were poor. Half of the children were placed in a preschool program, the other half were not. The preschool program consisted of a half-day program with intellectual (cognitive) and social development activities and home visitations for each school year for five years. A 20-year followup revealed that program participants as compared to nonparticipants had: higher high school graduation rates (32%), higher employment, vocational training and college attendance rates (50%), lower teen pregnancy rates (50%), and lower arrest rates (40%). The economic benefits were estimated at $1:4, that is every $1.00 invested saved $4.00.

A somewhat similar 15 year followup study (Lally & Mangione, 1986) conducted in Syracuse produced equally dramatic results. In this case, a followup of 65 participants in an early intervention preschool as compared to 54 children in a control group revealed dramatic differences in criminal justice costs, self-control, achievement, and positive attitude. The program participants significantly outperformed nonparticipants. The criminal justice cost difference was $10.00 for nonparticipants as compared to $1.00 for program participants.

A provocative study by Robledo (1986) on the cost for school dropouts provides compelling data for intervention. Basically, the study examined the social-welfare cost of 86,000 school dropouts in Texas as compared to the cost of providing intervention programs to keep them in school and sending a representative proportion to college. The social-welfare cost to the public for these students was: Criminal justice, $367.8 million; Welfare, $253.7 million; Remedial and Vocational Training, $12.9 million; Unemployment Insurance, $17.6 million; dollar loss in income taxes, $16.9 million—for a total of $17.5 billion or over $200,000 per dropout. School failure for whatever reason is an expensive proposition. The cost to help these students stay in school and go to college was $1.9 billion. In other words, the cost-benefit ratio of a comprehensive intervention program is $1:9. These studies and an increasing body of literature clearly suggest that early childhood intervention is a viable alternative to produce a literate and productive body of citizens.

DELIVERY SYSTEM ISSUES

The funding, oversight, and administration of child care and development programs from a state perspective invariably involve the so-called "delivery system"—that is, the structural or organizational configuration by which programs are funded and regulated, and services are delivered at the community level. The issue is important since a "delivery system" defines organizational relationships.

State Administration

In most states the administration of child care and development programs is part of either a social service or a state education department. Placement is strategic and often defines the visibility, priority, and thrust of local programs. In the case of California, subsidized child care and development are administered by the Department of Education. This has resulted over the years with strong emphasis on program content, particularly age and developmentally appropriate activities, prescriptive staffing ratios, high teacher qualifications, strong oversight and program quality, and articulation with schools. Nonsubsidized private programs fall under the jurisdiction of the Department of Social Services which limits oversight to licensing and complaint investigation. In the latter case there is no monitoring for program quality, staffing requirements and qualification are significantly less, and program technical assistance does not occur.

In California, the bifurcation between state subsidized child care and development programs under the Department of Education versus private-profit programs under the Department of Social Services is historical and unlikely to change given vested interest in early intervention versus a social service orientation. This need not be that way in other states. Optimally, a state "children's services" organization should be able to administer both subsidized and nonsubsidized programs. What is critical to that determination is a state's policy view of child care and development programs as either a "market services" program or an early education intervention program. The former concept lends itself to minimal oversight (generally licensing), while the latter requires extensive technical assistance, development of a variety of intervention strategies in instruction, curriculum and staffing and training. My experience has been that both types of nonsubsidized free market programs and state subsidized programs provide vital services. Subsidized programs, however, by definition focus on serving single working mothers, and providing badly needed early intervention services for at-risk children in locations unserved by private providers. In the latter case, programs with a strong educational component are a must and these children have been well served by our State Department of Education.

Funding

No issue hits at the heart (or more appropriately the purse strings) of public policy than funding. If social and economic lessons have taught us anything, it is that child care and child development programs are not cheap. The point in fact is that the public and policy makers alike must understand that they get what they pay for. Programs that are marginally funded invariably result in poor program quality, high staff turnover, and public dissatisfaction. Conversely, adequately funded programs are stable, continually build on their experience and program quality, and provide an array of support services to aid families' maintenance. High-quality programs generate their own success.

Determining adequate funding levels is a difficult task. A good baseline is to assess, via a survey, the "private market rates" accounting for variations in hours, part- and full-time care, child-to-adult ratios, and teacher backgrounds and education. Assessing program quality is also a must and a variety of observational instruments are available. These instruments generally assess the nature of the developmental program (i.e., curriculum), support services, teacher–child and adult–child ratios, health and safety, nutrition programs, parent education and the like. Programs that go beyond basic "child care" and provide an age and developmentally appropriate curriculum and these other services will cost more, but the benefit to the child and parents is significantly greater as evidenced by the research.

In California the funding rate for subsidized center-based programs is $20.53 per day (adjusted annually for the cost-of-living); the part-day program such as State Preschool and Campus program average $11 per day; Family Day Care averages $18 per day; and Latchkey programs about $15 per day. There are also funding adjustments for special needs children such as non-English speaking and exceptional-needs children such as physically handicapped. A recent comparison between publicly subsidized and private programs found little difference in rates. There is, however, great funding variability within programs. For example, school district operated programs pay higher salaries but also provide facilities and support services at no or reduced cost. By contrast, private programs pay teachers less, but have high facilities, insurance, and physical plant cost.

Affordability and Accessibility

The issue of funding aside for a moment, the companion issue of accessibility must be considered. The fact of the matter is that neither in California, nor anywhere else in the nation to my knowledge, are there sufficient programs in existence to meet the needs of the public. Programs are simply inaccessible because there are so few and many are expensive thus driving many desperate parents to use "underground" unregulated programs with often disastrous results.

In California only 9 percent of the children in need who meet the state income test are being served. This figure is arrived at by factoring out of the state's child population, birth to five years old, those served by federal Head Start, the private market programs, other social services, and those making self-care provisions. Three-year waiting lists are common. To effectively put in place a comprehensive delivery system would take another $2 billion, excluding facilities repair and renovation costs to meet local licensing standards and staff training costs.

The price of any state not having a comprehensive system in place is even more staggering, ranging as previously noted up to 10 times the cost in manifestation and treatment of social problems, economic losses, and educational failure that this nation can ill afford. This figure also belies the tragic human dramas of children and their parents.

Staffing

Another critical component to child care and/or child development programs is staff. A professional, highly trained cadre of staff is the most critical component of any delivery system accounting for some 80–90 percent of the cost. While the public expectations are high for child care providers and child development teachers, such expectations and demands are not matched by salaries. The fact of the matter is that the early childhood education pay is not commensurate to training. While school-based preschool teachers fare significantly better than their private-nonprofit counterparts it is because most school districts in California make a significant funding contribution in support of their preschool programs.

As previously noted, in California a site director must be a fully credentialed teacher. Site teachers must also have advanced training. There is a "career ladder" set of requirements beginning with a minimum of 12 semester units in early childhood education or child development that is valid for 2 years, then a Children's Center Instructional Permit consisting of 60 units, including 24 units in early childhood education, plus field experience and passage of a basic skills test, or a bachelor's degree. Also being implemented in California is a multiple subjects credential which allows holders significant flexibility in teaching opportunities.

Ratios

Another important quality indicator is that of teacher–child and adult–child ratios. Next to funding this is perhaps the most controversial issue facing policy makers. In California there is an annual debate

Table 4.2.   Licensing Ratios

Age Group	Department of Education		Department of Social Services
Infants (Birth to 2 years)	1:3	1:18	1:4
Infants/Toddlers (mixed) (Birth to 3 years)	1:4	1:16	N/A
Preschoolers (2 years to 6 years)	N/A	N/A	1:12 (or 1 teacher + 1 aide:15)
Preschoolers (3 years to 6 years)	1:8	1:24	N/A
School-Age (6 years to 14 years)	1:14	1:28	1:15 (1 teacher + 1 aide:28)

over ratios as it relates to cost and program quality with one faction arguing to increase ratios (that is "add a few more kids") to serve more children at the same cost. On the other hand, others (including myself) argue of the need to maintain low ratios and high quality particularly in view of the increasingly pervasive needs of children such as incidence of poverty, language needs, and effects of drugs.

California's ratios of state-funded child development programs administered by the Department of Education, and child care programs licensed by the Department of Social Services are contained in Table 4.2.

Curriculum

It is axiomatic to note that "children learn by doing." Enhancing the development of a child's attributes requires a clearly defined theory based curriculum to guide teaching practices, uniform standard of program quality, and caregiver practices. Such curriculum, based on developmental learning theory, will normally consist of instructional techniques which are age and developmentally appropriate. Translated, motor development, art activities, creative arts, language development activities such as small group story telling, letters and numbers, dramatic play, development of basic mathematical concepts through measurement activities such as cooking experiences, and a wide variety of other developmental activities. Language development through activities such as story telling, dramatic play, dictation, and drawing is particularly important. A curriculum that is multicultural, antibias, and nonsexist is also critical. A number of curriculum advisories and guidelines are readily available (National Association for the Education of Young Children, 1986; California State Department of Education, 1989). Inappropriate curriculum such as passive sitting and listening, rote memory drills, and excessive paper-and-pencil tasks should be avoided.

Tax Credits

An indirect way to support child care is through use of a combination of Federal and State tax credits. Federal tax credits enacted in 1976 for employment-related child care are on a sliding scale ranging from 20 percent to 30 percent. For a family with an income of less than $20,000 annually this means a tax credit of $1440 for two children. For a family with an income of over $28,000 the two-child tax credit is $960.

California's tax credit for child care also enacted in 1976 was 30 percent of the applicable Federal credit. Over the years, the State tax credit has undergone significant things. In 1986, the tax credit was changed from a sliding 5 percent to 10 percent of the Federal tax credit to a flat 30 percent which in 1987 amounted to $110 million.

Other types of tax credit such as for employers are also possible. The Federal Internal Revenue Code, for example, allows employers up to $5,000 in tax credit annually for dependent care. This tax credit is an employer-taxable deduction and in turn means lower payroll taxes for employers. To spur employers to provide child care, California enacted State tax credits up 30 percent of the cost for development of on-worksite child care, and a 50 percent tax credit for operating cost. While the new tax provision is still too new to ascertain its effectiveness, it holds great promise.

In brief, States could and should examine the possibility of combining both support of State-subsidized programs with some type of tax credit to benefit the broad spectrum of the taxpaying public.

SUMMARY

In summary, there are a multitude of policy and program issues confronting States contemplating the establishment of child care and/or child development programs. I have noted some significant issues that various states will confront. The extent to which states can be effective in resolving these issues and instituting programs depends upon their political will. Invariably states will be confronted with issues of funding, program content, staffing, ratios, administration, and oversight to note a few. But one thing is clear above all, what states elect to do in the form of child care and/or child development must be done well and without compromise or apology regarding program quality even if it means limited programs. Program quality is everything. Anything less would be a failure to reap full benefits of establishing child care and development programs.

A repertoire of resource materials and experiences are available from which states can draw. States also have tremendous flexibility in combining or leveraging state and federal funds and tax credits to design a stable funding base for their programs. The challenge is here and now. In the immortal words of Robin Williams in the film *Dead Poets' Society, carpe diem, carpe diem*—seize the day, seize the opportunity.

REFERENCES

Bates, T. (1987, Fall). *The changing family to the year 2000: Planning for our children's future.* Sacramento, CA: Assembly Human Service Committee.

California State Department of Education. (1987). *Triennial Report on Publicly Funded Child Development Programs: 1985–86.* Sacramento, CA: Author.

Cervantes, R. (1984, May). Ethnocentric pedagogy. In E. Zigler (Ed.), *The Common School.* Beverly Hills, CA: Sage.

Clements, J., Schweinhart, L., Barnett, S., et al. (1984). *Changed lives: The effects of the Perry program on youths through age nineteen.* Ypsilanti, MI: The High/Scope Press.

Committee for Economic Development. (1985). *Investing in our children.* New York: Author.

Hamburg, D. A. (1987). *Fundamental building blocks of early life.* New York: Carnegie Corporation.

Kirst, M. (1988). *The conditions of children in California.* Policy Analysis for California Education.

Lally, R., Mangione, P., & Honig, A. (1986). *The impact of intensive intervention (birth to five) on children from low income multi-risk families: The Syracuse University Children's Center findings 15 years later.* San Francisco, CA: Far West Research Laboratory.

National Association for the Education of Young Children. (1986). *Position statement on developmentally appropriate practice in early childhood education programs serving children from birth through age 8.*

National School Boards Association. (1987, September). *Report on the State Early Childhood Initiative meeting.* Alexandria, VA: Author.

Olsen, L. (1988). *Crossing the schoolhouse border: Immigrant students and California public schools.* San Francisco, CA: California Tomorrow.

Robledo, M. (1986). *Texas school dropout survey project: A summary of findings.* San Antonio, TX: Intercultural Development Research Association.

Weikart, D. (1987, December). *The cost-effectiveness of high quality early childhood programs.* Ypsilanti, MI: High/Scope Educational Research Foundation.

Chapter 5

The High/Scope Perry Preschool Study, Similar Studies, and Their Implications for Public Policy in the U.S.

Lawrence J. Schweinhart
David P. Weikart
High/Scope Educational Research Foundation, Ypsilanti, MI

A ROLE IN THE NATIONAL DEBATE

The High/Scope Perry Preschool study (Weikart, Deloria, Lawser, & Wiegerink, 1970; Weikart, Bond, & McNeil, 1978; Schweinhart & Weikart, 1980; Berrueta-Clement, Schweinhart, Barnett, Epstein, & Weikart, 1984) and similar studies have become part of the national debate about early childhood programs, cited repeatedly in the halls of Congress and the pages of the *New York Times*, even invoked in a political editorial in the *New Republic* ("Bring Back Big Spending," 1989). But brief citations easily lead to misunderstandings. Some people mistakenly conclude that good early childhood programs for poor children have only short-term effects. Others draw the overstated conclusion that such programs are a panacea, sufficient by themselves to solve the problems of poverty. Still others overgeneralize the findings, applying them to all Head Start or child care programs, regardless of the quality of these programs. The purpose of this chapter, then, is to contribute to the national debate by presenting, *in concise detail*, the design and findings of the High/Scope Perry Preschool study and similar studies and examining their implications for public policy in the United States.

DESIGN OF THE HIGH/SCOPE PERRY PRESCHOOL STUDY

The High/Scope Perry Preschool study identified young children living in poverty, randomly assigned them to preschool and no-preschool groups, operated a high-quality child development program for the preschool group at ages 3 and 4, and collected data on both groups of children throughout their childhood and adolescence.

The longitudinal sample consists of 123 persons who, at least during the 1960s, lived in the attendance area of the Perry Elementary School in Ypsilanti, Michigan. Although the study sample originally had 128 children, 4 children left and 1 died shortly after the study began. This sample was accumulated over the years, beginning with 28 4-year-olds and 17 3-year-olds in 1962, followed by 26 3-year-olds in 1963, 27 in 1964, and 25 in 1965. These children were invited to join the study sample because their families lived in poverty, as assessed by parents' years of schooling and employment status, and because the children had low intelligence-test scores at ages 3 or 4. Their mothers had completed a median of 9.7 years of schooling and their fathers, 8.8. In 58 percent of the families, at least one parent was employed, usually in unskilled labor. Half the families received welfare assistance; 47 percent had no father living with them. All members of the study sample were black, as was virtually everyone living in the attendance area of the Perry Elementary School at that time.

The internal validity of the study rests on the rare accomplishment of random assignment to groups: Neither parents nor teachers had a choice about which children did and did not attend the preschool program. Each year from 1962 to 1965, project staff randomly assigned members of the class of children who joined the study sample either to a "preschool group" who received the Perry Preschool Program or a "no-preschool group" who received no preschool program. Pairs of children with similar initial intelligence-test scores were randomly divided into two groups; these assignments were reversed as needed until the two groups had the same girl/boy ratio and the same average socioeconomic status. One group was randomly assigned to attend the preschool program and the other was designated the no-preschool group. As new classes were added to the study sample in 1963, 1964, and 1965, 23 younger siblings were assigned to the same group as their older siblings, to eliminate the possibility of the preschool program indirectly affecting a child in the no-preschool group. The preschool group had 58 members and the no-preschool group had 65. Confidence that postprogram group comparisons reflect preschool-program effects is justified also by the near absence of statistically significant group differences on background characteristics. There were no statistically significant differences (with a probability of less than .10) between the preschool group and the no-preschool group at project entry on mean Stanford-Binet intelligence test score, mean socioeconomic status, parental unemployment rates, percentage of fathers absent, mean school years completed by mothers and fathers, girl/boy ratio, mean family size, or mean birth order of the participating child. The only statistically significant difference between groups was in maternal employment rate at program entry (9% in the preschool group, 31% in the no-preschool group), but this difference did not recur when maternal employment was measured again 11 years later. Statistical tests have detected no bias attributable to maternal employment at project entry or to any other background characteristic.

The Perry Preschool program developed the High/Scope Curriculum—a child development curriculum approach that promotes intellectual, social, and physical development democratically by providing an open framework in which children initiate their own learning activities with teacher support (Weikart, Rogers, Adcock, & McClelland, 1971; Hohmann, Banet, & Weikart, 1979). Teachers help children plan their own activities and engage in key child development experiences. Each year, four teachers taught a class of 20 to 25 3- and 4-year-olds—one teacher for every five to six children. Although these group sizes exceeded the 16 to 20 children later found optimal by the National Day Care study (Ruopp, Travers, Glantz, & Coelen, 1979), the staff-child ratios were well below that study's recommended 8 to 10 children per adult. The program employed teachers certified both in special education and in early childhood education. In those days of teachers shortage, the first qualified persons who applied were hired. They received supportive supervision, studied early childhood development, brought in speakers, and together developed the High/Scope Curriculum. The school district paid them according to its teacher salary schedule. One teacher remained throughout the five years of the project; three remained 2–3 years; and six remained 1–2 years. Two of the teaching positions were consistently occupied by black females and two by white females. The project director was a white male and the school principal was a black male.

The teachers worked in partnership with the parents; a teacher visited each mother and child in their home once a week for an hour-

and-a-half to discuss the child's developmental progress and to model adult-child activities. The class sessions for children ran two-and-a-half hours on weekday mornings. The program year ran 30 weeks from mid-October to late May, once at age 4 for the 13 oldest children, twice at ages 3 and 4 for the remaining 45 preschool-group children. Since part-time programs of at least 30 weeks have been found effective, it is reasonable to assume that full-time programs over that period of time or longer would be at least as effective (Westinghouse Learning Corporation, 1969; Berrueta-Clement et al., 1984, pp. 94–105, 108).

Sources of data include parent interviews when children were 3 and 15; annual intelligence and language tests from ages 3 to 10 and at age 14; annual achievement tests from ages 7 to 11 and at ages 14 and 19; annual teacher ratings from ages 7 to 10; participant interviews at ages 15 and 19 and now at age 28; school record information collected at ages 11, 15, and 19; and police and social services records information collected at age 19 and now at age 28. Age-28 data are now being collected but have not yet been analyzed. The median percentage of missing cases across all data sources is under 5 percent, with only 4 measures exceeding 25 percent. Only 2 cases were missing for the crucial age-19 interview.

In this chapter, we report only those findings whose probability of chance occurrence is less than .05, based on the directional (one-tailed) hypothesis that the preschool group would do better than the no-preschool group; it should be noted that previous reports used the less appropriate, but more conservative, nondirectional two-tailed tests of statistical significance.

RESULTS OF THE HIGH/SCOPE PERRY PRESCHOOL STUDY

The preschool group surpassed the no-preschool group in intellectual performance from ages 4 to 7. Probably because of this intellectual boost, the preschool group achieved greater school success than the no-preschool group—higher school achievement and literacy, better placement in school, stronger commitment to schooling, and more years of school completed. Probably because of this greater school success, the preschool group surpassed the no-preschool group in teenage socio-economic success and social responsibility: higher rates of employment and self-support, a lower welfare rate, fewer acts of serious misconduct, and a lower arrest rate. Table 5.1 summarizes these findings of the Perry Preschool study. Analysis of financial costs and benefits re-

Table 5.1. Major Group Differences in the High/Scope Perry Preschool Study

Outcome[a]	Age at Measurement	Preschool Group	No-Preschool Group
Stanford-Binet mean IQs	4	96	83
	5	95	84
	6	91	86
	7	92	87
School performance			
School achievement (items passed)	14	36%	28%
Literacy (items passed)	19	62%	55%
School placement			
Ever mentally impaired (records)	19	15%	35%
Years in special education (records)	19	16%	28%
Commitment to schooling			
Value placed on schooling			
(23+ on 28-point scale)	15	75%	62%
Enjoy talking about school (parent)	15	65%	33%
Do homework	15	68%	40%
"Smarter than classmates"	15	85%	59%
Schooling completed			
High school graduation	19	67%	49%
Postsecondary education	19	38%	21%
Adolescent socioeconomic success			
Employment	19	50%	32%
Self-support	19	45%	25%
Welfare	19	18%	32%
General Assistance (records)	19	19%	41%
Adolescent social responsibility			
Mean acts of serious misconduct	15	2.3	3.2
Ever arrested (records)	19	31%	51%
Mean arrests (records)	19	1.3	2.3

[a]Self-report unless otherwise indicated. For all entries, the preschool group performed better than the no-preschool group, with a directional probability less than .05.

vealed that the program provided a substantial return on public investment.

Initial Boost in Intellectual Performance and Motivation

On the average, the preschool group outperformed the no-preschool group on the Stanford-Binet Intelligence Scale from ages 4 to 7, from after one program year up to two years after the program. The average intelligence test scores of the two groups differed by 13 points at age 4, 11 points at age 5, and 5 points at ages 6 and 7. The two groups had the same mean intelligence test scores prior to the preschool program and again at ages 8, 9, 10, and 14.

During (indeed, within two months of program entry) and immediately after the preschool program, the preschool group outscored the no-preschool group on the Leiter International Performance Scale, the Peabody Picture Vocabulary Test (PPVT), and the Illinois Test of Psycholinguistic Abilities (ITPA, especially its auditory-vocal association subtest). However, during this period, testers did know to which groups children belonged. The preschool group outscored the no-preschool group on the PPVT at age 6 and the ITPA and Leiter at age 9, but not on other administrations of these tests at ages 6, 7, 8, and 9.

The preschool group had a higher average—across ages 6, 7, 8, and 9—than the no-preschool group on teacher ratings of school motivation (such items as "shows initiative," "alert and interested in schoolwork," and "motivated toward academic performance"). In kindergarten through sixth grade, members of the preschool group averaged 11.9 days absent per school year, while members of the no-preschool group averaged 16.3.

Improved School Success

The average score of the preschool group on the California Achievement Test was statistically significantly higher than the average score of the no-preschool group at ages 6, 7, and 8; slightly but not statistically significantly higher at ages 9 and 10; and both statistically significantly and substantially higher at 14. Arithmetic subtests had the same pattern of differences; statistically significant reading subtest differences appeared at ages 6, 8, 9, and 14; and statistically significant language subtest differences appeared at ages 8, 9, and 14. The large achievement test differences at age 14 may be partly explained by its greater demand for task persistence than earlier tests. At age 14, the preschool group averaged 89 percent of test items completed while the no-preschool group averaged 82 percent.

At age 19, the preschool group outscored the no-preschool group in basic literacy on the Adult Performance Level Survey. According to the test's national norm, 62 percent of the no-preschool group, but only 39 percent of the preschool group, scored "below average." The preschool group outscored the no-preschool group in the content areas of occupational knowledge and health information, with nonsignificant trends in the same direction for community resources, consumer economics, and government and law. The preschool group outscored the no-preschool group in reading, writing, and identification of facts and terms, with similar but nonsignificant trends for computation and problem solving.

The preschool group's high school grade-point average of 2.1 exceeded the no-preschool group's average of 1.7. Members of the preschool group averaged .7 failing grades per school year; members of the no-preschool group averaged 1.0.

At ages 15 and 19, the preschool group attached greater importance to high school than did the no-preschool group. Also at age 15, only 23 percent of the preschool group had not thought of going to college, as compared to 40 percent of the no-preschool group; almost two-thirds of the preschool-group parents, but only one-third of no-preschool-group parents, reported that their children enjoyed talking about school; two-thirds of the preschool group reported doing homework, as compared to only two-fifths of the no-preschool group; and 85 percent of the preschool group, but only 59 percent of the no-preschool group, considered themselves smarter than their classmates.

Despite the fact that subjects' intelligence test scores at age 3 theoretically placed them on the borderline of mental impairment at that time, only 15 percent of the preschool group and 35 percent of the no-preschool group were subsequently classified as mentally impaired. Preschool-group members averaged only 2.0 school years in special education classes rather than regular education classes, as compared to 3.6 school years for no-preschool-group members. However, preschool-group members averaged 1.0 school year receiving supplementary compensatory education classes, in addition to regular education classes, as compared to 0.4 school year averaged by members of the no-preschool group. Combining the two types of extra educational services, preschool-group members averaged 3.0 school years in special and compensatory education, while no-preschool group members averaged 4.0 school years. These differences probably would have been even greater if the no-preschool group's high school graduation rate had been as high as the preschool group's.

Sixty-seven percent of the preschool group, but only 49 percent of the no-preschool group, graduated from high school. The preschool group's graduation rate equaled that of all black 19- and 20-year-olds in the United States in 1980 (U.S. Bureau of the Census, 1980). At age 19, 38 percent of the preschool group, but only 21 percent of the no-preschool group, were receiving either academic or vocational postsecondary education. Through age 19, the highest grade level completed by members of the preschool group averaged 11.5, while the highest grade level completed by members of the no-preschool group averaged 11.1.

Greater Success as Adolescents in the Community

Half of the preschool group, but only one-third of the no-preschool group, were employed when interviewed at age 19. Since leaving school, the preschool group had averaged 4.9 months without work, while the no-preschool group averaged 10.3; moreover, the preschool group reported greater job satisfaction than the no-preschool group. With job earnings averaging only $4,845 across groups, 45 percent of the preschool group, but only 25 percent of the no-preschool group, said they supported themselves by their own and/or their spouses' earnings.

When interviewed at age 19, 18 percent of the preschool group, but 32 percent of the no-preschool group, reported they were currently receiving welfare assistance. The average annual welfare payment was $633 per person in the preschool group and $1,509 per person in the no-preschool group. According to the records of the Michigan Department of Social Services, 19 percent of the preschool group, as compared to 41 percent of the no-preschool group, had ever received General Assistance (in poverty, but not qualified for AFDC—Aid to Families with Dependent Children) as an adult or principal grantee, with most of these people receiving Food Stamps as well. Groups did not differ to a statistically significant extent in their overall use of Food Stamps, AFDC, or Medicaid.

At age 15, the preschool group reported fewer acts of misconduct than did the no-preschool group, including fewer acts of *serious* misconduct—2.3 vs. 3.2 acts per person. At age 19, although similar differences in self-reported misconduct were not statistically significant, the preschool group reported fewer involvements in serious fights, gang fights, inflictions of injuries needing medical attention, and run-ins with the police than did the no-preschool group (Schweinhart, 1987, p. 141).

Police arrest records confirm this pattern. Only 31 percent of the preschool group, but 51 percent of the no-preschool group, were ever arrested as juveniles or as adults. Seven percent of the preschool group, as compared to 17 percent of the no-preschool group, had been arrested five or more times. The arrest rate of the no-preschool group, 2.3 arrests per person, was nearly twice that of the preschool group, which was only 1.3 arrests per person; there were statistically significant group differences in the numbers of both major and minor charges. The rate of property and violence charges was .8 per person in the preschool group, as compared to 1.2 per person in the no-preschool group (Schweinhart, 1987, p. 142).

Teen girls in the preschool group reported fewer pregnancies than did teen girls in the no-preschool group (.7 vs. 1.2 pregnancies per girl).

Substantial Return on Investment

Taxpayers received substantial returns on their investment in the Perry Preschool Program—$3.00 for every dollar invested in the 60-week program at ages 3 and 4 and $5.95 for every dollar invested in the 30-week program at age 4. The dollar figures reported in this section are the per-child costs and benefits expressed in 1988 constant dollars discounted at 3 percent annually. The ledgers of the Ypsilanti Public Schools provided a thorough accounting of *program costs* for personnel, overhead, supplies, child selection, and building space. Due largely to the high teacher–child ratios, the costs were high, about $6,500 per child-year. Reducing the ratios from 1:6 to 1:10 would have reduced the cost per child-year to $3,900.

The benefits of the program recounted herein generated $39,278 per child in financial benefits to taxpayers. Taxpayers saved $7,005 per child because of reduced special education costs, $4,252 because of reduced crime costs to victims and the criminal justice system, and $22,490 because of reduced welfare payments. It cost them $964 per child because more of the preschool group than the no-preschool group received postsecondary education, but this higher education attainment helped the preschool group would have higher lifetime earnings and therefore pay $6,495 in additional lifetime taxes.

Children who received the 30-week program generated essentially the same benefits as did children who received the 60-week program. Thus, the 30-week program was a better investment, at least for the 13 children whose program lasted this long in this study. Even if the investment return had been only dollar for dollar, the investment would have been made worthwhile by the obvious, nonfinancial benefits of preventing school failure, crime, and need for welfare assistance.

EVIDENCE FROM SIMILAR STUDIES

The Head Start Synthesis Project meta-analysis of all available studies of Head Start's effects identified 50 studies that found evidence of immediate improvements in children's intellectual performance, socio-emotional performance, and health that lasted several years (McKey et al., 1985). It also found that these Head Start programs provided and linked families with health, social, and educational services and influenced various institutions to provide such services (McKey et al., 1985, p. 1). Ramey, Bryant, and Suarez (1985) identified another 11 experimental studies in which the mean intelligence test score of children who participated in preschool programs was higher, or the same as, the mean intelligence test score of children in the study's control group.

In addition to the Perry study, 7 other long-term studies have found evidence that good programs for young children living in poverty produce statistically significant long-term benefits. Three of these studies followed participants to ages 18 to 21: the Early Training Project study (Gray, Ramsey, & Klaus, 1982), the Project HOPE study (Gotts, 1989), and a local Head Start study in Rome, Georgia (Monroe & McDonald, 1981). The remaining four studies followed participants to ages 9 to 15: the Syracuse study (Lally, Mangione, & Honig, 1988), the Harlem study (Palmer, 1983), the Milwaukee Project study (Garber, 1988), and the New York Department of Education's evaluation of the state's public school prekindergarten programs (Irvine, 1982).

All the programs examined in these longitudinal studies served young children living in poverty who were at special risk of school failure. Children entered the programs at some time between infancy and age 5 and remained in them for at least one or two school years. Of the 3,552 children who originally participated in these studies (including the Perry study), 74 percent provided information in the most recent follow-up surveys. The programs studied included a part-day preschool program, a summertime part-day preschool program combined with weekly home visits during the school year, a program of twice-weekly home visits to parents and children, and a program of twice-weekly one-on-one teacher–child sessions. The Consortium for Longitudinal Studies included some of these studies and others in a follow-up assessment in the late 1970s that reported findings of positive program effects on intelligence test scores at school entry, special education placement, and grade retention (Lazar, Darlington, Murray, Royce, & Snipper, 1982). The New York State Experimental Prekindergarten evaluation (Irvine, 1982), with 2,058 4-year-olds—white, black, and other—demonstrates that such results can be obtained in multi-site, service-oriented systems as well as in single-site demonstration programs.

When compared to their peers in similar circumstances who did not participate in good programs (differences identified with a probability of less than .05), young children living in poverty who attended good programs demonstrated the following characteristics:

- Seven of the eight studies with relevant data reported fewer students placed in special education or retained in grade.
- All four studies with relevant data reported more youths graduating from high school.
- Two of the three studies with relevant data reported that their groups averaged higher on achievement tests over the years.
- Two of the three studies with relevant data reported fewer youths arrested.

Thus, the Perry study's findings for grade placement and high school graduation are reasonably conclusive across studies. The economic value of these two benefits alone is sufficient to repay taxpayers for the cost of the early childhood programs. All of the long-term early childhood studies mentioned here—the only studies with adequate, relevant data—have reported statistically significant effects over time.

Although some have claimed that most effects of such programs fade away, there is virtually no evidence of fadeout for children's special education placement, high school graduation, delinquency, pregnancy, employment, or return on investment; fadeout evidence is mixed for children's socioemotional behavior and school achievement. Clear evidence of fadeout has been found only for children's intelligence-test scores. In the 1960s, the hypothesis was that even though educational programs were found to raise young children's scores, subsequent educational programs would not affect them. Instead, it may be argued, a difference in intelligence-test scores reflects a difference in educational settings. When children who had preschool programs and children who had not had preschool programs came together into the same elementary school classrooms, their intelligence-test scores also came together.

Early childhood education seems to produce its long-term effects not through sustained improvements in intelligence, as was once hoped, but by equipping children to be more successful students. Early childhood program experience enables children to achieve greater success during their first weeks in school. Their success breeds higher motivation, better performance, and higher regard from teachers and classmates. More successful school careers increase their chances of graduating from high school, holding jobs, and avoiding commission of crimes (Schweinhart & Weikart, 1980).

Early childhood program quality is also important for young children whose mothers are employed, both poor and nonpoor. Studies of these children, such as the National Day Care study (Ruopp et al., 1979) and the National Child Care Staffing study (Whitebook, Howes,

& Phillips, 1989) show that high-quality programs with low staff turnover make greater contributions to children's behavior and development than do low-quality programs with high staff turnover. Programs make greater contributions when group sizes are small, when there are enough adults, and when these adults are trained in early childhood development.

Put simply, good early childhood programs contribute to the development of young children who live in poverty and young children whose mothers are in the labor force; poor early childhood programs do not contribute and may even have negative effects on their development. Although longitudinal studies have examined a variety of programs for poor children and for children whose mothers are employed, the following generalizations may be made about the characteristics of effective programs, staff, and administrators (Schweinhart, 1988; Schweinhart & Weikart, 1988).

- Effective programs use explicitly stated, developmentally appropriate curricula that support children's self-initiated learning activities (Schweinhart, Weikart, & Larner, 1986).
- Effective teaching staff have been trained in early childhood education and staff turnover is low (Ruopp et al., 1979; Whitebook et al., 1989).
- Effective administrators provide inservice training and supervisory support for their staff's curriculum implementation.
- Effective programs maintain classes of fewer than 20 3- to 5-year-olds for every pair of teaching adults (Ruopp et al., 1979).
- Effective programs provide home visits at least monthly or support other forms of intensive parent involvement.

The accreditation criteria of the National Academy of Early Childhood Programs (National Association for the Education of Young Children, 1984) embody these quality characteristics. In addition, the NAEYC criteria require programs to comply with state and local health and safety requirements; train staff to detect illness and provide first aid; and ensure that children receive nutritious meals, health and social service referrals, and developmental assessments. Three program-quality categories have major effects on program cost: staff-child ratio, staff salaries and benefits, and supplementary services (home visits, staff development, meals, referrals, and assessments). Program quality is most dependent on program curriculum, but most of the curriculum cost appears indirectly, in staff salaries and benefits, with the direct cost of curriculum appearing as supplies and equipment.

IMPLICATIONS FOR U.S. POLICY

The public role in the United States is becoming one of targeting public funding to help families enroll their young children in good programs which they need but their families cannot otherwise afford. In concept, this role involves full public funding of good programs for young children living in poverty, whether or not their mothers are in the work force, and partial public funding to support the quality of programs for young children whose mothers are in the labor force or in school.

Populations in Need

Young children in poverty can attend good programs only when the public fully funds such programs for them. The research findings above make a compelling case that poor 3- and 4-year-olds whose mothers are not in the labor force need part-time programs. These findings combine with the child care need to make the case that poor children under 5 whose mothers are in the labor force need full-work-time programs.

Part-time programs would be appropriate for 1.2 million 3- and 4-year-olds in poverty with nonemployed mothers. Publicly funded part-time programs serve 500,000 3- and 4-year-olds in poverty, 31 percent of the total. Head Start programs serve 365,000 (U.S. Head Start Bureau, 1989) and public school prekindergarten programs serve 135,000 (Mitchell, Seligson, & Marx, 1989, p. 31); thus, 720,000 who need part-time programs are not now being served.

Of the 1.1 million children under age 5 in poverty with mothers who are employed, 570,000 are now in day care homes and centers; parents and relatives take care of the others. Federal and state governments provide some child care funds through the Title XX Social Services Block Grant.

Public funding is needed to subsidize good programs for nonpoor young children whose mothers are in the labor force. Of the 9.5 million nonpoor children under 5 with mothers in the labor force (U.S. Bureau of Labor Statistics, 1988), nonrelatives in homes take care of 2.7 million and day care centers and schools take care of 2.3 million; parents and relatives take care of the rest (U.S. Bureau of the Census, 1987). The unmet need for child care is unknown because mothers who cannot find good programs make other arrangements—placing their child in unsatisfactory programs, prevailing upon relatives for child care, or staying home and taking care of their young children themselves.

Mothers who do not live in poverty and are not in the labor force take care of 6.7 million children under 5, with 615,000 of these children enrolled in part-time nursery schools (National Center for Education Statistics, 1986). Thus, 6.7 million of the nation's 18.5 million children under 5, or 36 percent, are now enrolled in day care homes, day care centers, or nursery schools.

Early Childhood Program Costs

The nation now invests a total of 14.9 billion dollars a year in early childhood programs for poor children and nonpoor children whose mothers are in the labor force. Families with mothers employed outside the home spend $11.1 billion on child care each year (U.S. Bureau of the Census, 1987), subsidized by federal tax breaks for dependent care worth $4.0 billion. In FY 1988, the federal government spent $2.9 billion on support for early childhood programs (U.S. Department of Labor Secretary's Task Force, 1988). States spent $600 million on child care (Blank, Savage, & Wilkins, 1988) and $250 million on prekindergarten programs (Mitchell et al., 1989).

Current early-childhood-program costs in day care centers reflect a level of quality that has been called "barely adequate as evaluated by objective measures" (Whitebook et al., 1989). Families with employed mothers report spending $2,262 per child in day care centers, $2,137 per child in day care homes, and $1,477 per child in care by relatives (U.S. Bureau of the Census, 1987). Teachers in day care centers receive an average hourly wage of $5.35, or $9,363 annually (Whitebook et al., 1989). Forty-one percent of day care center staff leave their jobs each year.

In a study of 265 NAEYC-accredited full-time early childhood programs, the U.S. General Accounting Office (1989) found that the average annual per-child cost was $4,660, including $590 for the value of in-kind donations such as rent and labor. Programs had good staffing (one adult for every 4 infants or nine 4-year-olds), but provided low pay ($13,700 per teacher). Staff salaries would require a 46 percent increase for teachers to average $20,000 a year, which would increase the average cost per child to $6,075, or $5,585 without in-kind donations. Clifford and Russell (1989) estimate that with desirable staff pay (average teacher salary of $20,000) and staffing (1 adult for every 4 infants or 10 4-year-olds), the per-child cost of a good full-time early childhood program would be $5,268 a year.

Head Start programs, serving youngsters 20 hours a week for 34 weeks a year, spent an average $2,664 per child in 1988 (U.S. Head

Start Bureau, 1989). However, the average salary for Head Start teachers was $12,074 a year (1,300 hours), $15,403 a year for those with bachelors' degrees. If the salaries of all Head Start staff were increased by 25 percent, the average teacher salary would be $15,000, and the cost per child for the 34-week program would be $3,177. *Full-work-time* Head Start programs would cost about $5,900 per child, the same as the full-work-time programs cited above plus an additional $500 for supplementary services for children in poverty (Schweinhart, 1989).

Table 5.2 estimates the costs required for good early childhood programs in the United States, based on the information on populations and costs presented in this chapter. It assumes an average full-work-time teacher salary of $20,000 and an average "part-time" teacher salary of $15,000. Some would argue that such salary levels, more than double the current averages, are beyond reach; others would argue that the average early childhood teacher salary should be the same as the average public school teacher salary of $27,423 (National Center for Education Statistics, 1989). We believe that the proposed averages are reasonable, achievable, and essential to the stabilization of the early childhood teacher workforce and maintenance of quality in early childhood programs. However, it should be noted that both costs and population sizes will change over time. Indeed, the introduction of funding for good programs will inevitably cause increases in populations seeking these programs.

The total public and private cost to provide needed good early childhood programs in the United States is $37.3 billion; the nation now invests $14.9 billion. It needs to invest an additional $22.4 billion:

Table 5.2. Costs Required to Provide Good Early Childhood Programs in the U.S.

Cost Source	Number of Children ('000s)	Cost/Child	Total Cost (bill.)	Current Spending (bill.)	Additional Spending Needed (bill.)
Part-time programs for poor 3- and 4-year-olds	1,200	$3,177	$ 3.8	$ 1.5	$ 2.3
Full-time programs for poor children under 5	1,100	$5,900	$ 6.5	$ 2.3	$ 4.2
Full-time programs for nonpoor children under 5	5,000	$5,400	$27.0	$11.1	$15.9
Totals	7,300		$37.3	$14.9	$22.4

$2.3 billion more for part-time programs for poor 3- and 4-year-olds; $4.2 billion more for full-time programs for poor children under 5; and $15.9 billion more for full-time programs for nonpoor children under 5.

Additional investments in good early childhood programs for *poor* children must come from public sources and private sources acting in the public interest; such programs are too expensive for poor families and provide long-term benefits to taxpayers (Berrueta-Clement et al., 1984). Additional investments in good early childhood programs for *nonpoor* children will come from public, corporate, and family sources; all these sources have a vital interest in such programs. Besides providing funding directly, government can leverage additional funding by creating incentives for corporations and families to spend more.

The $37.3 billion cost of good early childhood programs for children under age 5 compares to a national expenditure of $11.5 billion per grade level for public schools in 1985–86 (National Center for Education Statistics, 1987, p. 36). It would cost the nation a total of $24.6 billion to provide the young children born in poverty each year with the good part-time and full-work-time early childhood programs they needed over the years. If these programs were as financially fruitful as the Perry Preschool program, the return to taxpayers on this investment would be $56.2 billion, a net annual profit of $31.6 billion.

Distinctions in family circumstances—between the poor and the nonpoor and between employed and nonemployed mothers—do not require distinct early childhood programs. In fact, society is better served when young children from varying family circumstances enroll together in the same programs—poor children with nonpoor children; children of employed mothers and children of nonemployed mothers; and, of course, white children with black, Hispanic, and other minority-ethnicity children. The only necessary program distinction is that children with employed mothers need full-work-time programs while children with nonemployed mothers need only part-time programs. Nothing prevents a home or center from providing both part-time and full-work-time programs. Yet it seems easier for the public and policy makers to understand a program with a distinct mission to a category of children, such as Head Start's part-time programs for poor young children.

The governance of early childhood programs needs to be more unified and better coordinated at federal, state, and local levels of government. The federal government and each state government should have a strong office of early childhood programs, located either in the state education agency or the state human services agency. Human services agencies have been responsible for the regulation of existing early childhood programs, but are associated with welfare assistance and poverty when most of the children served by early childhood programs are not poor or on welfare. Although education agencies have always focused on public schools, they are attractive locations for early-childhood-program offices because both education and early childhood programs are investments in people. Whichever agency houses an office of early childhood programs, that office needs strong ties with the other agencies that have various responsibilities for early childhood programs.

State policy makers sometimes single out public schools for funding because these sites already provide K-12 schooling. With qualified early childhood teachers, public schools should develop central roles in the early childhood provider community, as sites for demonstration programs, community-wide inservice training, and hubs for networking (Zigler, 1987; Schweinhart, 1989). However, adequately funded early-childhood-program licensing offices are the key to identifying suitable program sites not only in public schools, but also in community centers and homes. The variety of existing types of program sites better meets the variety of community needs. Any program site that can consistently provide good early childhood programs should be eligible for licensing and funding.

Public investment in early childhood programs, and public support for such spending, is increasing. Sixty-nine percent of the American public say they are willing to spend more taxes to pay for Head Start programs; 58 percent say they are willing to do the same to pay for day care for young children with working parents (Elam & Gallup, 1989, p. 52). At the Education Summit in Virginia, President Bush agreed with the nation's governors that "priority for any further [federal] spending increases be given to prepare young children to succeed in school" ("Text," 1989). State and local spending on early childhood programs also continues to increase.

Although the costs of good early childhood programs for the nation are great, the eventual costs of not providing them, in money and in decreased quality of life, are greater.

REFERENCES

Berrueta-Clement, J. R., Schweinhart, L. J., Barnett, W. S., Epstein, A. S., & Weikart, D. P. (1984). *Changed lives: The effects of the Perry Preschool Program on youths through age 19 (Monographs of the High/Scope Educational Research Foundation,* 8). Ypsilanti, MI: High/Scope Press.

Blank, H., Savage, J., & Wilkins, A. (1988). *State child care fact book 1988.* Washington, DC: Children's Defense Fund.

Bring back big spending. (1989, March 27). *The New Republic,* pp. 7–8.

Clifford, R. M., & Russell, S. D. (1989). Financing programs for preschool-aged children. *Theory into Practice, 28,* 19–27.

Elam, S. M., & Gallup, A. M. (1989, September). The 21st annual Gallup poll of the public's attitudes toward the public schools. *Phi Delta Kappan, 71,* 41–56.

Garber, H. L. (1988). *The Milwaukee Project: Preventing mental retardation in children at risk.* Washington, DC: American Association on Mental Retardation.

Gotts, E. E. (1989). *HOPE, preschool to graduation: Contributions to parenting and school-family relations theory and practice* (Final Report). Charleston, WV: Appalachia Educational Laboratory.

Gray, S. W., Ramsey, B. K., & Klaus, R. A. (1982). *From 3 to 20—The Early Training Project.* Baltimore, MD: University Park Press.

Grubb, W. N. (1987). *Young children face the states: Issues and options for early childhood programs.* New Brunswick, NJ: Center for Policy Research in Education.

Hohmann, M., Banet, B., & Weikart, D. P. (1979). *Young children in action: A manual for preschool educators.* Ypsilanti, MI: High/Scope Press.

Irvine, D. J. (1982). *Evaluation of the New York State Experimental Prekindergarten Program.* Paper presented at the annual meeting of the American Educational Research Association, New York City.

Lally, J. R., Mangione, P. L., & Honig, A. S. (1988). The Syracuse University Family Development Research Program: Long-range impact of an early intervention with low-income children and their families. In D. R. Powell (Ed.), *Parent education as early childhood intervention: Emerging directions in theory, research, and practice* (pp. 79–104). Norwood, NJ: Ablex.

Lazar, I., Darlington, R., Murray, H., Royce, J., & Snipper, A. (1982). Lasting effects of early education: A report from the Consortium for Longitudinal Studies. *Monographs of the Society for Research in Child Development, 47* (2-3, Serial No. 195), 1–151.

McKey, R. H., Condelli, L., Ganson, H., Barrett, B. J., McConkey, C., & Plantz, M. C. (1985). *The impact of Head Start on children, families and communities* (Final Report of the Head Start Evaluation, Synthesis, and Utilization Project). Washington, DC: CSR.

Mitchell, A., Seligson, M., & Marx, F. (1989). *Early childhood programs and the public schools: Between promise and practice.* Dover, MA: Auburn House.

Monroe, E., & McDonald, M. S. (1981). *A follow-up study of the 1966 Head Start program, Rome City Schools, Rome, Georgia.* Unpublished paper.

National Association for the Education of Young Children. (1984). *Accreditation criteria and procedures of the National Academy of Early Childhood Programs.* Washington, DC: Author.

National Center for Education Statistics. (1986). *The condition of education 1986 edition.* Washington, DC: U.S. Government Printing Office.

National Center for Education Statistics. (1987). *The condition of education 1987.* Washington, DC: U.S. Government Printing Office.

National Center for Education Statistics. (1989). *The condition of education 1989.* Washington, DC: U.S. Government Printing Office.

Palmer, F. H. (1983). The Harlem Study: Effects by type of training, age of training, and social class. In Consortium for Longitudinal Studies, *As the twig is bent . . . lasting effects of preschool programs* (pp. 201–236). Hillsdale, NJ: Erlbaum.

Ramey, C. T., Bryant, D. M., & Suarez, T. M. (1985). Preschool compensatory education and the modifiability of intelligence: A critical review. In D. Detterman (Ed.), *Current topics in human intelligence* (pp. 247–296). Norwood, NJ: Ablex.

Ruopp, R., Travers, J., Glantz, F., & Coelen, C. (1979). *Children at the center: Summary findings and their implications* (Final Report of the National Day Care Study, Volume 1). Cambridge, MA: Abt Associates.

Schweinhart, L. J. (1987). Can preschool programs help prevent delinquency? In J. Q. Wilson & G. C. Loury (Eds.), *From children to citizens: Families, schools, and delinquency prevention* (pp. 135–153). New York: Springer-Verlag.

Schweinhart, L. J. (1988). *A school administrator's guide to early childhood programs.* Ypsilanti, MI: High/Scope Press.

Schweinhart, L. J. (1989, Winter). Early childhood programs in the U.S. today. *High/Scope Resource,* pp. 1, 9–13.

Schweinhart, L. J., & Weikart, D. P. (1980). *Young children grow up: The effects of the Perry Preschool Program on youths through age 15* (Monographs of the High/Scope Educational Research Foundation, 7). Ypsilanti, MI: High/Scope Press.

Schweinhart, L. J., & Weikart, D. P. (1988). Education for young children living in poverty: Child-initiated learning or teacher-directed instruction? *Elementary School Journal, 89,* 213–225.

Schweinhart, L. J., Weikart, D. P., & Larner, M. B. (1986). Consequences of three preschool curriculum models through age 15, *Early Childhood Research Quarterly, 1,* 15–35.

Text of final summit statement issued by President, Governors. (1989, October 4). *Education Week,* p. 12.

U.S. Bureau of the Census. (1980). (October Current Population Survey). Unpublished data.

U.S. Bureau of the Census. (1987). *Who's minding the kids? Child care arrangements: Winter 1984–85* (Series P-70, No. 9). Washington, DC: U.S. Government Printing Office.

U.S. Bureau of Labor Statistics. (1988, November). Unpublished data.

U.S. Department of Labor Secretary's Task Force. (1988). *Child care: A workforce issue.* Washington, DC: Author.

U.S. General Accounting Office. (1989, July). *Early childhood education: Information on costs and services at high-quality centers; fact sheet for the Chairman, Committee on Labor and Human Resources, U.S. Senate* (GAO/HRD-89-130FS). Gaithersburg, MD: Author.

U.S. Head Start Bureau. (1989, October). Unpublished data.

Weikart, D. P., Bond, J. T., & McNeil, J. T. (1978). *The Ypsilanti Perry*

Preschool Project: Preschool years and longitudinal results through fourth grade (Monographs of the High/Scope Educational Research Foundation, 3). Ypsilanti, MI: High/Scope Press.

Weikart, D. P., Deloria, D., Lawser, S., & Wiegerink, R. (1970). *Longitudinal results of the Ypsilanti Perry Preschool Project* (Monographs of the High/Scope Educational Research Foundation, 1). Ypsilanti, MI: High/Scope Press.

Weikart, D. P., Rogers, L., Adcock, C., & McClelland, D. (1971). *The Cognitively Oriented Curriculum: A framework for preschool teachers.* Urbana, IL: University of Illinois.

Westinghouse Learning Corporation. (1969). *The impact of Head Start: An evaluation of the effects of Head Start on children's cognitive and affective development* (Vols. I–II). Athens, OH: Ohio University.

Whitebook, M., Howes, C., & Phillips, D. (1989). *Who cares? Child care teachers and the quality of care in America, executive summary, National Child Care Staffing study.* Oakland, CA: Child Care Employee Project.

Zigler, E. F. (1987). A solution to the nation's child care crisis: The school of the Twenty-First Century. Appendix to R. C. Granger with A. W. Mitchell, *Public schools and prekindergarten programs: An examination of six issues.* New York: Bank Street College of Education.

Part II
Policy Issues Related to Child Care

Chapter 6

Issues Related to Infant Child Care Policy

Eleanor Stokes Szanton
National Center for Clinical Infant Programs, Arlington, VA

Day care for infants and toddlers has become a highly charged issue. The awkward term of art, "infant child care," is itself suggestive of ambivalence regarding the activity it describes. It makes infants seem a special case, a rarified form of childhood, when in fact children under age three comprise more than half of the population eligible for full-day child care (Bureau of Labor Statistics, 1988).

THREE VIEWS OF INFANT CARE

The issue of infants in child care raises three of our nation's most frequently debated domestic policy concerns: (a) work and family issues, (b) efforts to reduce the number of families on welfare, and (c) concerns about an educable labor force for the economy of the 21st century.

Work and family issues. Since 1987 over 50 percent of mothers of infants are in the labor force (Bureau of Labor Statistics, 1988). Though a substantial number are not working full time, it is clear that many more than ever before are leaving their babies and toddlers in out-of-home care by nonfamily members. Whether this situation is through choice or necessity, it makes parents unusually anxious. It is more of a wrench to be separated from an infant than from an older child (Moen, 1989). Furthermore, infants are more vulnerable to mishandling than older children (American Association for Protecting Children, Inc., 1987, p. 20). Yet they are without means to resist or reveal maltreatment. As Edward Zigler has characterized it, "Parents are uncomfortable about having their children cared for in ways they were not" (Zigler & Finn-Stevenson, 1989; *The Washington Post*, 1989).

Reducing the welfare rolls. There has been an unexpectedly broad consensus among federal and state policy makers behind the provisions of the Family Support Act of 1988 requiring mothers on welfare (AFDC) whose children are age three or over to accept training in preparation or employment. Furthermore, the legislation was designed to require teenage mothers on AFDC to continue schooling regardless of their children's age. (States have the option to require *all* AFDC mothers of babies over age one to take part.) These women are reimbursed for their child care expenses during the period of their training and the first six months of their employment. However, reimbursement ceilings are very low. Child care advocates worry that the level of reimbursement is not nearly sufficient to pay for quality child care for children who may already be at risk for other reasons. Nor are there strong regulations outlining the quality of the child care to be used. In this context, then, child care for infants and toddlers had been transformed in the minds of policy makers from "a possibly dangerous new way to care for our nation's infants" to "an important back-up for a much-needed program" with little regard for the quality of that back-up.

Assuring our economy an educated work force. Others in this book speak more fully about the many new initiatives designed to give young children a better educational start, so that they will be ready and eager to learn in school. The unanimity on this matter among governors, business leaders, and educators has been gratifying. And though the bulk of programmatic initiatives related to this movement are in enriched prekindergarten or expanded Head Start, a significant number do focus on the uses of family resource/parent education programs and day care as a locus for improving young children's development and for identifying health and developmental problems in the earlier years.

Readers should be experiencing triple vision by now as they consider these three distinct views of infant day care: the worrisome new institution vs. the offhand back-up to a parental program vs. a key feature of "the right start" for members of our future labor force.

CHILD CARE ISSUES WRIT LARGE

"Infant child care" suffers not only from society's blurred vision of what it is, but also from the fact that all problems of child care are heightened for infant care. Thus the supply of infant care is even smaller compared to demand than is the supply of care for older children (U.S. Department of Labor, 1988); the adult/child ratios must be even lower; the cost per child is higher; caregivers are less well trained; staff turnover is greater; and regulation is less widespread. In many cases we do not know what kind of care infants and toddlers are receiving, since most who are in family day care are in unlicensed, unregulated homes (Hofferth & Phillips, 1987; Kahn & Kamerman, 1987). It is no overstatement to say that infant care is in a state of crisis. Care of acceptable quality, where ratios are low and group sizes small, is simply not affordable for most families.

There is now disturbing new evidence that the old way of "affording" infant day care—by underpaying caregivers—is no longer working. The recent Child Care Staffing Study undertaken by the Child Care Employee Project, gathering data from 227 child care centers (of diverse sponsorship) serving children of all socioeconomic strata in five geographically diffuse metropolitan areas found that staff turnover has almost tripled in the past decade, jumping from 15 percent in 1977 to 41 percent in 1988. In fact, the odds are almost fifty-fifty that a baby will have to become accustomed to a new caregiver in each of the first three years of life. Child care workers, even those with training, typically earned not much more than the minimum wage (Whitebook, Howes, & Phillips, 1989).

Public policy makers' ambivalence about this problem is perhaps at its most extreme with respect to the issues of paid parental leave at childbirth or adoption. The broad availability of paid parental leave would greatly reduce the pressure of numbers in infant day care. It would also provide parents and their babies the time they need to become firmly attached to each other—for parents to know the child's individual sensitivities and possible special needs in order to make a more intelligent placement into child care. Yet policy makers, many of whom express concern about the possible ill effects of early child care, have not adopted the measure that would most powerfully alleviate that concern, and which is law in 80 countries and all developed countries, except South Africa and the United States (Kamerman, Kahn, & Kingston, 1983).

THE SAFETY OF INFANT CARE:
CONTROVERSY AMONG THE EXPERTS

To add to the problems besetting infant care, there has been no unanimity within the child development field itself as to the effects of more than half-time care for infants under one year of age. It is claimed that certain studies show that children who have been in care more than 20 hours per week prior to age one are less securely attached to their parents, more aggressive in primary school, and less liked by schoolmates (Belsky, 1986). But a number of researchers take strong issue with these conclusions. They point out that the studies Belsky cites were retrospective rather than prospective, did not control for quality, and were strongly confounded with family variables, including maternal attitude toward employment and child care (Phillips, McCartney, Scarr, & Howes, 1987).

Concerned about the effect of this dispute which has been fully aired in the media and is ever more visible to concerned parents, the National Center for Clinical Infant Programs (NCCIP) in October 1987 called a "summit meeting" of top-level researchers in infant day care. The meeting, co-hosted by the National Academy of Sciences and the Institute of Medicine, was designed to determine what all could agree on and, where disagreement remained, what were the most important avenues for future research. The group agreed that:

> When parents have choices about selection and utilization of supplementary care for their infants and toddlers and have access to stable child care arrangements featuring skilled, sensitive and motivated care givers, there is every reason to believe that both children and families can thrive. Such choices do not exist for many families in America today, and inadequate care poses risks to the current well-being and future development of infants, toddlers and their families, on whose productivity the country depends. (National Center for Clinical Infant Programs, 1988)

The recent report of the National Academy of Sciences makes the same point (1990).

UNRESOLVED QUESTIONS ABOUT
INFANT DAY CARE

Nevertheless, there remain some unanswered questions about infants and toddlers in child care: For example, what kinds of children, from what kinds of families do *not* typically fare well, and what kinds of care do they need? The research "summit meeting" suggested that a group of small parallel, prospective, longitudinal studies be undertaken to compare groups of children who experience a variety of early child care circumstances. The goal of these research efforts would be to see how various factors contribute to developmental outcome in unique, shared, and/or interactive ways, and the relative contributions of various factors to developmental outcome. Factors such as socioeconomic status; family composition; maternal level of education; amount and sources of family stress and family social support; parental feelings and attitudes about separation and supplemental care for infants; parents' sensitivity to their infants' cues; parents' satisfaction in parenthood; the infant's temperament, activity level, and other individual characteristics, including any factors likely to pose a risk to optimal development; the quality of the child care, including the amount and characteristics of interaction between adults and infants; the stability and continuity of care; the temperament of the caregivers; the level of education and specific knowledge of child development of the caregivers; the characteristics of the caregiving environment including health and safety, noise level, visual appeal, amount of space and number of children and adults typically present; the type of care, the adult/child ratio, the size of the group in which the child was cared for; and the relationship between child care providers and parents should all be looked at for their potential impact on very young children (National Center for Clinical Infant Programs, 1988; National Academy of Sciences, 1990).

The U.S. Public Health Service's National Institute of Child Health and Human Development, already interested in supporting a major collaborative, longitudinal study of infant day care, used the recommendations of the "summit meeting" in designing its own request for proposals for the study (Friedman, 1990). One hopes that this National Study of Young Children's Lives will help untangle the variables presently confounded and that it will show what elements are essential to quality infant care and what elements are detrimental to healthy growth and development.

These research studies will be helpful in the first of the volitile issues raised at the beginning of this chapter: the work/family issue. They may be able to illuminate the second and third issues as well.

Furthermore, the collaborative research, as well as certain pilot initiatives presently being conducted around the nation, are likely to highlight ways in which infant day care can be used as a *positive* force in the healthy development of infants and toddlers. These include the use of child care for much more widespread immunization of infants, the training of child care workers in the detection and referral of developmental delays, handicapping conditions, and developing emotional or behavioral problems (Pizzo, 1990; Johnston, 1990). One hopes they will highlight the importance of caregiver-parent relationships, of cultural sensitivity, and of the opportunities to detect potentially severely damaging environmental problems. Child care is a window through which to spot and treat emerging health, developmental, and interactional problems before they become major disorders.

SPECIAL CHARACTERISTICS OF INFANT AND TODDLER CHILD CARE

Infant care is a highly distinct form of child care. To quote members of NCCIP's Day Care Committee:

> Developmentally appropriate programs for children from birth to age 3 are distinctly different from all other types of programs—they are *not* a scaled-down version of a good program for preschool children. These program differences are determined by the unique characteristics and needs of children during the first 3 years:
>
> - changes take place far more rapidly in infancy than during any other period in life
> - during infancy, as at every other age, all areas of development—cognitive, social, emotional, and physical—are intertwined (This author would add, even more intertwined.)
> - infants are totally dependent on adults to meet their needs
> - very young children are especially vulnerable to adversity because they are less able to cope actively with discomfort or stress. (Lally, Provence, Szanton, & Weissbourd, 1986, p. 17)

For all these reasons, infants require caregivers who demonstrate affection even as they offer a stimulating environment; responsive caregiving, sensitive to individual differences between children and to changes in each child's state; an environment in which they can explore the real objects that make up daily living; a caregiver who elaborates verbally on what they are attempting to do, understanding that they need to hear language pitched at them long before they are able to respond verbally themselves. Infants and toddlers require very close consultation between caregiver and family about recent events in the child's day or night. They require a caregiver with particular sensitivity to cultural differences, if any, since this is a time in which very deep cultural patterns are being formed. Most of these required competencies are important for all children in daycare. For infants they are essential. Furthermore, a number of them are not at all intuitive, even to an individual who may have been a highly successful parent; they require training.

Quality Infant Care: Its Relationship to Caregiver Training

The training of infant and toddler caregivers is at best an afterthought on public policy agendas. This is surprising, since almost without exception studies that have examined the elements of quality child care in relation to child competence have found that children who were rated as more highly competent had caregivers who had had job-related training (Ruopp, Travers, Glantz, & Coelen, 1979; Phillips et al., 1987; Weikart, 1989; Whitebrook et al., 1989). Yet training seems to keep falling off the list of what policy makers believe they can afford or legislate. Why should this be so? To begin with, there appears to be a residual belief that the care of infants and toddlers is "just babysitting" or "just comes naturally." Thus, in 1989, 7 states had no educational requirements of center-based classroom teachers; 30 states had no requirements for family day care providers (Adams, 1990).

Interestingly, resistance to expenditures for the training of providers of infant and toddler child care draws on child development research, as well. Research showing the degree to which traits are heritable, as in the studies of twins from behavioral genetics (Plomin, 1989), as well as research showing the degree to which infants and those who take care of them are "preprogrammed" have led some to take the position that it is very hard to do developmental harm to a child in the first years of life. Therefore, it is important to tease out what does come naturally from what does not. (Of course, those behaviors that come naturally do so only to some caregivers and some infants.) And which nonintuitive caregiver behaviors are subject to change through training and greater knowledge of child development? In other words, it is vital to describe those caregiver behaviors and knowledge that probably account for a significant share of the correlation between adult training and child competence. (This is not by any means to imply that a lot of formal education-based learning is important. Competency-based training, such as the CDA credential, is an example of training that is excellent but not necessarily offered by institutions of higher education.)

Key Caregiver Behaviors and Knowledge Which are Not Intuitive

The importance of receptive language. The history of research in infant development over the past 20 years is almost synonymous with new discoveries concerning the degree to which babies, even *in utero*, can distinguish and begin to discriminate among sounds (Friedlander, 1970; Eimas, Sigueland, Jusczyk, & Vigorito, 1971). Language aimed slowly, distinctly, directly at a baby in the context of a social relationship has been shown to enhance the development of a child's ability to communicate long before the infant or toddler is actually using language herself. Recent research also has brought to light in fascinating detail the degree to which adult baby talk seems to be universal and thus probably prewired (Fernald et al., in press), one example of the "what-comes-naturally" research cited above. Nonetheless, it is startling how many adults believe that a child begins to understand language only when he begins to speak. Knowledge of what does and does *not* constitute a stimulating linguistic environment is a critical factor, especially for family day care providers tempted to leave the television running.

Health and safety of infants in groups. Individuals who have enjoyed and who have been successful at parenting their own small children are often potentially excellent caregivers in infant day care. However, by and large, they have had no experience in the important area of caring for babies in groups. Their own children are likely to have been of disparate ages. Untrained caregivers may be totally unprepared for the kinds of public health practices necessary when several children at once are in diapers, are still lacking in many kinds of immunities, and are totally innocent of basic sanitary behaviors (American Academy of Pediatrics, 1986).

Learning by doing: The responsive environment

The child. It is apparently not intuitive to give a baby space to explore, following her lead, letting her bring things to show. Yet this kind of sensitive, responsive caregiving appears to be a key to emotional attachment (Ainsworth, 1973; Stern, 1985), and cognitive development (Beckwirth, Cohen, Kopp, Parmelee, & Marcy, 1976; Emde, 1980). Even an impoverished home is relatively full of fascinating shapes, sounds, smells, patterns of color, pots, clothing, human beings, available for discovery. However, caregivers who ignore or discourage exploration or who believe themselves to be administering a "curriculum" frequently lose this rhythm of allowing the child to explore, elaborating verbally on what the *child* is focusing on. Without training, observation, and practice, they may overwhelm the toddler with directions and suggestions. As one writer observing a child care worker has described it, "She told the observer she was becoming frustrated trying to keep the children entertained. She said she had been letting them watch more TV, even though she didn't like it, because she'd done everything she could think of to entertain them" (Eheart & Leavitt, 1989).

The caregiver. It is also not intuitively understood, without training or careful discussion, how much a baby learns from the simple routines of child care and therefore how much of an opportunity these can be for caregivers.

> Gina lifted Jackie from the water and placed him on the counter to be dried. He seemed to enjoy being rubbed with the towel. He smiled at Gina, and made happy squeals and a "da da" sound. He remained inactive, lying on his back while his diaper and shirt were put on. Gina talked with him frequently while she bathed and dressed him and Jackie responded by making soft, pleasant sounds. When placed in a sitting position to have the rest of his clothes put on, he did not try to move away, nor did he actively enter the dressing process. When he was dressed, Gina helped him stand up and invited him to look at himself in the mirror. He smiled, babbled, and waved his hand at the observer, whose reflection he could also see. He then looked at his own reflection, smiled broadly, and bounced up and down as though charmed with what he saw. (Lally et al., 1986, p. 26)

This caregiver has made the most of a bath, and the child has learned a lot at his own speed and in his own style, probably more than he would have from imitating the actions of a caregiver working with a "curriculum." Yet without training, caregivers—particularly those who are depressed, anxious, angry, or bored—can easily lose these opportunities for learning mixed with warmth and practical routines. In fact, they may turn these necessary routines into negative experiences.

The importance of state. Surprisingly, it is not altogether intuitively understood that the infant or toddler's state is of the utmost importance in considering how to interact with her. For although it is part of time-honored childrearing lore that a baby may be too fussy or sleepy or hungry to appreciate her surroundings, it is only in the past 15 years that researchers have learned the positive side of this wisdom—just how responsive an infant can be at the teachable moment (Brazelton & Yogman, 1986; Tronick & Gianino, 1986). Caregivers with a number of children to attend to are not in a position to be entirely responsive to each child's state at all times, though the need to be so a relatively high proportion of the time is one of the chief reasons why the infant:adult ratio must be lower than for other children. Nonetheless, training for and modeling behavior which keeps state in mind—showing the possibilities—can make a great difference, both for infant and caregiver.

The importance of individual differences. Another set of very important insights gained by developmental and clinical research of the past two decades yet which does not come naturally to many caregivers are the implications for caregiving of individual differences in central nervous system processing of stimuli. These lie in two major categories.

The overstimulated child. The first category is of infants who, because of premature birth or some other cause, have hypersensitive nervous systems. These children, easily overstimulated, must defend themselves by either shutting out the world or overreacting—for example, averting their eyes or screaming when picked up. They seem unable to buffer themselves or sort out multiple stimuli to the degree other children are able to do. These are children who will probably do better in an individual or small group setting such as family day care. (They are also children for whom parental leave at childbirth may be particularly important.) They are children for whom special caregiver/ parent training is extremely important. Learning to stimulate only one source of sensory input at a time requires coaching for caregivers as much as for parents (Brazelton & Yogman, 1986). Furthermore, staff in a larger child care center need advice about more sheltered environments for such children.

The timid toddler. A second category of individual differences among children is in their physiological (and emotional) reaction to new or strange situations. Longitudinal research shows the stability of stress reactions over a lifetime in both humans and other primates (Champoux & Suomi, 1988; Kagan, Reznick, & Snidman, 1987). An understanding of this basic element in some children may be recognized in the popular lore of childrearing but often as something a child is to be jollied or shamed out of. Understanding of the nature and source of this individual trait is another important piece of a caregiver's training.

The importance of training for staff morale. There is yet another reason staff training is of utmost importance. That is to dignify and enliven the work of the caregiver. As fascinating as infants can be, their care for many hours on end in the same environment can lead to burnout. Therefore, it is important for their own morale that caregivers understand the meaning of the behavior they observe. It provides a fascination that otherwise might be missing (Provence, Naylor, & Patterson, 1977, pp. 204–205).

The importance of self-awareness. Finally, caregivers trained to understand their own feelings in dealing with infants and with their parents are much better prepared to provide high quality care. Babies evoke strong emotions. Caregivers need to have thought about, and discussed in training, their feelings in relation to a fussy baby; a baby who won't eat; a young child who seems to be resisting toilet training; a beautiful, cuddly infant whose parents seem to ignore or abuse him.

Parents of infants often exhibit guilt about leaving their child and jealousy of the caregiver. Caregivers need the opportunity to explore their reactions to these feelings in the safety of a training situation. The resulting insights can make all the difference between a negative, competitive situation and one which utilizes the parents' strength of emotion about their child in a positive way.

Cultural differences in the childrearing context are a third area in which one should have practice in self-awareness. In this case, self-awareness is training about ethnocentricity. Learning important features of another culture—particularly ones which impinge on childrearing—are essential to developing respect for parents and teamwork with them, should they be of a different cultural background. Conversely, since these earliest years are ones when the most basic cultural patterns are developing, parents have a right to be comfortable in the knowledge that the practices they follow at home are not scorned during the day.

TRAINING ESSENTIAL FOR ALL THOSE
WHO WORK WITH INFANTS AND TODDLERS
AND THEIR FAMILIES

The National Center for Clinical Infant Programs has recently developed a set of recommendations for educators, for policy makers, for parents, and for professional groups, which outline elements that ANY individual being trained to work with ANY infant or toddler in ANY discipline should have as part of their training background. Entitled *Preparing Practitioners to Work with Infants, Toddlers and Their Families*, these call for:

- knowledge of certain core concepts that integrate information from many disciplines about early child development
- opportunities for direct observation and interaction with infants and toddlers and their families
- individualized supervision that allows for the exploration of one's own feelings
- collegial support, both within and across disciplines (National Center for Clinical Infant Programs, 1990, a,b,c,d).

These are part of every good training program for those seeking to work in infant and toddler child care—no doubt more so than for a number of other disciplines working with infants and toddlers and their families. However, if training is a low priority for the expenditure of funds or time, caregivers may not have had these experiences.

SUMMARY

The issue of infant and toddler child care is entangled with some of the major domestic issues facing this country. It is viewed very differently depending on which of these issues is the context of the moment. Yet it presents problems to an even greater degree than those facing child care in general, as certain recent demographic studies have shown.

Researchers agree there is no reason to believe infants under one year of age suffer in child care, provided their parents have freely chosen it and that it is a quality program. However, many parents today do not have the opportunity to choose and to choose quality. Furthermore, certain questions remain about who is most vulnerable, in what kind of care. These will continue to be researched, in a new collaborative study, among others.

Nonetheless, there should be no controversy about the need for training of infant and toddler caregivers. A number of features are distinctive to infant care and are, by and large, not intuitively understood. Quality care requires training for them.

REFERENCES

Adams, G. C. (1990). *Who knows how safe?* Washington, DC: Children's Defense Fund.

Ainsworth, M. D. S. (1973). The development of infant-mother attachment. In B. M. Caldwell & H. N. Ricciuti (Eds.), *Review of child development research III* (pp. 1–94). Chicago, IL: University of Chicago Press.

American Academy of Pediatrics. (1986). *Report of the Committee of Infectious Diseases* (P. Georges, ed.). Elk Grove, IL: Author.

American Association for Protecting Children, Inc. (1987). *Highlights of official child neglect and abuse reporting, 1985.* Denver, CO: The American Humane Association.

Beckwith, L., Cohen, S. E., Kopp, C. B., Parmelee, A. H., & Marcy, T. G. (1976). Caregiver–infant interaction and early cognitive development in preterm infants. *Child Development, 47,* 579–587.

Belsky, J. (1986). Infant day care: A cause for concern? *Zero to Three, VII* (1).

Brazelton, T. B., & Yogman, M. W. (Eds.). (1986). *Affective development in infancy.* Norwood, NJ: Ablex.

Bureau of Labor Statistics. (1988). *Marital and family characteristics of the labor force: March 1988.* Unpublished data. Washington, DC: U.S. Department of Labor.

Champoux, M., & Suomi, S. J. (1988). Behavioral development of nursery-reared rhesus macaque neonates. *Infant Behavior and Development, 11,* 363–367.

Eheart, B. K., & Leavitt, R. L. (1989). Family day care: Discrepancies between intended and observed caregiving practices. *Early Childhood Research Quarterly, IV*(1), 145–162.

Eimas, P. D., Sigueland, E. R., Jusczyk, P., & Vigorito, J. (1971). Speech perception in infants. *Science.* Washington, DC: The American Association for the Advancement of Science.

Emde, R. N. (1980). Emotion availability: A reciprocal reward system for infants and parents with implications for prevention of psychosocial disorders. In P. M. Taylor (Ed.), *Parent–infant relationship* (pp. 87–115). New York: Grune & Stratton.

Fernald, A., Taeschner, T., Dunn, J., Papousek, M., Boysson Bardies, B., & Faukui, I. (in press). A cross-language study of prosodic modifications in mothers' and fathers' speech to preverbal infants. *Journal of Child Language.*

Friedlander, B. Z. (1970). Receptive language development in infancy: Issues and problems. *Merrill-Palmer Quarterly*. Detroit, MI: Merrill-Palmer Institute.

Friedman, S. L. (1990). NICHD infant child-care network: The National Study of Young Children's Lives. *Zero to Three, X*(3).

Hofferth, S., & Phillips, D. (1987). Child care in the United States, 1970–1995. *Journal of Marriage and the Family, 49*, 559–571.

Johnston, K. (1990). Mental health consultation today care providers: The San Francisco daycare consultants program. *Zero to Three, X*(3).

Kagan, J., Reznick, J. S., & Snidman, N. (1987). The physiology and psychology of behavioral inhibition in children. *Child Development, 58*, 1459–1473.

Kahn, A., & Kamerman, S. (1987). *Child care: Facing the hard choices*. Dover, MA: Auburn House.

Kamerman, S. B., Kahn, A. J., & Kingston, P. (1983). *Maternity policies and working women*. New York: Columbia University Press.

Lally, J. R., Provence, S., Szanton, E., & Weissbourd, B. (1986). Developmentally appropriate care for children from birth to age 3. *Developmentally appropriate practice*. Washington, DC: National Association for the Education of Young Children.

Moen, P. (1989). *Working parents: Transformations in gender roles and public policies in Sweden*. Madison, WI: University of Wisconsin Press.

National Academy of Sciences. (1990). *Who cares for America's children? Child care policy for the 1990s*. Washington, D.C.

National Center for Clinical Infant Programs. (1988). *Infants, families and child care: Toward a research agenda*. Washington, DC: Author.

National Center for Clinical Infant Programs. (1990a). *Preparing practitioners to work with infants, toddlers and their families: Issues and recommendations for educators and trainers*. Washington, DC: Author.

National Center for Clinical Infant Programs. (1990b). *Preparing practitioners to work with infants, toddlers and their families: Issues and recommendations for parents*. Washington, DC: Author.

National Center for Clinical Infant Programs. (1990c). *Preparing practitioners to work with infants, toddlers and their families: Issues and recommendations for policymakers*. Washington, DC: Author

National Center for Clinical Infant Programs. (1990d). *Preparing practitioners to work with infants, toddlers and their families: Issues and recommendations for professions*. Washington, DC: Author.

Phillips, D., McCartney, K., Scarr, S., & Howes, C. (1987). Selective review of infant day care research: A cause for concern! *Zero to Three, VII*(3).

Pizzo, P. D. (1990). Whole babies, parents and pieces of funds: Creating comprehensive programs for infants and toddlers. *Zero to Three, X*(3).

Plomin, R. (1989). Environment and genes: Determinants of behavior. *American Psychologist, 44*, 105–111.

Provence, S., Naylor, A., & Patterson, J. (1977). *The challenge of daycare*. New Haven, CT: Yale University Press.

Ruopp, R., Travers, F., Glantz, F., & Coelen, C. (1979). *Children at the center:*

Final results of the National Day Care Study. Boston, MA: Abt Associates.

Stern, D. M. (1985). *The interpersonal world of the infant.* New York: Basic Books.

Tronick, E. Z., & Gianino, A. (1986). Interactive mismatch and repair: Challenges to the coping infant. *Zero to Three, VI*(3), pp. 1–6.

U.S. Department of Labor. (1988). *Child care—a work force issue. Report of the secretary's task force.* Washington, DC: U.S. Government Printing Office.

The Washington Post. (1989, September 3). Area parents torn by day-care angst.

Weikart, D. P. (1989). *Quality preschool programs: A long-term social investment.* New York: Ford Foundation.

Whitebook, M., Howes, C., & Phillips, D. (1989). *Who cares? Child Care Teachers and the Quality of Care in America* (Executive Summary, National Child Care Staffing Study). Oakland, CA: Child Care Employee Project.

Zigler, E. F., & Finn-Stevenson, M. (1989). Child care in America: from problem to solution. *Educational Policy, 3*(4), 313–329.

Chapter 7
Emerging Child Care Policy Issues

Helen Blank
Children's Defense Fund, Washington, DC

A child care crisis confronts this nation. It grows more severe every day and will intensify further as America approaches the new century. Policy changes to address American families' child care concerns must take into account the various gaps in the existing system. Many families cannot choose safe child care without financial assistance to cover the costs. All families face difficulties in searching for a quality child care arrangement that leaves them free from concern about their children's well-being. Finally, the growing demand for child care in many communities results in a lack of a child care search that is frustrating. This chapter examines the issues that must be addressed to make safe child care more easily available to America's families and discusses the consequences of inadequate child care both for children and their families. It also considers the role that child care plays in keeping the country economically competitive. Policies are recommended that are essential to building a responsive child care system.

Demand for child care is climbing rapidly. As recently as 1970, only three out of 10 preschool-aged children in America had mothers in the work force. Today, five out of 10 do and the proportion will climb still further, to seven out of 10 by the year 2000, if current trends continue. At the turn of the century, four out of five women in America ages 25 to 54 will be working.

For more and more families, child care spells work and self-sufficiency. Two-parent families increasingly need two incomes to provide for their children. Between 1973 and 1986, median annual earnings of men ages 20 to 30 plummeted by 28 percent. Many young families can only cushion the impact of this drop if mothers bring home a second paycheck (Children's Defense Fund, 1988). At the same time, more and more families are headed by single parents who need child care to work at all. Families without two wage-earners face a high risk of sinking into poverty: Almost half of those headed by a single mother aged 25 to 44 are poor today. For growing numbers of American working families struggling to make ends meet—whether on one income or two—child care has become a necessity of economic survival (Bureau of the Census, 1989).

The quality of child care will help shape the work force of the next century. The millions of American children who will spend a significant part of their childhood in child care are vital to the nation's future economic health and competitiveness. To prepare the next generation to be productive workers, the nation must ensure that every child gets a strong early foundation for learning. For most children who need child care, this means access to care that is safe, affordable, and high quality. For disadvantaged youngsters, who need extra help to compensate for poverty's deprivations, it means offering a chance to experience the extra boost provided by comprehensive early childhood programs such as Head Start.

America's patchwork child care system—already swamped by existing demands—is ill-equipped to cope with stepped-up pressures. Unless the nation acts now, the future will only bring longer day care waiting lists and more children left in substandard day care or waiting home alone because no affordable care is available.

TWENTY-SIX MILLION AMERICAN CHILDREN IN SEARCH OF A CHILD CARE SOLUTION

Every day, millions of children—infants, preschoolers, and school-agers—are affected directly by the nation's child care dilemma. This is because the sole parent living with them, or both parents, are in the work force.

Five million infants and toddlers. The past few years have witnessed a surge in demand for child care for an especially vulnerable group: babies and one- and two-year-old youngsters.

Because this nation's employment policies have not kept pace with changing realities, many parents who would like to stay home with their infants cannot do so. They cannot afford the economic risk. Unlike all other Western industrialized nations except South Africa, the United States does not have a parental leave policy that guarantees new parents a leave of absence and job security when they return to work. In the absence of such protections, and with more and more mothers of infants having to work, more working families must seek infant care (Kamerman, Kahn, & Kingston, 1983).

Fifty percent of mothers of babies one year old or younger are working. They find the costs of infant care especially high and the choices few. In Arizona, for example, less than 3 percent of licensed child care centers offer slots for infants (Governor's Office for Children, 1986). Nearly half of the women who went back to work four to seven months after childbirth faced significant problems finding child care, according to Mothers in the Workplace, a 1987 study conducted by the National Council of Jewish Women's Center for the Child (National Council for Jewish Women Center for the Child, 1987).

Around the country, parents are competing just to get their infants and toddlers on child care waiting lists. At the Children's Edition, a child care center in Louisville, Kentucky, for example, 96 youngsters younger than two are among the 130 children on the waiting list for the center's 86 child care slots. The average wait is nine months to a year (Locke, 1988).

Five million 3- to 5-year-olds. Although more programs are available for preschoolers than for infants, many for 3-and 4-year-olds are run on a part-day basis. Most parents, however, do not work part-time. As a result, bewildered youngsters must shuttle among as many as three care-giving situations in a single day, increasing their anxiety and disrupting their normal learning and play patterns. Only the luckiest children are placed in a single stable arrangement. In Vermont, for example, only one out of four preschool children with working parents is cared for in a regulated full-time day care slot (The Governor's Commission on the Status of Women's Child Care Task Force, 1985).

Sixteen million 6- to 13-year-old youngsters. The dearth of after-school care for school-age youngsters leaves them to loiter in streets or playgrounds, or go home alone or with other children to an empty house.

• A survey in Los Angeles, California, found nearly one-quarter of 7-

to 9-year-olds in self-care after school (Wellesley College Center for Research on Women, 1987).

- In Columbus, Ohio, one-fourth of the 500 households surveyed relied on self-care for school-age children age 12 and younger. Not surprisingly, half of these families said they were uncomfortable with their child care arrangements (Wellesley College Center for Research on Women, 1987).
- In a 1987 study conducted by Louis Harris and Associates for the Metropolitan Life Insurance Company, a majority of more than 1,000 teachers interviewed cited isolation and lack of supervision after school as the major reasons children have difficulty in school (Metropolitan Life Survey, 1987).

In 1984, when children were invited by the language arts magazine *Sprint* to write about a situation they find scary, the editors were stunned by the response. Nearly 70 percent of the 7,000 letters that poured in from fourth-, fifth-, and sixth-graders from across the United States described fears of being home alone, mostly while parents were working.

THE QUALITY OF CHILD CARE MAKES A DIFFERENCE

Parents, teachers, and child development experts agree that good child care makes a positive and permanent difference to a child's development. Child care that works for children is that which keeps group sizes small and has fewer children per adult caregiver. Children in such settings receive more attention and get more chances to improve their cognitive, social, and language skills. In addition, good child care is staffed by caregivers with solid training and has low caregiver turnover, qualities that can best be achieved by paying employees decent wages.

Parents want their children to have a good child care experience. They know that the current system does not provide adequate assurance of that outcome. That is why they overwhelmingly support minimum national standards for child care. In a survey conducted by *NBC News* and *The Wall Street Journal*, for example, 69 percent of the surveyed public backed such standards (*National Journal*, 1988).

Today, millions of children live in states that do not adequately protect them against unsafe or low-quality child care:

- South Carolina allows one caregiver to care for as many as eight infants. In Georgia and North Carolina, one caregiver may care for seven infants. Nineteen states allow staff-to-infant ratios of one to five or worse.
- Thirty-five states and the District of Columbia have such low expectations of family day care providers that they require no training in child development. Thirty-two states require no training before teachers come to work at day care centers.
- Twenty-nine states and the District of Columbia do not protect parents' right to drop in unannounced in family day care homes to check on their children.
- In Colorado, each case worker on the state's licensing staff monitors an average of 211 child care facilities. While the day care licensing caseload has nearly tripled since 1971, the licensing staff has declined from 8.5 positions to 6.5 (Carahan & Jones, 1988).

WHEN PARENTS CANNOT AFFORD QUALITY CHILD CARE, CHILDREN PAY THE PRICE

Recently, in a community near Chicago, 47 youngsters—half of them younger than two—were discovered being cared for in a basement by only one adult. At $25 a week, the program was one-third of the cost of most child care in the community. When the state closed this "center," many of the parents objected. No concerned parent would happily put a child in such a child care situation. But the parents could afford no better. When parents cannot afford decent child care, children suffer and often are placed in care that is dangerous (Enstad, 1988).

It costs an average of $3,500 a year to send one child to full-time child care—money that is getting harder to find in many families' budgets. The median income of America's families with children fell 4 percent between 1973 and 1987 and would have fallen more except for increased numbers of working mothers (U.S. Congress, 1986). For younger families with children the child care burden is greater still, because they have suffered a 26 percent income drop since 1973 (Children's Defense Fund, 1988).

While purchasing child care is a struggle for many working families, poor and near-poor families cannot afford decent child care at all unless they stop eating, buying shoes, or paying the rent. For example, America's single mothers who are raising one or more children younger than six have a median income of $7,013 (as of 1987). The annual cost of child care for one child would eat up nearly half their entire income (Bureau of the Census, 1989).

THE GAPS IN AMERICA'S CHILD CARE SYSTEM

Meeting the nation's child care crisis calls for a working partnership among the federal government, the states, the private sector, and America's families to assure an adequate supply of quality child care and to provide help to lower-income families so they can keep working. But the federal government has walked away from any significant role in improving quality or expanding supply, and has provided scant help to lower income families that are working hard to provide good child care for their children.

The federal government has been the missing partner. Despite the demographic and economic convulsions that make child care a pressing national concern, the nation still has no broad federal policy or program that addresses the availability, affordability, and quality of child care.

Federal child care help through the Title XX Social Services Block Grant has dwindled. On average, states use about 18 percent of their allotment of Title XX funds—funds that must meet a broad range of human service needs—to help lower-income families pay for child care. But Title XX funding never has come close to meeting the need. In FY 1977 the program served only 12 percent of the 3.3 million poor children younger than six. Today the money is stretched even more thinly. The overall Title XX appropriation for FY 1989 is less than half of what it was in FY 1977 (after adjusting for inflation), while the number of preschool children in poverty has soared to almost 5 million (CDF, 1989).

Federal tax breaks do not build a good child care system. The dependent care tax credit is the only federal source of child care help that has increased significantly in recent years. The credit allows families to offset some of their federal tax bill by claiming a portion of their child care expenses. More than 8.4 million families received $3.127 billion of credits in 1985 (Internal Revenue Service, 1987–1988). But the credit does little for the lower-income families that most desperately need child care assistance, because these families have little or no federal income tax liability to offset, and because the credit covers only a fraction of the cost of care. Nor does the tax credit have any impact on the two other key child care problems: availability and quality of care.

Under the Family Support Act of 1988, AFDC families will receive federal child care help. The welfare reform bill is expected to provide $1 billion over five years to defray child care costs for AFDC parents who participate in education and work preparation programs, work, or are in a one-year transitional period after their earnings make them ineligible for AFDC. But millions of poor and near-poor working families who do receive AFDC benefits are still without child care help (Family Support Act, 1988).

States cannot handle the child care crisis alone. Some states are struggling to address the child care crisis by boosting state contributions to Title XX-funded child care or by launching new child care programs. But more states are sliding backward. In 1988, 26 states spent less in real dollars for child care funded through the Title XX Social Services Block Grant than they did in FY 1981. Only 20 states are serving more children than they did in 1981, while 23 states are serving fewer (Blank, 1988). Even California, which annually invests more than $300 million in child care, serves only 7 percent of the children eligible for child care assistance.

These numbers mean that children are at risk. Lashwana, a two-year-old toddler who lives in Broward County, Florida, is one of close to 33,000 on the state's waiting lists for child care help. Lashwana is often left in the care of her seven-year-old sister, who stays home from school to babysit so their mother can go to work (Weinstein, 1989).

Private sector efforts are growing, but still very scarce. While employers are increasing their involvement in child care, only approximately 4,500 employers out of 6 million across the United States provide any child care help to their employees. Very few of even these 4,100 employers provide the most needed help: assistance to families in paying their child care bills (Weinstein, 1989).

HEAD START: AN EARLY CHILDHOOD PROGRAM THAT HELPS OUR NEEDIEST CHILDREN

All children need a strong early childhood experience as a foundation for later learning. But disadvantaged 3- and 4-year-olds, struggling under the hardships of poverty, need something extra before they go to school: the comprehensive services provided by the federal Head Start program.

Head Start, however, only has the funds to serve one out of five eligible children (Turner, 1990). As a result, poor children are far less likely than more affluent children to have the opportunity to enroll in an early childhood development program. In 1986 fewer than four out of every ten 4-year-olds with family incomes below $10,000 a year were enrolled in a preschool program. In contrast, two out of three 4-year-olds whose families had incomes of $35,000 a year or more attended such programs (Kamerman, et al., 1983).

The shortage of help to poor preschoolers is extremely short-sighted. The business-led Committee for Economic Development (CED), in its 1987 report, *Children in Need: Investment Strategies for the Educationally Disadvantaged*, stated that such programs represent a "superior educational investment for society." CED recommends that the nation expand the Head Start program until every eligible child has an opportunity to participate (Committee for Economic Development, 1988).

Research shows that the benefits of early education programs last through school and into adulthood.

The hallmark of Head Start's effectiveness is its multifaceted approach to helping children learn, develop, and grow. Head Start succeeds by:

- *Providing a broad range of needed services:* "Head Start is much more than just preschool education," Sharon Glynne, a Fairfax County Head Start coordinator, told Lisbeth Schorr, author of *Within Our Reach: Breaking the Cycle of Disadvantage.* "Our new child-initiated learning curriculum is exciting, it works, but it wouldn't work without the health and nutrition and social services we also provide. . . . Our teachers understand that a child whose family got evicted that day can't pay a lot of attention to classroom routines." Head Start addresses a broad range of children's needs. In 1988, for example, almost 100 percent of all Head Start children received vaccinations, medical screening, dental checkups, and needed treatment (Turner, 1990).
- *Involving and energizing families:* Four out of five Head Start parents volunteer in the program, helping youngsters and learning new skills and new self-respect. More than one-third of all Head Start employees are parents of current or former Head Start children (Turner, 1990).

Although 2.5 million disadvantaged youngsters are potentially eligible for Head Start, approximately one-in-five of those children are lucky enough to be admitted (Turner, 1990). Many of the others are waiting for an open slot:

- In Bath, New York, where the Head Start program has an enrollment of 119, 90 remain on waiting lists (Hurt).
- In Phipsburg, Pennsylvania, 313 children receive services, while 188 children wait for a slot to open up (Levin, 1988).

These children have to wait because federal funding for Head Start has not kept pace with spreading child poverty during the 1980s. But inadequate funding also has meant that program quality has been harder to maintain. All around the country, Head Start programs are struggling to attract and retain qualified staff, to maintain or renovate their facilities, and to provide preschoolers with transportation to the programs. While some states have boosted their investment in early childhood programs for youngsters, their total spending on such programs was less than $250 million in 1988 (Blank, 1988).

A FEDERAL AND STATE ACTION AGENDA

The Federal Government
Congress should:

- Appropriate $925 million to fund the Child Care and Development Block Grant for FY 1993 and $50 million authorized to help states improve the quality of child care in the Licensing and Monitoring Grant Program.
- Pass S. 911 which would ensure that full funding was available by 1997 to provide Head Start for all eligible children.

State Governments
Each state should:

- Carefully implement the two new federal child care programs—the Child Care and Development Block Grant and the "At-Risk" Child Care Program.
- Ensure that new federal child care funds not be used to supplant existing state child care investments and consider supplementing these federal funds with additional state money. Since no federal program will be able to reach all families that need assistance, states must continue to assist low- and moderate-income families in paying for child care.
- Supplement Head Start or support state-initiated programs that

114   BLANK

provide comprehensive services to preschool children and operate full days throughout the year.

- Put into place strong health and safety standards that are monitored carefully regardless of the sponsor of the child care program or the numbers of children served.
- Make sure all programs comply with state regulations by investing the necessary resources in monitoring and enforcement efforts.
- Adopt standards and policies that ensure quality care. These include standards that keep group sizes and child-to-staff ratios low and ensure an adequate and stable supply of trained early childhood teachers and administrators. They also include policies that promote the active involvement of parents.
- Increase the amount of good quality child care by establishing state grants and revolving loan funds to cover start-up and expansion costs and quality improvements, as well as recruitment and training efforts for new child care providers. These efforts should be targeted to those areas and communities in greatest need of financial assistance.
- Expand the supply of trained child care workers by establishing scholarships and loan forgiveness programs for individuals seeking early childhood development credentials. Significantly improve the quality and supply of training opportunities.
- Implement the child care provisions of the Family Support Act in a manner that ensures that families are offered high quality child care. Effective implementation should include adequate rates and payment mechanisms, meaningful standards, and child care counseling services.

REFERENCES

Blank, H. (1988). *State child care fact book*. Washington, DC: Children's Defense Fund.

Carahan, A., & Jones, V. N. (1988, June 26). Day Care Experience May Scar: Caseload, Understaffing Impede State Inspectors' Watchdog Role. *Rocky Mountain News*.

Children's Defense Fund. (1988). *A Children's Defense Fund Budget 1989*. Washington, DC: Author.

Children's Defense Fund and Center for Labor Market Studies. (1988). *Vanishing dreams: The growing economic plight of American families*. Washington, DC: Northeastern University.

Enstad, R. (1988, April 6). Crowded Day Care Facility Closed. *Chicago Tribune*.

Governor's Child Care Coalition; Governor's Office for Children. (1986, November). *Child Care in Arizona: Putting the Pieces Together*.

Governor's Commission on the Status of Women's Child Care Task Force. (1985, October). *The economics of child care: Taking care of Vermont's most valuable natural resource.*

Internal Revenue Service. (1987–1988, Winter). Statistics of Income Division, 501 Bulletin. Washington, DC.

Kamerman, S., Kahn, A., & Kingston, P. (1983). *Maternity policies and working women.* New York: Columbia University Press.

Metropolitan Life Survey of *The American Teacher 1987: Strengthening Links Between Home and School.* (1987, May/June). New York: Louis Harris & Associates.

Morgan, G. (1987). *The National State of Child Care Regulations 1986.* Watertown & 174 Work/Family Directions, Inc. 3-3, 5-1, 7-2.

National Council for Jewish Women Center for the Child. (1987, March). Mothers in the Workplace. *The medical and family leave: Benefits available to female workers in the United States.* New York: Author.

Opinion outline: Views on the scene. (1988, September 17). *National Journal, 38,* 2344.

Research & Policy Committee for Economic Development, a statement. (1987). *Children in need: Investment strategies for the educationally disadvantaged.* Washington, DC: Author.

U.S. Department of Commerce, Bureau of the Census. (1989). *Current Population Reports,* Series P-60, No. 163, Poverty in the United States: Table 15.

Weinstein, B. (1989, Spring). Brighter beginnings for Broward and beyond. *Florida's Child, 1*(1).

Wellesley College, Center for Research on Women. (1987, July). Columbus Explores Child Care Territory. *School-age Child Care Project Newsletter, 4* (3),

The Role of the Corporation in Promoting Early Childhood Education and Care and Family Support Systems

Ellen Galinsky

Families and Work Institute, New York, NY

A nursery school teacher calls an early childhood educator who works regularly with corporations. "I think it's time for me to make a career change," she said. "I want to work with corporations, helping them set up child care centers for their own employees."

This conversation indicates an important new trend: Over the past decade corporate involvement in the field of early childhood education and care has become increasingly commonplace. Thus, it is not at all surprising that a nursery school teacher would see working with corporations as a legitimate avenue for a career change. Her belief that companies are routinely providing on-site centers, however, is erroneous. As this chapter will reveal, providing on-site care is only one of the numerous roles that corporations have assumed in promoting early childhood education and care as well as family support. This chapter will review the development of each of these roles (using case studies as illustrations), delineate obstacles, and discuss the impact of these roles. Finally, we will draw some conclusions from our discussion. Because there has been a greater corporate involvement in child care than in family support, these examples will predominate.

PROVIDING GENERAL FINANCIAL ASSISTANCE

For many years, much of the corporate giving to child care has been channeled through the United Way, whose mission is "to increase the organized capacity of people to care for one another." Company volunteers seek donations from individual co-workers. In addition, individual community members are also solicited. The resulting monies are distributed among designated member agencies to "address unmet needs in the community."

For example, the United Way of Rockland (New York) was founded in 1964 by 12 core volunteers. That year six companies, with the assistance of fewer than 100 volunteers, raised $190,000 for member agencies, or $55,000 more than the agencies had been able to raise alone. In 1989, $1,050,000 was raised and over 295 local companies participated. Four day care centers and the local child care resource and referral agency were among the numerous recipients of these funds (United Way of Rockland County, n.d.).

Nationwide, the funds given to child care programs through United Way have increased. According to a survey of 375 United Ways, in 1983 over $40 million were distributed; in 1987, that amount had topped $66 million. The amount targeted to child care centers represented 2.9 percent of their total giving and a 1986 record of fund distribution indicates that 890 centers had been served nationwide (United Way of America, 1987).

United Way agencies determine giving by establishing a "priority basis." The latest survey of 451 United Ways indicated that 21 percent see child care as a priority. Within this general rating, some United Ways designate a specific aspect of child care. United Ways in Lehigh, Northhampton, and Warren Counties (Pennsylvania) established a Child Care Advisory Committee to investigate the prevalence of local latchkey children. Upon finding that many children were left alone while their parents worked, they targeted giving to programs to serve these children.

Numerous corporate foundations have also made individual donations to child care and family support programs. Until recently, most corporate donations to education were concentrated on universities and high schools and were clearly intended to bolster students' preparation for labor force entry. As it has become evident that problems of literacy and scientific achievement have their roots in early childhood, and as the rate of high school dropouts rises, some foundations have begun exploring the possibility of funding local child care and family support programs. It is, however, still unusual for the individual child care or family support program to receive general support from corporate foundations. The National Child/Care Staffing Study found that, on average, only 6 percent of centers' budgets came from donated monies (Whitebook, Howes, & Phillips, 1989).

DONATING EXPERTISE AND PRODUCTS

Another longstanding corporate role is that of benefactor. When I visited exemplary child care programs in the mid-1970s for my book, *The New Extended Family: Day Care That Works* (Galinsky & Hooks, 1977), I found that many directors tried to tap local corporations for castoffs. Surplus paper was used for drawing, packing crates for makeshift buildings in house corners, and plastic scraps for collage materials.

The use of donated materials reaches a pinnacle in the Maryland Committee for Children's office building in downtown Baltimore. The ground floor is filled with beautifully designed displays heaped with buttons, scraps of materials, and intriguing industrial parts, all for the use of local child care centers and family day care homes.

Corporations have also donated expertise. The graphics art department at Orange and Rockland, a New York State utility, has designed brochures for the Rockland Council for Young Children. Lederle Labs printed a calendar illustrated with children's photographs; the proceeds from the calendar sales went to support child care in Rockland County.

Child care and family support programs have also sought business assistance in marketing and fiscal management. Most frequently, they receive this help by inviting corporate managers to serve on their boards, but occasionally companies have loaned executives to help manage a fiscal crisis or develop a strategic plan. Some programs seek out the assistance of retired executives. For example, Family Focus, a parent support program in the Chicago area, contacted Executive Service Corporation. For a small fee that went to maintain the services of this agency, a volunteer spent hours working with the Executive Director of Family Focus, reviewing their bookkeeping procedures and helping to devise a workable system for financial management.

SCRUTINIZING THE DELIVERY SYSTEM

Approximately 5,500 American companies provide some form of child care assistance for their employees (Friedman, 1990). Many have gone through a careful planning phase to select the kinds of programs they want to offer their employees. This planning typically includes an analysis of employees' needs and a corresponding review of the community resources available to meet those needs. Although intended to help employers select child care options, these community assessments also function as a market analysis of the local child care delivery system. In this process, gaps in service as well as strengths are identified (McConaghy & Siegel, 1988).

The experiences of Johnson & Johnson can serve as an example. Johnson & Johnson contracted with Resources for Child Care Management (RCCM) to assist their Work/Family Task Force in arriving at recommendations. RCCM conducted a community assessment at J&J's various locations. This review revealed, for example, that in the State of New Jersey only 15 percent of needed care was provided by regulated child care programs; most parents used underground, unlicensed, and unregulated care. Accordingly, most parents found it difficult to find care, especially for infants and school-age children, and many were leaving their children at home alone. Inclement weather caused particular problems. While the cost of care was high (between $110 and $150 a week for infant care in one county), caregiver salaries were low ($12,000–$17,000 for assistants and teachers, respectively). Thus, staff turnover was high, exceeding 50 percent in some locations. This community analysis was helpful in leading Johnson & Johnson to make the decision to establish at least two on-site centers.

With money from corporate contracts, over 200 child care resource and referral agencies nationwide serve as what McConaghy and Siegel (1988) term "data librarians." In the course of helping to match parents with child care, they tabulate the relation of parent need and preference for care in specific neighborhoods to the availability of openings. In this way, supply and demand ratios can be tracked.

This activity in the child care marketplace is a relatively new phenomenon. Because the child care system is largely home-based and informal, it has lacked both analysis and planned growth. It is not uncommon for large gaps between supply and demand to exist. In *The New Extended Family: Day Care That Works*, William Hooks and I compared the growth of child care to a field filled with weeds and flowers, springing up willy-nilly. Obviously, there are exceptions— Kinder Care's selection of the morning side of the highway (the route most frequently used for parent employees to get to work) as sites for their centers is one—but until the infusion of corporate needs assessments and corporate-supported resource and referral analyses, the child care marketplace was largely unmonitored.

PROVIDING INFORMATION
AND FINANCIAL RESOURCE

The three most frequent solutions to helping employees solve work/family problems have been (a) the provision of information and financial assistance through corporate child care resource and referral (CCR&R) programs, (b) Flexible Spending Accounts (FSAs), and (c) parent seminars at the workplace.

Child Care Resource and Referral is a counseling program to help parent employees find and judge child care. By 1990, 1,500 companies provided CCR&R programs (Friedman, 1990). These services are either contracted out to a national R&R organization such as Work/Family Directions in Boston, Massachusetts, who subcontracts to local agencies, or directly to local agencies. A few companies like the Lincoln National Corporation run their own in-house R&R service. When employees need child care, they telephone a counselor (or meet in person if the service is in-house) who obtains information about the child's age, cost requirements, and the parents' preference for type of care and location. The counselor then provides information on how to select quality care and, after the conversation, selects several options that meet the parents' criteria, calls to see if there are openings, and forwards the information to the parent. The CCR&R counselor does not make the selection for the parent but merely provides suitable alternatives for the parent to select among. After several weeks, the counselor calls the parent to determine if care has been obtained and if so, how satisfied the parent is both with the child care and with the R&R service. Almost all CCR&R agencies also provide assistance in locating child care free of charge to the general public. This service is usually subsidized by state contracts and foundations. The corporate service, called "enhanced resource and referral," is more personalized than the services received by the general public.

A *Flexible Spending Account (FSA)* is a salary reduction plan made possible by Section 125 of the IRS Code. Employees can reduce their salaries by up to $5,000 and be reimbursed for child care and certain other expenses with these pretax dollars. There are certain restrictions on FSAs. First, employees can use either an FSA or the Dependent Care Tax Credit but not both, and providers being reimbursed are required to claim the income on their own taxes, disallowing any use of the underground child care market. Furthermore, if the funds in the account are not used up by the end of the first year, it must be forfeited. In 1990, approximately 2,500 companies had established FSAs (Friedman, 1990).

Although the pervasive image of corporate involvement in child care is that of on-site child care centers, most companies encourage their employees to buy into local child care systems, through corporate assistance in both finding and paying for local care. Many corporate executives do not want to be in the child care business. As one said, "We're in the pharmaceutical business, not the day care business and we ought to stick with the business we know." Company executives also note that pumping money into their own community child care system is a "good neighbor thing to do." Rather than set up a competing service, they are trying to improve local child care. Presumably, more information on how to select quality care and more money to purchase it will stimulate the American free enterprise system.

The impact of this type of involvement has been impressive. Largely with corporate dollars, a child care resource and referral system has been forged across America. Where CCR&R agencies did not exist, companies such as IBM (and more recently, AT&T) have provided seed money to create them. Where they did exist, corporate money has helped them achieve greater fiscal and operational stability. An increasing number of states are now funding these agencies; California, Massachusetts, Michigan, Maryland, and New Jersey have statewide CCR&R coverage (McConaghy & Siegel, 1988). CCR&R is becoming the hub of the child care system, helping to monitor and plan its growth, to broker among the various constituent groups, and, as I describe later, to recruit and train new providers.

Taking a nationwide view of the impact of corporate involvement in the child care system, a problem becomes readily apparent. As the New York State Task Force on Work and Family observed, companies tend to become involved in local child care in parts of the country where the care is of higher quality (New York State, 1989). Furthermore, the locations of the Fortune 500 companies that have pioneered these services tend to be in the prosperous parts of the country. By these well-meaning efforts, the gap between the more affluent, successful communities and those less so is widening. Furthermore, even within those communities served, the corporate employees who receive "enhanced R&R" are entitled to a more customized service than the parents who don't work for one of these employees. In fact, one CCR&R in Portland, Oregon, serves only employees of subscribing companies and is not available to the general population. It may be that companies are sapping the best care for their employees, leaving the lesser quality care for other parent employees who may also receive less pay and have fewer benefits.

Analysis of FSA usage also shows they serve more well-off employees. Parents need a sufficiently high income to be able to afford to cut half their salaries, pay for child care with a smaller salary check, and wait to be reimbursed (Friedman, 1985).

Parent Seminars at the Workplace are workshops or lectures giving parents information and support to enable them to achieve a better balance between their job and family responsibilities. A 1984 study by Catalyst estimated that over 1,000 employers were conducting seminars at the workplace for employed parents. These seminars provide family support, although they are more likely to be organized by CCR&R agencies than parent educators or family support programs. For example, IBM contracted with Work/Family Directions to develop a curriculum for work/family seminars and to conduct these programs through their network of CCR&R agencies in their over 200 locations. In some corporations, a specific vendor conducts the majority of their work/family seminars, as has been the case for Bristol-Myers and Bank Street College. In other cases, each seminar is contracted to different experts as has been the custom at Time, Warner Inc. Some companies use in-house experts who convene regular support groups.

In professional conferences on this subject, the providers of lunchtime seminars express frustration that the typical pattern of holding one session ever few months or even once a year in a superficial approach to family support. A subject such as single parents is introduced; participants become involved and eager for more depth and then the allotted hour-and-a-half is up and the company representatives feel that they have "fully covered" the topic and go on to the next one. The pattern followed by Merck & Co., Inc. provides much more depth. A several-week series on a specific topic is offered. The participants can return to the subject of parenting preschool children or managing time after exploring some of the concepts at home.

PROVIDING DIRECT SERVICE

Approximately 250 corporations have created child care centers. Management schemes range from complete to very little corporate control:

Company-owned and operated. The company is fully responsible for the daily operation and management of the center. Since 1980, Hoffman-La Roche has operated a child care center for 60 children at its Nutley, New Jersey, headquarters. The staff at the center are employees of Hoffman-La Roche and thus receive above-market wages and benefits. The company also subsidizes the program to the amount of $1,000 per child. In response to long waiting lists at the center and the perceived benefit that Hoffman-La Roche has been deriving from this initiative, they have budgeted $1 million for expansion so that twice as many children can be served. Such generous subsidies enable less highly paid employees to afford the service.

Company-owned, contracted service. Under this fiscal arrangement, the company contracts a vendor to provide the child care service and can change vendors if there is dissatisfaction. Such was the scenario at Campbell Soup Company in Camden, New Jersey, in mid-1980s. The company was using a large, for-profit chain to operate its center. When parents' complaints about the high rate of staff turnover began to surface, the company hired a consultant from Resources for Child Care Management to evaluate the service and eventually hired Resources for Child Care Management to run the center. The center now serves 110 children and receives a 40 percent subsidy, which makes it possible for employees at all income levels to enroll their children.

MacCare, an on-site center serving McDonnell Douglas employees in St. Louis, has a slightly different arrangement. While the center is under the auspices of the company, it is a separate subsidiary, responsible for its own budget. The company provided the start-up cost and donates the cost of the space, a rambling, spacious old elementary school, minutes away from headquarters.

Employee-owned and operated. Several corporations have provided start-up money for on- or near-site programs to be owned and operated by employees. The Employee Center for Young Children serving Merck in Rahway, New Jersey, and the center that serves World Bank employees in Washington, DC, are two examples of this management form. At Merck, the center was established with a $100,000 grant. The long waiting list recently prompted the company to donate the land and provide major funding for a new center closer to the Rahway facility that will be twice as large as the current program (150 children).

The problem with this management arrangement is that parent fees must cover the full costs of care. If the program is to serve less well-off employees, there is constant pressure to raise funds, to crowd the classrooms with more children, or to pay lower salaries. These potential compromises in quality are draining to the directors who voice their concerns at conferences, stating that the companies get a lot of positive public relations for these programs but don't understand the day-to-day struggle to assure quality.

The centers at Merck, Hoffman-La Roche, and McDonnell Douglas are all expanding because employee demand far outstrips the number of children that can be served. Most employee centers have long wait-

ing lists, especially for infant care. In such a situation, difficult decisions must be made. If there is an opening, does the program take the
renowned Ph.D. job candidate that the company is trying to recruit or
the secretary who has had her name on the list close to since her child's
conception? Expanding the center is clearly not the only solution to
this problem. While there has been talk of creating a network of family
child care providers clustered around the on-site center, this initiative
has rarely materialized.

Prior to creating an on-site program, a common obstacle is a concern
about equity. The provision of a program that by its very nature serves
only one select group of employees flies in the face of a corporate
commitment to providing benefits that serve all employees equally.
When need outpaces supply, as is frequently the case at on-site centers,
employees on the waiting list do feel disgruntled. In contrast, employees without children or those who choose a different form of care rarely
complain about the center. Most employees are said to be glad to work
for a company that has an on- or near-site child care center.

Another inhibiting factor is the fear of liability suits. Companies
worry that parent employees will go after the corporations as the "deep
pockets" if an accident at the program occurs. Employers who sponsor
centers report that the cost of insurance is not at all prohibitive and
that perhaps because of an insistence upon quality, suits are almost
non-existent. When risk-management training for insured providers
becomes more commonplace, the hype surrounding liability insurance
should subside. A new report commissioned by the Department of
Labor should also help dispel the myths around this problem (Friedman, 1989a).

A third obstacle to on-site centers is their cost. Start-up costs and
ongoing subsidies are expensive. Companies justify this expenditure
by saying that if just a handful of employees are retained as a result of
the center, the cost is worthwhile.

A recent review of the research on the benefits of an on-site care by
Friedman (1989b) indicates that on-site programs do not affect absen-
teeism (perhaps because of more stringent policies for sick children at
on-site centers) as much as recruitment and retention. In view of
impending labor shortages, this is an interesting finding. Although the
benefits of on- or near-site centers are being revealed by research,
corporate child care consultants have made numerous, and to some
extent, exaggerated claims over the years. The past decade has seen
only marginal growth in the provision of direct service. The growth
that has occurred has been an expansion of centers in hospitals (800
centers) and federal agencies (250 centers). Nevertheless, some companies who originally rejected this option are currently reconsidering,

and real estate developers are beginning to offer child care centers as an amenity within office park complexes.

The impact of on- and near-site care on the community child care system is complex. Some claim that a corporate center, with its increased visibility and higher salaries, will cream off some of the best local teachers. If the center is open to nonemployee parents, there is fear that the parents most committed to quality will be drawn to the program, thus again, siphoning off individuals who could serve as catalysts to improving the community system. Local providers, particularly the mom-and-pop businesses, claim that the corporate center skews competition, giving the corporate center an unfair advantage.

There are others who argue just the opposite: that better salaries and better quality will "trickle down" into the community, serving as models and inspirations. Without research on these issues, the impact of on-site care is unclear. I suspect, however, that the impact partially varies as a function of how involved the staff of the center is with other local providers and how cooperatively they all work together.

INCREASING THE SUPPLY AND IMPROVING THE QUALITY OF CHILD CARE

When corporate representatives begin to investigate the local child care system, they often discover its unwieldy intricacies. Needs assessments reveal that approximately one in two employed parents have difficulty finding child care, that the multiple arrangements parents put together are tenuous, and finally that the range of quality runs the entire gamut (Galinsky, 1988; Whitebrook, Howes, & Phillips, 1989). Companies thus recognize that if they establish CCR&Rs or FSAs but local care is inadequate, these services could provoke more dissatisfaction than satisfaction. Furthermore, they realize that corporate-sponsored centers might drain the local system. In response, an increasing number of companies have begun to develop initiatives to increase the supply and improve the quality of child care services through a variety of means: CCR&Rs, individual or collaborative corporate contributions, special funds, and sponsorship of NAEYC accreditation efforts.

Recruiting and Training Through CCR&Rs

In 1984, IBM established an important precedent in corporate involvement in child care by targeting a percentage of their CCR&R fee for efforts to increase the supply and improve the quality of local child care. Since that time, Work/Family Directions, the IBM contractor, has made this function a part of its service for other corporate clients. To date, over 55,000 new providers have been recruited. Of these, 45,000 are family child care homes. Work/Family Directions estimates that approximately 20 percent of the per-employee fee paid by companies is used for recruitment. A nationwide survey of the services that CCR&Rs provide found that 93 percent of the 200 agencies recruit family day care providers (Friedman, 1989c).

Another feature of CCR&R's services is training. Work/Family Directions also give special grants for this purpose. Local agencies provide ongoing training and hold conferences with the express purpose of improving the quality of local services.

Corporate Contributions

Corporate giving has slowly begun to identify the need to increase supply and enhance quality. One of the most innovative grants was made by 3M's McKnight Foundation. These funders recognized the havoc that low caregiver salaries were creating, contributing to staff turnover and the inevitable erosion of quality. They gave a $468,000 grant to improve salaries in the Minneapolis/St. Paul area, including minigrants to programs and intensive training in such matters as budgeting.

A number of recent efforts to increase the supply of better quality care has been directed specifically at family day care in response to the fact that most children are in family child care settings. For example, American Express funded Child Care, Inc., a CCR&R agency in New York City, to recruit and train providers.

In March 1988, Mervyn's, a division of Dayton Hudson, launched a program entitled Family-to-Family. The intent of this four-year, $3,714,800 initiative is to increase the quality of family day care in 15 communities where Mervyn's stores are located. Their goals are:

- A potential accreditation model will be developed establishing quality standards for family child care.
- Nine funded providers in 15 communities will be accredited.
- Fifteen local family child care home training institutes will be established.
- Four thousand family child care home providers, of which 2,000 will be newly recruited, will be trained, providing 20,000 children with a quality family day care environment.

In 1989, Target Stores joined this effort, dedicated to similar goals. They will launch a major consumer education effort to increase parents' awareness and expectations of quality in family child care. In addition, these companies are providing a real service to other potential funders in this area by funding an evaluation of Family-to-Family.

Collaborative Funding Efforts

The California Child Care Initiative Project (CCCIP), one of the most comprehensive efforts to increase the supply of high-quality child care, was spearheaded by the BankAmerica Foundation and eventually involved a collaboration of 33 organizations, including 23 businesses and 10 public agencies. Overall, $3.2 million has been raised since 1985. By the middle of 1988, 1,600 licensed new homes were established, serving 6,500 children (Friedman, 1989c). A 1987 evaluation comparing providers recruited by CCCIP with other providers found the recruited group more likely to avail themselves of training opportunities and less likely to quit or leave the field (Friedman, 1989c). The Ford Foundation has now funded replication of CCCIP in other states.

Child Care Funds

AT&T pioneered this type of corporate assistance with its ground-breaking union-negotiated Family Care Development Fund in the summer of 1989. Beginning in the spring of 1990, $10 million grants have become available for local AT&T sites to engage in efforts to increase the supply and improve the quality of local child care for their employees. A local individual or group of employees sponsor proposals to be considered by boards specifically created to award these grants.

Since the AT&T initiative is just beginning, it will be some time before the results of this intervention can be ascertained. Given that the fund is specifically aimed at addressing AT&T's employees' problems, it will be interesting to evaluate the impact on local child care: Will this effort siphon off the best community child care for AT&T employees, or will the fund stimulate a general improvement of quality?

Accreditation Efforts

The National Association for the Education of Young Children (NAEYC), the largest professional organization of early childhood educators, with 76,000 members and 400 affiliate groups nationwide, has developed a program to accredit high-quality early childhood centers. Since this program was launched in 1986, 1400 programs have been accredited and close to 4000 are enrolled (NAEYC, 1990). In the fall of 1989, several major corporations asked NAEYC to help them fund the accreditation fees of programs in their communities (whether or not employees' children were served) in order to increase the number of high quality local programs. IBM, one of these companies, announced a $250,000 effort (as one part of a $22 million child care fund) to assist programs to become accredited. Such initiatives, if they become more widespread, could have considerable impact on elevating the standards of center-based programs.

Local or State Task Forces

As individuals, a number of business executives have pledged to assume leadership on task forces to identify and solve local child care problems. Although there has been no systematic analysis of the origins and prevalence of these efforts, there seem to be four major conveners:

The United Way. In locations as diverse as central Massachusetts, Danbury (Connecticut), Alexandria (Virginia), Dade County (Florida), and Minneapolis (Minnesota), the United Way has assembled task forces on the crisis in early education and care. An inspiring example occurred in Minneapolis. Chaired by the CEO of Honeywell, this United Way Task Force was named Success by Six. Its intent was to identify the obstacles that prevented children from entering first grade as successes and to eliminate these roadblocks, a strategy now being replicated in other communities.

Resource and referral agencies. The Maryland Committee for Children assisted in the formation of a public/private partnership whose aim was "to increase workforce productivity and promote economic development by strengthening the child care delivery system." The Maryland Employers Advisory Council on Child Care was chaired by the CEO of Commercial Credit Group, Inc. Their concluding recommendation (now becoming a reality) was the creation of the Maryland Child Care Resource Network, a network of CCR&Rs, coordinated by a statewide Resource Center that is to maintain a statewide database, provide training and technical assistance to the CCR&Rs, coordinate public policy efforts, raise funds for the network, broker contracts, and serve as a liaison with child care delivery systems in other states.

Chambers of Commerce. The St. Paul Chamber of Commerce convened a Child Care Task Force to assemble data about their community and brought in local and national experts. A notable feature of this task force was that it didn't conclude with a report bound to grow dusty on the bookshelf. They not only outlined what they planned to accomplish, they set objectives, timelines, and strategies. Many of their goals have since been enacted.

The State Executive Office. Numerous governors and lieutenant governors across the country have developed mechanisms to address the child care crisis. Their strategies include conferences (e.g., in Virginia and Indiana), task forces (e.g., in Tennessee and Oregon), and CEO breakfasts (e.g., in New York). In some states (e.g., Wisconsin) and cities (e.g., Los Angeles), an employer-supported child care coordinator job has been created. The purpose of these efforts is to involve the business community in formulating community solutions to local child care problems or in the provision of services for their employees.

The Coalition for Utah's Future serves as an interesting example of this trend. Originally established by one Governor, but supported by the next, the coalition was directed to help "the state plan and implement its future." According to former Governor Scott H. Matheson, "the basic commitment of the coalition would have to be to ensure that its goal would be fully and effectively implemented in the shortest possible time." One of its subgroups, the Task Force on Children, constituted of many business leaders, has conducted a comprehensive study of Utah's problems. They found that 149,412 children between the ages of 0–13 need care and have no relatives to care for them and that the average child care employee's salary was $4.08 in 1988, a significant factor in the 46 percent turnover rate. This self-study culminated in a conference in September 1989 and recommendations.

Although there has been no formal evaluation of these various efforts, it appears that these action-oriented task forces have the potential to bring about change. Occasionally, the recommendations are ignored or dropped due to a change in state leadership or other factors, but generally they are a catalyst (albeit sometimes slower than advocates would like) to a number of well-conceived and integrated proposals to bring about improvement.

ADVOCATING THROUGH THE LEGISLATIVE PROCESS

The results of corporate involvement in the legislative process have been more mixed than the other corporate roles. Historically, corporations have been reluctant to testify for child care legislation, feeling that it falls beyond their direct business purview. However, as the links between child care problems and productivity, child care and economic development, and early education and later school and employment success have become more evident, several corporations have stepped across that barrier and used their clout in Congress to urge government action. The CEO of the Port Authority of New York and New Jersey testified in June of 1989 for increased funding for Head Start. Representatives from Mervyn's and American Express testified for the child care bill known as ABC (the 100th Congress). American Express, in fact, surprised observers by taking a stand in favor of national standards governing child care.

On the other hand, corporate involvement in the legislative process has also been aimed, perhaps unintentionally, at reducing quality. These incidents seem to follow the same pattern: While trying to establish on-site centers, high-ranking business representatives find the bureaucratic maze and strict standards inhibiting and press their legislators either to drop all legislation affecting corporate programs and rewrite new policies, as was the case in Colorado, or to reduce existing standards, as happened in California. The bill in Colorado passed both houses of the legislature but was vetoed in 1989 by Governor Roy Romer. In 1990, the same bill was passed.

In these episodes, protection is confused with bureaucracy. It is true that becoming licensed can be difficult and that some existing standard may be ill-founded, but discarding the whole procedure or gutting their protective clauses is not the solution. Perhaps some procedures could be eliminated and/or simplified, and an ombudsperson could be appointed to help companies (and other providers) through the licensing maze. However, laissez-faire thinking has led to proposals (in California) that allow infants to be placed in a tiny room with no available outdoor space in the care of a virtually untrained provider—because, after all, "their parents are nearby" and "babies sleep all day." This is outrageous. In Washington State, corporations defeated child care legislation for fear of raising taxes. If this trend continues, companies will have taken on the role of advocating against quality care.

THE IMPACT OF CORPORATE INVOLVEMENT

The fact that the corporate community has increasingly become concerned with the field of child care has meant a great deal to many providers. Laboring under difficult working conditions, earning poverty-level salaries, watching their co-workers "vote with their feet" and leave the field despite a desire to stay, and being labeled "babysitters" is extremely disheartening. As President of the National Association for the Education of Young Children, I meet with affiliate groups weekly throughout the country. When I report on corporate interest in child care, they feel encouraged. Knowing that business executives take their work seriously has been an inducement to stay in the field and attempt to bring about needed reform.

In addition, corporate involvement in child care has created a career path for a small group of early childhood professionals. Unfortunately, there is little training or preparation for this role. Teachers, tired of the classroom, often assume they can jump in and help corporations start on-site centers. They don't realize that employers and employees may not want this form of corporate assistance and that consultants must be well versed in all forms of corporate initiatives (including time policies and benefits), designing and analyzing needs assessments, conducting focus groups, and working with the corporate community. Although visions of making money lead some educators to consider this path, such jobs are few and far between. It takes a long time to break into the corporate network—companies tend to select consultants on the basis of other executive referrals.

As the preceding review has revealed, the major impact of corporate involvement has been to strengthen community child care by increasing its supply and improving its quality. Yet, as this is such a new endeavor, many questions bear addressing:

1. The companies that pioneered child care initiatives have used a very thoughtful process in identifying their employees' problems and creating innovative solutions. As corporate involvement becomes more mainstream, will programs be crafted with the same thoughtfulness and care?
2. A select few pioneering companies have not only developed programs to serve their own employees but have also invested time and money in improving the community system. Will this trend continue or will corporate involvement serve as a siphon, depleting the community of its best resources?
3. Will companies strive to improve quality or will they endorse efforts to lower standards?
4. Since companies have become involved in child care for business reasons (to improve the productivity of their current workforce and the skill of the future workforce), will they be attracted to family support programs at the workplace or will they see these efforts as peripheral?

It seems hard to remember a time when business was uninvolved in early childhood issues, yet this involvement has come about in less than a decade. Although in sheer numbers, the participating companies represent a small fraction of corporate America, the scope of the various roles they have taken is wide. As a movement, however, its direction and effect are yet to be determined.

REFERENCES

Friedman, D. E. (1985). *Corporate financial assistance for child care.* New York: The Conference Board.

Friedman, D. E. (1989a, July). *Perceptions and realities of child care liabiity insurance.* Report prepared for the Department of Labor.

Friedman, D. E. (1989b, June 7). *The productivity effects of workplace centers.* Paper presented at Child Care Center at the Workplace, Resources for Child Care Management (RCCM) Conference, Chicago, IL.

Friedman, D. E. (1989c, July). *Addressing the supply problem: The family day care approach.* Report prepared for the Department of Labor.

Friedman, D. E. (1990). *Estimates from national monitors of employer-supported child care.* Unpublished memo. New York: Families and Work Institute.

Galinsky, E. (1988). *Child care and productivity.* Paper prepared for Child Care Action Campaign conference, "Child Care: The Bottom Line," New York, NY.

Galinsky, E., & Hooks, W. H. (1977). *The new extended family: Day care that works.* Boston: Houghton Mifflen.

McConaghy, E., & Siegel, P. (1988, November 10–13). *The challenge for child care resource and referral services.* Paper presented at the NACCRA preconference session, 1988 NAEYC Annual Conference, Anaheim, CA.

Smith, M. (1988, October 1–1989, September 30). Confronting tough issues. *Young Children, 45*(1), 32–38.

[New York State] Governor's Task Force on Work and Family. (1989, March). Final Report. Albany, NY: Governor's Task Force.

United Way of America. (1987, March). *Child care* (The Action Series). Alexandria, VA: Author.

Whitebook, M., Howes, C., & Phillips, D. (1989). *Who cares? Child care teachers and the quality of care in America* (Executive Summary, National Child Care Staffing Study). Oakland, CA: Child Care Employee Project.

Part III

Policy Issues Related to Public School Early Childhood Programs

Chapter 9
Developmentally Appropriate Practice and the Challenge of Public School Reform

Thomas Schultz

National Association of State Boards of Education, Alexandria, VA

The worlds of early childhood education and the public schools are intertwined in several ways. For instance, one important part of the mission of early childhood programs is to prepare children for success in school. In the minds of parents, the "proof of the pudding" for a successful early childhood program lies in the reception of its "graduates" by the public school. This expectation is shared by policy makers choosing to invest public dollars in early childhood services. In another fashion, recent enthusiasm for preschool programs has given rise to a host of institutional tensions between early childhood programs and the public schools in competing for funding and the opportunity to sponsor services. At the federal level, debates on child care legislation have included questions of whether a portion of funds should be "earmarked" for programs in the public schools. At the state level, Head Start programs are strongly concerned with a pattern of establishing public school programs for low-income preschoolers rather than choosing to expand enrollments in Head Start. At the local level, competition between public schools and other early childhood programs encompasses staff, facilities, and children.

A third facet of the early childhood–public school relationship relates to the agenda of promoting "developmentally appropriate practice" in kindergarten and the primary grades. While the laity commonly assume that early childhood education is defined by the years prior to the onset of public education, child development experts and the early childhood professional community lay claim to the years from birth to age 8 as their rightful institutional turf. Based on this presumption, the major national organization representing the early childhood community, the National Association for the Education of Young Children (NAEYC) has developed and promoted a detailed and comprehensive set of prescriptions for curriculum, assessment, and pedagogy in kindergarten and the primary grades of elementary school (Bredekamp, 1987). In this respect, early childhood educators take issue with the practices of most public school classrooms and seek to change them.

These three different relationships define three different roles for early childhood educators. In the first case, early childhood leaders are in a responsive relationship to public schools; in the second, the role is one of competitor; in the third, a change agent or advocate role vis-á-vis public school practices is called for. My argument is that this third relationship, that of promoting change in public school policies, routines, and practices should receive increased attention as a policy challenge for early childhood educators in the 1990s. In this chapter I first establish the significance of the agenda of developmentally appropriate practice within the present policy context for public education. Second, I analyze the "degree of difficulty" of implementing these concepts in the public schools, both in terms of present helpful and hindering forces, and in terms of lessons from past efforts on the problems of changing classroom practice. Third, I advance a set of possible strategies for promoting the agenda of "developmentally appropriate practice" in the public schools.

CONVERGING AGENDAS: POLICY CHALLENGES FOR EARLY CHILDHOOD AND PUBLIC EDUCATION

For public education, the past decade of national commissions and reports have led to a consensus around two central performance problems: reducing the gap in educational outcomes between low income and minority students (who will constitute an increasing proportion of public school students) and their more advantaged counterparts, and improving the overall abilities of students to apply knowledge and skills, solve problems, and communicate effectively. On the one hand we are struggling to eliminate a persistent dropout rate of approximately 25 percent; on the other hand we are concerned with the students who successfully stick with the public schools but who graduate with minimal skills in terms of their preparation for the workforce, for higher education, or for citizenship.

During the past decade, early childhood education has been predominantly viewed as a solution to the first of these difficulties. That is, early childhood education has been promoted and perceived as a targeted intervention for "at-risk" populations, designed to equalize their chances to compete with middle- and upper-class children. Project Head Start, by its very title, exemplifies this set of assumptions. The implication is that if poor children receive preventive assistance before beginning the competitive race of public education, they will be more nearly able to end up in the front ranks of runners, or at least to finish the race without falling by the wayside.

This formulation of early childhood education is relatively attractive to educators for a number of reasons. First, the parameters and costs of implementing these programs appear to be well established (if often ignored in large-scale state and local programs). Second, the implementation task is in the form of a discrete, new program which requires and brings with it new resources, rather than calling on redirection/competition for existing funds (although some educators are wary about assuming any increased responsibility and rue the "opportunity costs" if new dollars are spent on preschool education rather than to bolster existing salaries and services). Over the years schools have become relatively adept at adding on new programs. Third, progress on the agenda of expanding preschool opportunities is easily measurable in terms of funding and enrollment.

However, there are a growing series of misgivings within the early childhood community regarding this pattern of new preschool programs. First is the concern that a dominant pattern of funding part-day programs is unresponsive to the needs of working parents and to the likely demands of welfare reform legislation on low-income parents. Second is a concern that tenets of quality are not being followed with sufficient rigor. Third is a concern that a dominant pattern of funding through public schools is at best ignoring the experience of Head Start and other community-based programs, and at worst is attacking the capacity of these other providers by competing for space, staff, and ultimately children. Fourth is the observation that funding priorities and eligibility criteria for these programs lead to a pattern of programs that are segregated by income and often by race as well.

Finally is the question of whether even a high-quality preschool experience is sufficiently powerful to ensure the outcomes we are after. For example, data from Head Start and other programs consistently show a "drop-off" effect in academic benefits from preschool services, with significant differences between enrolled and unserved children at age 5 eroding as the students continue their school careers. And even within the widely trumpeted success of the Perry Preschool endeavor we can see absolute rates of delinquency and failure to complete school that are alarming and unacceptable within the present climate of concern regarding economic and social needs. For example, while graduates of the High/Scope Foundation's Perry Preschool were more likely to complete school than peers who did not participate in preschool, they still experienced a dropout rate of 33 percent (Berrueta-Clement, Schweinhart, Barnett, Epstein, & Weikart, 1984, p. 31).

In summary, while the match between promoting preschool services and the schools need to address "at-risk" populations has served the interests and agendas of both early childhood and public school communities, there are substantial limits to this solution. For early childhood advocates, school-based part-day programs for low-income populations are only a small piece of the system of comprehensive services that they wish to create. For public education leaders, the preschool component is a significant but apparently only partial response to the challenge of serving at-risk students.

In addition, adding on a special program limited to low-income students offers no response to the second challenge for public education, that of the promotion of much higher levels of academic performance for all students. Can early childhood education contibute to the second preoccupation of education reformers, namely the enhancement of student performance in thinking and performance across a wide range of subject areas? My contention is that the agenda of developmentally appropriate practice offers substantial promise to respond to this concern.

The key deficiency in this instance is the limited abilities of students to move beyond ability to simply recall facts, to demonstrate abilities to apply and utilize knowledge. For example, in the most recent reports of the National Assessment of Educational Progress, the majority of 17-year-old students could not read at a level of difficulty similar to that of a newspaper editorial, only about one-third of this age group could write a persuasive letter, and fewer than 10 percent could solve multistep problems in mathematics (Applebee, Langer, & Mullis, 1989). These deficiencies are regarded as serious obstacles to our national economic health:

> An economy based on students who think for a living requires schools dedicated to the creation of environments in which students become very adept at thinking for themselves, places where they master the art of learning and acquire a strong taste for it. (A Nation Prepared, 1986, p. 21)

This intellectual performance crisis demands a different shape of response than the problems of "at-risk" student populations. Rather than narrowing a gap in performance between specific groups of students, we need strategies to raise overall performance levels for all students. We need to create a recipe for improvement that can alter two key qualities of the public school experience. First, we need to help teachers change the way they teach, the materials they utilize, and the way they work with students. Second, we need to provide incentives for all students to engage in more intellectually challenging work.

The agenda of developmentally appropriate practice meets the test of face validity in several respects. First, it is a comprehensive prescription that includes elements of instruction, materials, assessment, and social organization across all areas of curriculum content. Second, it fits the concern that students improve in their ability to make sense out of experience and to solve problems, since a principle of activities is to involve children in active engagement with a variety of materials. If students engage in problem solving from the beginning of their school careers, they are more likely to gain success and confidence in this mode of learning.

In sum, while the 1980s have seen a successful accomodation between the interests of early childhood educators and the public schools to promote programs for disadvantaged students, there are several looming limits on this strategy. Early childhood services may well prove to be inadequate in and of themselves to ensure school success for disadvantaged students, and may demand a complementary effort within early elementary grades to sustain the gains/benefits of early childhood experience. Further, if public support for early childhood services is limited to a low-income population, there are natural limits on long-term support and likely levels of quality and funding. By contrast the agenda of developmentally appropriate practice offers a universal prescription for improving the intellectual performance of America's students. A further advantage of the potential of developmentally appropriate practice is that if all schools begin to change in this direction, students will gain the benefits of greater continuity of curriculum and pedagogy as they move from high quality preschool programs into the public schools.

CHALLENGES IN PROMOTING
DEVELOPMENTALLY APPROPRIATE PRACTICE

NAEYC's publication of *Developmentally Appropriate Practice in Early Childhood Programs Serving Children From Birth Through Age 8* in late 1987 was followed in rapid succession by endorsement of these principles in major task forces initiated by the California State Department of Education (*Here They Come, Ready or Not*, 1988), and the National Association of State Boards of Education (*Right From the Start*, 1988). An April 1989 cover story on "How Young Children Learn" in *Newsweek* magazine exemplified favorable media attention to concerns regarding inappropriate testing and teaching in the early school years, and a positive treatment of the early childhood community's agenda for change (Kantrowitz & Wingert, 1989). Another positive sign is the nearly universal adoption of this phrase by policy makers and educators during discussions of preschool programs. Thus we can chart a very successful initial campaign to introduce a new term and set of concepts into the educational debate, a relative lack of any direct opposition to the principles, and an extension of the definition of early childhood education upwards into kindergarten and the primary grades. At the same time, it is difficult to know whether this rhetorical endorsement is leading to major changes in policy, to new resources, or to actual movement of classroom practices away from inappropriate practice and towards appropriate practice.

What are some key inhibiting forces on the education landscape which consitute substantial barriers to implementation of developmentally appropriate practice? To begin, the difficulty of the task is heightened by the simple size and complexity of the public education system. We have over 15,000 school districts, school boards, and superintendents; 58,000 elementary schools and principals; 1.5 million elementary school teachers and roughly 3 million students at each grade level. This is a big audience to reach with a consistent message.

A second structural fact of life in public education is complexity of decision making. Classroom practice can and is powerfully influenced by federal and state program guidelines, judicial rulings, and funding decisions. The tastes and preferences of school board members, superintendents, principals, curriculum directors, and parent groups influence local classroom practice as well. Thus, a single aspect of school practice, such as testing of young children, may be influenced by federal guidelines to determine eligibility for compensatory and special education services, decisions by the state legislature regarding accountability of local schools, and local school board policy regarding standards for school entry and promotion of students from one grade to the next. By contrast, Project Head Start, while serving over 400,000 children through a network of 1400 local programs has a much simpler authority structure. Policy decisions are basically made in Washington, DC and applied in a reasonably uniform fashion throughout the country. Due to these attributes of scale and complexity, advocates for developmentally appropriate practice must translate their message into a variety of forms for different audiences and broadcast it widely and persistently. Many different parties must at least acquiesce to a trial run for this concept or agree to refrain from actions/decision that would hinder implementation.

A third dimension of difficulty for implementation is the scope and tone of the developmentally appropriate practice recommendations. Simply put, the developmentally appropriate practice agenda calls for comprehensive and radical change in the core areas of school practice. By this I mean these principles apply across all areas of curriculum, teaching, and assessment for 4–5 years of public schooling, and that they are considerably divergent from the way teachers and schools currently operate. By contrast, many other proposals for school reform are more modest and conventional in their aims, seeking for example to require more quantity of the same type of schooling, or intensifying an existing form of instruction.

Fourth, I believe a significant impediment to prospects for developmentally appropriate practice is the accountability theme in current education policy. Many policy analysts and their audiences in legislatures, governor's offices, and local districts are enthused about the benefits of intensifying pressures on schools and teachers to produce improvements in achievement test scores. In some instances, this approach is offered to educators in return for a reduction in bureaucratic controls. In other cases, the assumption is that incentives in the form of more money, or threats of embarrassment or loss of control to higher authorities will make teachers and thus students work harder and more productively.

As testing becomes increasingly viewed as the coin of the realm, at least three possible implications can be forecast. First, practitioners will inquire of early childhood advocates, "what is the evidence that implementation of developmentally appropriate practice will increase test scores, or at least insure that kids will score no worse than conventional methods?" Second, some schools may be pressured into a desperate search for more radical alternatives and be willing to entertain solutions from the early childhood community. Third, heightened pressure may have a deadening effect on prospects for innovation, acting essentially to make pedagogy more traditional and conservative. Teachers who lack confidence in their ability to meet expectations for test score leaps will protect themselves by scrupulously adhering to traditional forms of instruction and classroom management.

A final barrier to receptivity towards developmentally appropriate practice is simply the crowded and constantly shifting environment of educational reform and school improvement. Because schools are always subject to a rhetoric of criticism and reform and because the notions of how and what to change seem to be always shifting, it is hard for any single agenda to be taken seriously. Teachers and principals are likely to listen with half an ear, trim their course slightly to the prevailing winds, or adopt only those features of current reform plans that serve their own agendas. Paradoxically, if schools are always being urged to change, they are unlikely to change in any substantial fashion.

In addition, one must admit there are competing ideas and packages of curriculum and staff development services that clutter the landscape. There are large bodies of research and rhetoric on effective teaching practices that are not congenial to the assumptions of developmentally appropriate practice. There are people who believe that more time on task and more active, teacher-directed drill and practice will lead to mastery and fluency of important knowledge and skills. These ideas and approaches are cleverly packaged and marketed relentlessly to school administrators and teachers.

In summary, while the notion of developmentally appropriate practice appears to match up well with a prime concern for enhancing intellectual performance of students, and it has enjoyed a remarkably positive initial reception, there are substantial barriers to quick implementation of these ideas. Some of these problems derive from the scope and scale of the early childhood reform agenda, some from the scale and complexity of America's public schools, and some with conflicting or competing ideas, such as an enthusiasm for accountability and a set of advocates for classroom practices that diverge from the desires of early childhood leaders. Based on this analysis, the task of implementing developmentally appropriate practice is large, complex, and daunting. One source of hints in responding to these challenges may come from a review of efforts to implement substantial change in classroom practice.

LESSONS FROM RELATED EXPERIENCE

While the principles and research base for developmentally appropriate practice represent state-of-the-art knowledge, there is a rich history of past efforts to change teaching practice in the public schools. Many of these reform efforts derived from a critique of existing practice that was remarkably similar to the present concerns of the early childhood community. I believe we can benefit from careful analysis of the strategies employed by groups with similar aims and intentions to those of advocates for developmentally appropriate practice. Fortunately, historians, policy analysts, and experts in the evaluation of implementation of educational innovations have produced a substantial body of work on these questions.

To illustrate the relevance of this work, consider the conclusions of Michael Fullan, who has synthesized a great deal of research on the problems of educational change. Fullan writes on the centrality of classroom teachers in implementing innovations and the importance of understanding their perspectives in assessing proposals for change. He posits three central concerns of teachers:

1. Does the change potentially address a need? Will students be interested? Will they learn?
2. How clear is the change, in terms of what the teacher must do?
3. How will it affect the teacher personally in terms of time, energy, new skill, sense of excitement and competence, and interference with existing priorities? (Fullan, 1982, p. 113)

Thus, in designing strategies to promote ideas of developmentally appropriate practice to teachers, early childhood advocates may work on responding to these three core concerns, to wit, constructing arguments and gathering evidence that more developmentally appropriate methods do produce greater student engagement and learning; preparing resources to guide teachers in daily routines, activities, and tactics; and finding ways to build support for teachers as they seek to implement these changes.

To amplify and add to these lessons, we next turn to work of a historian of education, Larry Cuban, who investigated the outcomes of a succession of efforts to alter classroom practice, from the Progressive Education Movement of the 1920s and 1930s to curriculum reform and open education initiatives in the 1960s and 1970s. He argues that each of these reform efforts was an endeavor to change classroom practice from a teacher-centered process to a student-centered process. He defines teacher-centered instruction as a teacher controlling what is taught, when, and under what conditions, through indicators such as:

* Teacher talk exceeds student talk
* Instruction involves the whole class
* Use of class time is determined by the teacher
* The classroom is arranged into rows of desks

By contrast, student-centered involves the following characteristics:

* Student talk equals or exceeds teacher talk
* Most instruction occurs individually or in small groups

- Students help to choose and organize the content and rules of behavior
- Varied materials are available for student selection and use
- At least half of the academic time is devoted to activities that allow student choice, and space allows for individual and small group work (Cuban, 1984, p. 3).

Using a wide range of evidence from over 1900 classrooms over the last 80 years, Cuban's conclusions paint a mixed picture of success for past reform efforts. To highlight the positive, he finds the greatest receptivity and holding power to implementing these notions in the early grades of elementary schools. Second, he documents a general trend in classroom practice in the direction of more diverse and varied methods, with a growing proportion of teachers employing a blend or synthesis of teacher-centered and student-centered activities and pedagogy. Third, he notes that some teachers in all types of schools and communities have been successful at sustaining a more student-centered approach to education. In other respects, Cuban's evidence is quite sobering. Even in instances where substantial resources and strong leadership from superintendents and school boards was in evidence, Cuban finds a maximum estimate of impact of student-centered practices in no more than 25 percent of a system's classrooms, and an even lower estimate of long-term, sustained adherence to those modes of operation. In addition, he finds that certain aspects of student-centered instruction are much less likely to be adopted and continued—notably those principles which involve shift in authority from the teacher to the students, whether the issue is rules of behavior or choice of activities.

Cuban explains this pattern of results as a combination of (a) structural features of the public schools, (b) the beliefs, experiences, and training of individual teachers, and (c) the demands of more innovative teaching. On the first factor he stresses that classrooms are:

> crowded settings in which the teacher has to manage 25–40 or more students . . . in a space no larger than a luxurious master bedroom. Amidst up to 1000 daily exchanges with individual students and groups, the teacher is expected to maintain control, teach a prescribed content, capture student interest in the subject matter, vary levels of instruction according to student differences, and show tangible evidence that students have performed satisfactorily. (Cuban, 1984, p. 242)

Under these conditions, teacher-centered instruction is an efficient and convenient way for teachers to maintain control and cover mandated content.

Secondly, Cuban notes that many teachers may hold to a set of beliefs supportive of more traditional practices and uncongenial to the principles of developmentally appropriate practice, for example:

> [K]nowledge must be transmitted to young people, . . . students learn best in a well-managed, quiet classroom where limits are made plain, academic rigor is prized, and rules are equitably enforced by the teachers; and the teachers' authority, rooted in institutional legitimacy and knowledge must be paid respectful attention. (Cuban, 1984, p. 245)

Third, Cuban joins with Fullan in stressing that a major constraint limiting teacher implementation of more student-centered practices is the personal cost in time and energy of changing routines:

> The time and effort burden falls directly and solely upon the teacher's shoulders. No professor, reformer, principal, or superintendent had to stay after 4 o'clock in the afternoon to put up learning centers. What clear and consistent yield could teachers count upon for their students and themselves from the additional exertion? What amount of work taken home and periodic rearrangement of the classroom? What problems with students, other colleagues, and school administrators might occur as a result of classroom changes? Are the inner rewards worth the tradeoff in potential problems and additional work? No unambiguous answers existed to these questions. (Cuban, 1984, p. 256)

A final example of scholarship on the process of changing teacher practice is the work of David Cohen. In a recent essay he advances an analysis of the challenges of what he describes as "adventurous" instruction, which he defines as follows:

> [It] assumes school instruction can be exciting, and must be if children are to learn; that instruction also should be intellectually challenging; that to be either exciting or challenging it must be attuned to children's ways of thinking, to their experience, and to their own efforts to make sense of experience. . . . (Cohen, 1988, p. 7)

Within this paradigm learning is seen as an active process of constructing and reconstructing knowledge in which teachers guide student inquiry and knowledge is seen as emergent, uncertain, and subject to revision. He contrasts this view to more traditional assumptions about education in which active teachers convey knowledge to relatively passive students, and in which learning occurs by listening, reading, practicing, and remembering, based on an assumption that knowledge is objective, stable, and authoritative.

Cohen raises a number of concerns regarding the difficulties of implementing developmentally appropriate practice, or adventurous instruction. For example, he joins Cuban and Fullan in highlighting the importance of time and effort requirements for teachers. Cohen's specific concern on this factor relates to the knowledge and capabilities that are demanded of teachers, for example:

> [T]eachers must take on a large agenda; to help students abandon the safety of rote learning, to instruct them in framing and testing hypotheses; and to build a climate of tolerance for others' ideas, and curiosity about unusual answers, among other things. Teachers who take this path must work harder, concentrate more, and embrace larger pedagogical responsibilities than if they only assigned text chapters and seatwork. . . . They require, for instance, a deep understanding of the material and modes of discourse about it. They must be able to comprehend students' thinking, their interpretations of problems, their mistakes, and their puzzles. (Cohen, 1988, p. 61)

Cohen also questions the assumption that by using more "appropriate" methods teachers can make learning enjoyable and effortless by appealing to children's natural curiosity and motivation. Rather he argues that simple memorization of facts may be less demanding for children than attempting to understand varied ways of solving problems. He suggests that "adventurous" teaching may entail more complex and ambiguous aims, and more skill, effort, and willingness to take risks from both teachers and students. He notes that rote learning may be boring and superficial, but it may be easier for all parties.

In summary, past efforts to alter classroom practice in the direction of "student-centered," or more "adventurous" instruction hold a number of lessons for advocates of developmentally appropriate practice. Perhaps the key point to ponder is the need to understand and respond to the realities and the perspectives of classroom teachers in any implementation efforts. From Fullan, we note the importance of presenting the potential of developmentally appropriate practice in terms that connect to teachers' perceptions of the needs of their own students (rather than in more abstract or academic terms), the need for precision in terms of how teachers carry out these concepts and principles, and for time and help in the tasks of developing materials and activities. From Cuban, we add the need to recognize the complex and crowded realities of classroom life, and the need for realistic expectations regarding teaching strategies given numbers of students, physical space and equipment, and the pace of social interaction. Cuban also notes the role of teacher belief on issues as basic as adult authority and the nature of knowledge, which need to be respected and accomodated by agents seeking to alter classroom practice in fundamental ways.

Cohen, speaking for himself but perhaps reflecting questions that teachers may raise, points out the risky and demanding expectations inherent in classroom strategies that focus on intellectual challenge and greater student autonomy. Against the backdrop of Cuban's reminders on the crowded and competitive reality of public school classrooms, Cohen's questions are sobering indeed.

Finally, the common factor from our survey of analysts is the importance of the workload demanded from teachers by developmentally appropriate practice. Cuban argues that teacher-centered practices have endured at least in part because they comprise economical, manageable strategies for coping with the realities of classroom life. Because this paradigm of schooling is old and pervasive, it is supported by a large repertoire of activities, tactics, routines, and scripts for teachers and students to follow. Thus we should not assume that rapid, wholesale change in the direction of more developmentally appropriate practice can take place without substantial support for teachers.

SUPPORTS AND PROMISING STRATEGIES

Up to this point, my analysis of prospects for implementation of developmentally appropriate practice may seem to have a gloomy cast. While the purpose and key features of NAEYC's document respond directly and persuasively to the dominant concerns of policy makers and citizens for enhancing students' problem-solving and thinking skills, the job of implementing these ideas is large and difficult. Similarly, while the concepts of developmentally appropriate practice have been favorably received and widely endorsed by national organizations and in the media, a study of past efforts to implement similar agendas for altering classroom practice reveals at best a mixed record of success. However, thinking clearly and critically about the existing challenges to implementation and the lessons of past experience should be helpful in devising strategies for advocacy of developmentally appropriate practice. Before moving to these suggestions, it is appropriate to take note of some additional sources of support for developmentally appropriate practice on the present scene.

First, a key dimension of support for developmentally appropriate practice comes from other proposals for curriculum reform. Scholars in cognitive psychology and content area learning are producing a range of studies that support the tenets and assuptions of developmentally appropriate practice. National curriculum reform efforts are emerging with recommendations that echo the precepts of the early childhood community. These reports emphasize themes such as integrating curricula, increasing attention to thinking skills and problem-solving, and strengthening the quality of instruction for all students.

For example, in the area of mathematics learning, research is enriching our understanding of how young children bring prior knowledge to early school learning and how they solve arithmetic problems in a variety of ways. Models of staff development for primary grade teachers based on this research have been developed by Carpenter and colleagues (Carpenter, Fennema, Peterson, Chiang, & Loeb, 1988) (Cognitively Guided Instruction), Cobb (Cobb, Yackel, & Wood, 1988) (Constructivist Teaching), and Lampert (1988) (Mathematical Discourse). And guidelines for reform by the National Council of Teachers of Mathematics and the Mathematical Sciences Education Board include recommendations for kindergarten through fourth-grade methods which are remarkably similar to the concepts of the NAEYC. In the area of science education, reports from the American Association for the Advancement of Science and the Center for the Improvement of Science Education recommend hands-on experience in the early grades, a more conceptual and enriched approach to assessment, and more varied classroom methods and materials. In writing and reading instruction, the whole language and emergent literacy movements are receiving support on a broad scale.

This pattern of converging recommendations and a broad consensus on needed improvements is reassuring to practitioners and policy makers. The early childhood community gains sympathy for its cause by highlighting the stultifying effects of teacher-directed instruction and the costs of inappropriate academic expectations on the learning of young children. Expert opinion on promoting content-area learning adds credibility to the promise that more developmentally appropriate methods will lead to valued educational outcomes.

A second arena of support for the ideas of developmentally appropriate practice is the area of plans to reform educational assessment. The testing community is moving toward performance-based and observational methods and toward the assessment of higher-order skills and problem solving. State and local testing directors are moving beyond a sole reliance on standardized multiple-choice format tests. As these forms of assessment make their way into practice, they will provide incentives for teaching methods that are attuned to broader aspects of student performance, and they will reduce presently powerful pressures on primary grade teachers to emphasize drilling students on factual material and specific skills more amenable to multiple-choice tests.

A third reservoir of support for the early childhood pedagogical agenda is existing teachers in public schools. Particularly among kindergarten teachers, one senses that teacher preparation experiences involved socialization into a developmental approach and that their personal beliefs still support this direction. Kindergarten teachers are frequently quoted as lamenting the perceived shifts in policy and practice in the direction of more drill-and-practice, less time available for teacher-initiated or child-initiated activities, and an increased emphasis on using tests of academic achievement with younger children. In addition, experienced teachers in the primary grade levels who are unsatisfied with the results of traditional methods and activities are a receptive audience for the ideas of developmentally appropriate practice. This sizeable group of staff within public schools represent powerful allies in advocacy efforts with their colleagues, with school principals, and with parents.

Within this context of contemporary forces and with our enlightened understanding of the lessons of past efforts to change teaching practice, I see four areas that represent promising strategies for promoting the developmentally appropriate practice agenda:

First, there are several challenges in presenting the rationale and content of developmentally appropriate practice. One problem is "premature rejection" of these ideas, often due to a belief that early childhood leaders are reviving the ideals of open education that are viewed as having been tried and failed, or are advocating an abdication of professional/adult responsibility for determining curriculum goals and for classroom management. Similarly, terms such as "teacher-directed instruction" are polluted by past history. For example, staff development and programs based on notions of effective teaching put forward a positive image of what is described as "active teaching." Another problem may lie in the format of the developmentally appropriate publication that contrasts "appropriate" and "inappropriate" practice. When teachers see many of their own habits and routines characterized as "inappropriate," they are often understandably defensive.

Presentational strategies may need to be tailored to specific types of audiences in public education. For example, for policy makers and administrators, the key arguments to stress may be the "fit" between the principles of developmentally appropriate practice and the high value being placed on thinking and problem solving as outcomes for education. For teachers, an important tactic may be to stress the positive promise of more appropriate methods to promote student success and accomplishment, rather than beginning with an extended critique of existing practice. Another suggestion is to find ways to provide more detailed portraits of what developmentally appropriate practice looks like and guidance on how to move in the direction of more appropriate practice in incremental ways. In particular, teachers need to understand how to alter their own behavior and routines, through more extended examples of developmentally appropriate methods in action.

A second major challenge is to generate, garner, and convey evidence regarding the outcomes of developmentally appropriate practice on student learning, to respond to questions on the relative effectiveness of this approach when compared with more traditional methods. A major effort is needed to synthesize the wide range of material available on teaching and learning of specific subject areas in the early elementary years.

A third challenge relates to issues of implementation. A central lesson from past efforts to move to more student-centered learning relates to the time and effort required of individual teachers. To be blunt, we cannot expect teachers to discard the existing curriculum, materials, tests, schedules, and classroom routines and develop a totally new set of these resources on their own time. An organizational challenge for the early childhood field is to become competitive in the market of materials, staff development services, and technical assistance. A related task is to gather examples of varied approaches to staff support and staff development, such as partnerships between higher education institutions and local schools, differentiated staffing arrangements that allow greater collaboration among teachers, and approaches to schoolwide planning and decision making that enhance teacher autonomy and promote collective efforts to solve problems.

A fourth dimension for professional leadership relates to refining and debating the content of developmentally appropriate practice. We need to address questions regarding the core vs. peripheral dimensions of this agenda. Is an ungraded early primary unit the ultimate, purist version of developmentally appropriate practice, or are self-contained classrooms also healthy environments for this philosophy? What more can be said regarding communication with and involvement of parents in developmentally appropriate classrooms and adaptation of developmentally appropriate principles for minority and non-English speaking children and families? To what extent is an integrated, project-type approach to curriculum vital or desirable?

CONCLUSION

My analysis rests on two fundamental assumptions. The first is that public schools need to take the agenda of developmentally appropriate practice more seriously, because it represents a comprehensive vision of classroom practice that can bring greater success and higher levels of intellectual performance for all children. The second is that advocates for developmentally appropriate practice need to take the task of promoting change in public education more seriously. This means learning more about decision making in public schools, more about the lessons of past efforts to improve classroom practice, more about the interests and agendas of public school teachers, and more about competing and congenial forces in the school reform arena. Developing and articulating the principles of developmentally appropriate practice was a magnificent first step for the early childhood community. Now it is time to step up to the larger, messier, and longer-term task of implementing this vision.

REFERENCES

A nation prepared: Teachers for the 21st century. (1986). New York: Carnegie Forum on Education and the Economy.

Applebee, A., Langer, J., & Mullis, I. (1989). *Crossroads in American education: A summary of findings.* Princeton, NJ: National Assessment of Educational Progress and the Education Testing Service.

Berrueta-Clement, J., Schweinhart, L., Barnett, W., Epstein, A., & Weikart, D. (1984). *Changed lives: The effects of the Perry Preschool Program on youths through age 19.* Ypsilanti, MI: High/Scope Educational Research Foundation.

Bredekamp, S. (1987). *Developmentally appropriate practice in early childhood programs service children from birth through age 8.* Washington, DC: National Association for the Education of Young Children.

Carpenter, T., Fennema, E., Peterson, P., Chiang, C., & Loeb, M. (1988, April). *Using knowledge of children's mathematical thinking in classroom teaching: An experimental study.* Paper presented at the annual meeting of the American Educational Research Association, New Orleans, LA.

Cobb, P., Yackel, E., & Wood, T. (1988). Curriculum and teacher development: Psychological and anthropological perspectives. In E. Fennema, T. Carpenter, & S. Lamon (Eds.), *Integrating research on teaching and learning mathematics: Papers from the First Wisconsin Symposium for Research on Teaching and Learning Mathematics* (pp. 92–130). Madison: University of Wisconsin Center for Education Research.

Cohen, D. (1988). *Teaching practice: Plus can change . . .* (Issue Paper 88–3). Lansing, MI: The National Center for Research on Teacher Education.

Cuban, L. (1984). *How teachers taught: Constancy and change in American classrooms, 1890–1980.* New York: Longman Press.

Fullan, M. (1982). *The meaning of educational change.* New York: Teachers College Press.

Here they come: Ready or not! A report of the school readiness task force. (1988). Sacramento: California State Department of Eudcation.

Kantrowitz, B., & Wingert, P. (1989, April 17). How kids learn. *Newsweek Magazine*, pp. 50–57.

Lampert, M. (1988). Connecting mathematical teaching and learning. In E. Fennema, T. Carpenter, & S. Lamon (Eds.), *Integrating research on teaching and learning mathematics: Papers from the first Wisconsin symposium for Research on Teaching and Learning Mathematics* (pp. 132–165). Madison: University of Wisconsin Center for Education Research.

Mathematical Sciences Education Board. (1989). *Everybody counts: A report to the nation on the future of mathematics education.* Washington, DC: National Academy Press.

National Council of Teachers of Mathematics. (1989). *Curriculum and evaluation standards for school mathematics.* Reston, VA: Author.

Right from the start. (1988). Washington, DC: National Association of State Boards of Education.

The reform of science education in elementary school. (1989). Washington, DC: National Center for Improving Science Education.

Science for all Americans: Summary. (1989, January). Washington, DC: American Association for the Advancement of Science.

Chapter 10

Creating Change with the Public Schools: Reflections of an Early Childhood Teacher Educator

Stacie G. Goffin
University of Missouri-Kansas City

Concerns about public schools as providers of early childhood education have come from various quarters, but most especially from early childhood educators concerned about the transformation of early childhood programs into havens for inappropriate practices and expectations. The critical challenge is translating the ideals presented in reports, such as *Right From the Start* (National Association of State Boards of Education [NASBE], 1988), into schools and classrooms.

One strategy employed by public schools seeking to develop appropriate early childhood programs is collaboration with area universities and colleges. This chapter describes one such effort, known as the Turner Project. The Turner Project, which began in the fall of 1988, supplies an informative example for highlighting some of the challenges involved in creating public school environments hospitable to appropriate early childhood curriculum and practices. Experiences associated with the Project also suggest policy issues for public schools, teacher preparation programs, and certification standards promulgated by state departments of education.

The Turner Project was a collaborative effort between the Turner Unified School District and the School of Education of the University of Missouri-Kansas City. It was initiated at the invitation of early childhood teachers[1] and the assistant superintendent of curriculum and instruction. I served as the consultant to, and facilitator of, the school district's efforts to reassess its early childhood programs. The assistant superintendent's interest in early childhood education, and teachers' concerns that the district's early childhood programs had become overly academic and stressful for children, sparked the program's initiation.

The school district purchased one-third of my time from the University (basically one course release time) for the program's development and implementation. This arrangement appeared not only to enhance the credibility of my efforts, but provided an opportunity to examine the costs and benefits of such a relationship. From my perspective, one of the most important aspects of this structural relationship was the legitimization it provided in the eyes of my academic superiors for the extensive time and effort devoted to the Project.

The Turner Project officially concluded in February 1990, 18 months following its initiation. The decision to conclude the collaboration was informed not only by a personal assessment that teachers were no longer in need of such intensive support, but also the necessity of reducing demand on my time. Far more than the time required to teach one university course was committed to the Project. An invitation to return and continue with the process during the 1990–1991 school year was accepted with trepidation, as I internally debated the costs and benefits of continuing with a project of vital importance that was extremely demanding of time and commitment.

THE TURNER PROJECT

When the Project began, early childhood classrooms were dominated by pencil-and-paper activities, such as workbooks and teacher-directed instructional activities with academic outcomes. Eighteen months later, when the Project officially concluded, classrooms included more opportunities for child-initiated learning, less whole-group instruction, and less reliance upon workbooks and teacher guides.

I conceptualized my role as a catalyst for instigating, promoting, and supporting reflection about the nature of teaching and learning within the context of early childhood education. The components of the

---

[1] In reference to the Project's participants, early childhood education refers to schooling prior to first grade.

Project established a structure within which teachers could construct a personal philosophy of teaching in early childhood education.

It was presumed that teachers who understood developmentally and educationally appropriate programs could make better informed decisions about their teaching and discriminate among alternative strategies. Although I eventually came to recognize the interventionist stance inherent in my role (see Goffin, 1991), there was no attempt to endorse or promote any particular set of teaching strategies or curriculum models. Nor were there expectations that teachers would apply, in any linear or direct fashion, information discussed during meetings or found in readings. Rather, discussions and interactions were intended as informants for teachers' reflections about their practice. This decision is consistent with Elliott's (1989) contention that, "The authority of the teacher educator does not rest on some 'infallible' educational theory but on his or her ability to utilise that theory as a resource for enabling practitioners to construct their own professional knowledge" (p. 84).

Emphasis was placed on exploring teaching and learning as a dynamic, continuously developing enterprise, and teachers were urged to recognize their opportunity to actively inform the teaching and learning occurring in their classrooms (versus passively implementing the strategies presented by teacher guides and workbooks). Within this context, teachers were assured the freedom to choose to change in ways they saw as meaningful.

Participants

The Project involved 14 teachers from the district's five elementary schools. The Turner Unified School District, located in Kansas City, Kansas, is a suburban-rural, primarily blue-collar community, with a high incidence of low-income families. Ten of the fourteen teachers taught either half-day or extended-day kindergartens. Two teachers taught early childhood-special education, and the remaining two teachers taught in newly created transitional first-grade classrooms.

The teachers brought a wide range of teaching experiences from various grade levels. Years of teaching spanned from 3 to 24 years. Years teaching early childhood education ranged from 0 to 20 years, including four teachers who were teaching early childhood education for the first time.

Only one of the teachers had any extensive, formal course work in early childhood education, which, in this instance, was in the Montessori Method. None of the teachers held a teaching certificate specific to early childhood education, which is consistent with certification requirements in the state of Kansas, where teachers are certified to teach grades K through 8.

The Structure of the Process

The Project was comprised of three main components: biweekly meetings of the early childhood teachers, informal, weekly classroom observations by me, and journals completed weekly by the participating teachers. The biweekly meetings were convened by alternately cancelling morning and afternoon sessions of half-day kindergartens. Meetings attempted to facilitate teacher discussions about teaching beliefs and practices and share information about early childhood education.

Readings, which were informed by teacher interests, provided focus for each session. The selection of readings was based upon their potential to challenge teachers to think about the differences between what was being espoused and their own practices. Meeting location rotated through each of the teacher's classrooms, enabling teachers, for the first time, to observe and question each other's teaching and learning environments. (For a more detailed description of the Project, see Goffin, 1991.)

These various components were unified by six "operating assumptions" and six goals, which are outlined in Figure 10.1. These assumptions and goals transcended the teachers' and district's specific request for support in rethinking their early childhood practices. Rather, they were personal statements, formulated prior to the Project's initiation, reflecting beliefs about change, teaching, and learning. They rendered an invisible conceptual coherence to the process, and provided a structure for integrating what appeared to be a loosely organized series of interactions.

Although these goals and assumptions recognized that significant change would result only if there were modifications in the system as well as individual teachers, my efforts focused primarily on helping teachers rethink their assumptions about learning and teaching in early childhood education. This decision assumed that, strategically, this was the best starting point for change. As will be seen, however, this interpretation unintentionally limited the scope of the Project's impact.

The nature of the process was evolutionary, evolving in relation to teacher input and personal assessment of the Project's development. A lecture was never delivered, and whole-group sessions, although framed by planned objectives, were never prescriptive. Classroom ob-

Figure 10.1.   Project Goals

1. Teachers will realize teaching is an intentional activity and their responsibility for organizing experiences that propel learning.
2. Teachers will feel more confident in their decisions and able to justify them.
3. Teacher practices will become more appropriate.
4. Teachers will become more reflective about their teaching.
5. Teachers will become more aware of themselves as agents for change.
6. The "system" will become more sensitive to what it needs to do to support early childhood education (i.e., building principals, first grade teachers, parents).

Operating Assumptions

1. As a change process, this *is* an evolving, creative enterprise and will require time.
2. Changes must come from teachers. The process is a catalyst to encourage professional thinking. Therefore, I cannot personally "promise" how classrooms will change. The specific outcome is unknown. Teachers determine how they will change.
3. Teachers can learn from each other. The process needs to encourage collaborative problem solving and encourage teachers to see each other—as well as me—as resources.
4. Change must be supported by different expectations from parents, community early childhood programs, building principals, and first-grade teachers. All these groups, therefore, must be participants in the process.
5. An important component in the process will be my ability to develop a relationship with teachers so they will risk change and be willing to consider new ideas; I need to avoid telling teachers "What and How."
6. What one thinks about the activity of teaching influences *how* one teaches.

servations were conducted on a revolving schedule. Visits, which were emphasized as nonevaluative and private, were crafted as opportunities to serve as personal consultant to interested teachers. "Consultations" often occurred during lunch and after afternoon children were dismissed. When teachers did not seek input, however, it was not offered.

The journals were initially developed to serve as a means for teachers to reflect upon their teaching, and to help inform my questions regarding teacher thinking about early childhood education and teaching practices, and their feelings about the change process. However, the journals quickly developed into an important device for permitting personal responses to the interests and concerns of individual teachers. They became a tool for individualizing the change process for each teacher and evolved into personalized technical assistance plans. They also provided a mechanism for connecting teachers with similar concerns.

Unexpectedly, teachers viewed my comments and attached articles as evidence of my interest in their teaching, and support for their risk taking. As expressed by one teacher, "It was through the journal entries and classroom observations that (the facilitator) became one of my main support system resources."

Teacher questions about "how to teach" were consistently deflected. Instead, teachers were provoked to think through issues for themselves, either individually or as a group. In this way, responsibility for decision making about curriculum and appropriate teaching practices were returned to the teachers. This practice also helped minimize the facilitator's label as "the expert" and inadvertantly becoming a substitute for district directives about what and how to teach. I hoped this strategy would strengthen teachers' awareness of their roles as decision makers in ways consistent with Darling-Hammond's (1985) contention that professionalization is marked, in part, by the extent to which members of an occupation maintain control over the content of their own work.

This nondirective stance, however, frequently provoked frustrations in the early phase of the Project. As expressed by one teacher:[2]

Teacher: What should I do?
Me: I don't know; I can't tell you what to do. I don't know your children, your classroom, or even you well enough.
Teacher: I understand your caution, but just tell me what to do on Monday.
Me: What do you want the children to be learning?
Teacher: I don't know!! Just tell me!!

Although biweekly meetings, journals, and classroom observations formed the Project's core, opportunities to promote appropriate early childhood education were seized whenever possible. Schorr (1988), in her identification of factors characteristic of successful intervention programs for children and families at risk, concluded that staff of successful programs had the time and skill to develop relationships based on mutual respect and trust, and willingly crossed traditional role boundaries. My experience suggests that the same conclusion might be applicable to successful interventions with early childhood public school programs.

Willingness to assume additional responsibilities extending beyond the three Project components positioned me to advocate for early childhood education at a variety of levels. In this way, I gained access to opportunities to serve as a change agent and early childhood advocate within the school district.

For example, the assistant superintendent freely offered my ser-

---

[2] Anecdotes are derived from audiotapes of the biweekly sessions, teacher journals, and questionnaires distributed by the author.

vices to district personnel whenever approached about issues related to early childhood education, leading to discussions with staff such as the district psychologist and the staff person responsible for developing a parent education program. When other grade-level teachers observed early childhood teachers' new room arrangements, many asked for and received similar "consultation." When teachers complained about a perceived lack of support for developmentally appropriate practice from their principals, they were prompted to request a meeting with the principals to share their concerns, and then assisted in developing their presentations. Discussions were held with individual teachers whenever requested. The assistant superintendent's casual suggestion to invite the mayor to the district during NAEYC's Week of the Young Child was nurtured into actuality. The six operating assumptions and six Project goals provided ongoing conceptual consistency to these various interactions and provided the thread that integrated these activities with the main components of the Project.

These additional responsibilities were willingly assumed because, as a teacher educator, I see myself as an early childhood advocate. The quality of children's early education and teachers' abilities to implement appropriate early childhood education matter to me as more than just a subject of scholarly investigation. Even though I had research questions I hoped the Project would help address, my identity as an early childhood teacher educator and advocate significantly informed my interactions.

Consequently, this collaboration appears to differ from collaborative efforts described or encouraged in the research literature (see, for example, Lieberman, 1990; Wood, Cobb, & Yackel, 1990). The Turner Project extended beyond the joint construction of knowledge to struggle with the issues of implementation of appropriate early childhood education in public school settings.

This overview hopefully conveys the Project as dynamic, evolutionary, and responsive. Because Project decisions were so contextualized, its story lacks an orderly, sequential framework. This makes the complete story of the Turner Project almost impossible to retell in its entirety. As a result, it is the principles and key elements of the process, rather than the process itself, which lend themselves to replication (Goffin, 1990).

Project Results

Based upon classroom observations and teacher reports, when the project officially concluded in February 1989, at least eight significant changes were observable in the way teaching and learning occurred.

There was (a) less reliance upon whole group instruction (b) decreased dependence upon workbooks and dittoes, (c) increased usage of activities associated with a whole-language and child-centered approach, (d) more relaxed classroom climates, (e) increased teacher interaction with individual children, (f) less fragmented scheduling, permitting children more time for involvement with learning, (g) more social interaction among children, and (h) increased teacher satisfaction with teaching (Goffin, 1991).

Significantly, although the extent of change varied tremendously among teachers, *every* teacher changed, and did so in ways that made their classroom practices more consistent with the norms of developmentally appropriate practice. These changes appeared to be accompanied by teachers' growing sense of professionalism. Many teachers became more reflective about their practice and assumed more responsibility for their classroom learning environments. As expressed by one teacher, approximately halfway through the Project:

> With all the information I have tried to take in over the past seven to eight months, I have honestly begun to want to become more aware of early childhood education, and I have gone to the library to begin my own research on the subject. I can say that I have never done this with my experience of the past. Hopefully, I am becoming more professional, and I am truly trying to become an advocate for children.

A year later, the teacher, who early in the Project demanded that I tell her what to do, revealed:

> Am I thinking any differently? I should hope so. I am changing every day. My main difference this year is I'm always asking myself if what we are doing has an appropriate outcome. That's why I've eliminated so many of the activities. They were "cute" but had no meaningful outcome. The words "developmentally appropriate" are always with me as I go from week to week.

POLICY IMPLICATIONS

My experiences with the Turner Project connect with three policy issues:

1. The role of public schools as catalysts for expanding the quantity and quality of appropriate early childhood programs.
2. Needed changes in university expectations, in general, and teacher preparation programs, in particular, in promoting school-uni-

versity collaborations on behalf of appropriate early childhood education.
3. The need for state certifications targeted to early childhood education, birth through age 8.

These policy issues are sequenced to reflect the order in which my experiences with Turner Project serve as an informant. The sequence also infers the nested relationship among policies. Creating substantive change with public schools in the area of early childhood education will necessitate policy changes at multiple levels.

Public Schools as Catalysts for Expanding Appropriate Early Childhood Education

Public schools can significantly influence the expansion of appropriate early childhood programs in at least two ways: (a) by supporting their own teachers' abilities to deliver developmentally and educationally appropriate programs, and (b) by working to strengthen the quality of early childhood programs within their communities. The latter leadership role is one receiving increasing attention (see, for example, NASBE, 1988; National Association of Elementary School Principals [NAESP], 1990), yet leadership and innovative thinking will be required in both arenas if children are to receive consistent, high-quality early education, regardless of program sponsorship.

Supporting the growth of early childhood teachers. A major challenge to efforts focused on increasing the availability of appropriate early childhood programs is the complexity of developmentally appropriate practice (Goffin, 1990). Teachers participating in the Turner Project seemed to assume that developmentally appropriate practice would be a "packaged" substitute for their current teaching practices. This understanding of developmentally appropriate practice appeared to exist, at some level, for almost all teachers, throughout the life of the Project.

In the eyes of most participants, the Project was viewed more as a "treatment" than as a catalyst for continuing growth and change. Naming our collaborative effort *The Turner Project* was an unfortunate misnomer. I suspect I succeeded in helping only a few of the participating teachers to recognize teaching as a learning enterprise.

A majority of teachers seemed to narrowly conceive developmentally appropriate practice as a methodology, versus a dynamic conceptual framework, that, once learned, would provide a replacement for their existing practices. A technological view of teaching dominated. Teachers had expected me to provide the newest "right" answers.

This way of thinking appeared to fuel their persistent search for "answers." As plaintively expressed by one teacher halfway through the Project; "There's so much I don't know. I don't know how you feel about Weekly Readers." Teacher expectations that they would be given a new teaching methodology, and that their learning would have a conclusive ending, seems uncomfortably consistent with the socialization provided by many teacher preparation programs.

This frame of reference perhaps led many teachers to expect their teaching could change quickly and to be unprepared for the challenges and frustrations that frequently accompany significant change. This way of thinking may also have contributed to the high level of defensiveness expressed by teachers. Challenges to one's teaching, in the context of believing there is a single right way to teach, logically implies one is currently teaching incorrectly.

As expressed by one teacher, "If I accept this developmentally appropriate approach, then I must reject everything I presently do and admit I am wrong." Not surprisingly, such interpretations generate a high degree of anxiety. Furthermore, this anxiety appears to be exacerbated by "admitting" one is wrong. Following their admissions, teachers frantically tried to "redo" their entire classrooms, tremendously adding to the demands upon their time, energy, and personal equilibrium. As summarized by the same teacher, "I can emphatically tell you that this change process has been an intensely unsettling experience that I can only describe as emotional chaos."

This apparent difficulty in understanding the dynamic quality of teaching also appeared to affect teachers' understanding of developmentally appropriate practice. They struggled with the distinction between the concepts of developmental and maturational. Their confusion appeared to be reinforced by concern with pressure being placed upon children to succeed academically, popular conceptions of readiness, and a focus on classrooms as a cohort of children versus individuals. Such misinterpretations hindered understanding of the dynamic, individual character of developmental classrooms and of children's growth.

Understanding developmentally appropriate practice also appeared to be complicated by the continuing assumption that children learned primarily through the process of being told. Teachers struggled to understand how children were learning if teachers weren't "teaching." As stated by one teacher, "I feel as if I am not always teaching because of the way I was used to."

On the other hand, teachers who abandoned their reliance upon direct instruction, questioned their usefulness as children became increasingly independent in their learning. Teachers' delicately balanced responsibilities as facilitator and guide were difficult to grasp. This was exacerbated by their uncertainty about what to teach if they were not following teaching guides and workbooks. This appeared to reflect not only teachers' insufficient knowledge of content, but also their struggle with expanding the purpose of early childhood education beyond preparation for first grade (Goffin, 1990).

Many intense exchanges debated the distinction between educational outcomes and the means used to achieve them—that, for example, the issue was not one of giving up phonics or teaching alphabet letters per se but rather recognizing phonics and letter recognition as means to a desired educational end. An attempt to have teachers develop an early childhood curriculum guide, which was chosen as a strategy to help teachers collaboratively become better informed about meaningful content that could substitute for a skills-based curriculum, failed to gain momentum because teachers became overwhelmed by the struggle of focusing on what they wanted children to learn. By substituting the word *teacher* for advocates, I can easily empathize with Sarason's (1987) declaration that he "continue(s) to be disheartened and amazed at how hard it is for advocates of change to state an overarching goal, a vision that says that all goals are instrumental to achieving a superordinate one" (p.120).

The potential exception was teacher interest in Whole Language. Because of its conceptual compatibility with developmentally appropriate practice, and the high level of interest in whole language being expressed by teachers of other grade levels, the assistant superintendent accepted my suggestion that whole language might be a strategic vehicle for extending the change process to other grade levels. Many teachers actively sought additional understandings about whole language and became "whole language teachers." Their classrooms quickly offered children many more opportunities for child-initiated learning.

Ironically, the success of this strategy complicated, to some extent, the process of creating more appropriate learning environments. Classrooms appeared to become victims of what Frank Smith (1989) called "overselling literacy." Although early childhood education includes more than literacy development, teachers' growing enthusiasm for whole language appeared to overwhelm other curriculum possibilities.

The fact that a whole-language approach doesn't directly contradict teachers' beliefs that early childhood education should prepare children for reading in first grade suggests a possible explanation for this enthusiasm. Additionally, a whole-language approach provides teachers a clear linkage between content and developmentally appropriate practice, a linkage not as easily available to them in other curriculum areas. However, teacher acceptance of the constructive nature of literacy development rarely seemed to generalize to other areas of the curriculum (see Wood, Cobb, & Yackel, 1990, for empirical documentation of a similar conclusion, and Green, 1973, for an analytic rationale for why such inconsistencies can coexist) or to their own professional growth.

These complexities and misconceptions highlight that helping teachers reconceptualize their roles as early childhood educators are not likely to be accomplished through 3-credit courses, brief in-service programs that attempt to add onto teachers' previous knowledge, or directives to disregard previous practices. The long-term commitment made by the Turner School District appears to be a critical factor in understanding the degree of success experienced in the Turner Project. Discussion of these challenges, however, is not intended to distract from the individual growth achieved by many teachers.

However, at the Project's conclusion, I felt anxious about how teachers, who were just beginning their risk taking, would be challenged and supported, and whether their current practices would simply become the new status quo. A critical policy issue for public schools, therefore, is how they can integrate such supportive staff development opportunities into their systems.

Implementing developmentally appropriate practice requires many teachers to effect paradigm shifts in their thinking. Such shifts require enormous teacher energy, emotional and intellectual courage and commitment, and perhaps, compatible teacher attitudes about the nature of teaching and learning (Staton, 1990). Teacher educators who attempt to assist teachers in making the shift, therefore, not only must be well informed about early childhood education, but they must also be knowledgeable about how to stimulate teachers to dismantle their existing paradigm, while providing support for teachers willing to accept the risk.

Providing leadership to the early childhood community. Because of the stature and resources of the public school system, many groups are suggesting that public schools assume a leadership position in increasing the availability of quality early childhood programs (NASBE, 1988; NAESP; 1990). I intended to seize this opportunity, not only for this purpose, but in order to try and create linkages among the various sponsors of early childhood education in the Turner community, ease transitions between programs by facilitating communication among teachers, and undermine the assumption perpetuated by many nonpublic school early childhood programs that their programs needed to be academically oriented in order to prepare children for kindergartens.

The process, however, never extended into the community, although initially efforts were made to invite members of the surrounding early childhood community to biweekly meetings. In part, these attempts failed because target teachers were in their classrooms teaching. A more significant explanation, however, was that no one assumed responsibility for fostering the relationship. Implementing the Turner Project, as idealized in Figure 10.1, would have promoted a multidimensional thrust, which I continue to believe is necessary. It would also have demanded considerably more planning, time, and effort than available from one course release time.

Changing Expectations for Early Childhood Teacher Educators

Public schools are increasingly regarding themselves as significant providers of early childhood education and are framing their discussions about programs for young children in the context of early childhood education. This extends earlier deliberations that centered on specific, isolated programs, such as kindergartens or programs for 4-year-olds, and suggests that public schools are beginning to think of themselves as early childhood as well as elementary school educators.

Although this expansion often still excludes the primary grades, this changing frame of reference bodes well for public schools' meaningful acceptance of appropriate educational programs for young children. To fully realize recommendations for developmentally appropriate practice (Bredekamp, 1987), the establishment of distinctive early childhood units (NASBE, 1988), and more appropriate assessment measures (National Association of Early Childhood Specialists in State Departments of Education, 1987), public schools will need to cultivate their new identity and provide teachers and children working and learning environments hospitable to educationally and developmentally appropriate programs. The need for this resocialization becomes more pressing as groups such as the National Education Association (NEA) resolve to place all 4-year-olds in public schools and the National Governor's Association focuses on early childhood education as a way to help all children "start school ready to learn."

These circumstances place early childhood teacher educators in an optimum position to take a leadership role in sharing their knowledge with public schools and promoting appropriate early childhood programs. As a result, early childhood teacher educators have the opportunity to function in the change agent role advocated by Schultz (see Chapter 9, this volume). A critical concern, however, is whether early childhood teacher educators can and will seize this opportunity.

Early childhood teacher educators are increasingly being asked to accept the responsibility of advocating the kinds of programs they know to be most beneficial for young children (Almy, 1985; Katz & Goffin, 1990). Extending this advocacy effort beyond teacher preparation programs to public schools and practicing early childhood teachers, however, may be perceived as an additional burden by teacher educators already encumbered with heavy course loads and supervision responsibility.

Even with a formalized agreement, which I helped negotiate, I still lacked sufficient time, resources, and, frankly, expertise to accomplish all the goals I set forth for myself. This admission points to a critical policy issue for teacher preparation programs in universities and colleges.

During the first nine months of the Turner Project, I conservatively clocked 234 hours for the effort. Release time from one course each semester was helpful, but clearly insufficient. This revelation is not meant to discourage school-university collaborations. The Turner Project was a successful collaboration and a personally meaningful learning experience. In retrospect, the effort could be classified as a successful example of action-based research at the level of teacher education. But, in conjunction with the increasing number of public schools that might be interested in such collaborations, quantifying the commitment helps highlight the potential time drain on early childhood teacher educators. It also points to the impact on departmental units. In early childhood programs staffed by only one or two faculty (such as my own), release time from teaching significantly affects the number of courses that can be taught. Under such circumstances, supporting the professional growth of practicing early childhood educators occurs at the expense of preservice teachers.

The demands placed upon early childhood teacher educators active in promoting appropriate early childhood curriculum and practices in public schools challenges the legitimacy of continuing to staff early childhood programs with one or two individuals. This policy perhaps needs no new circumstances to be questioned, but it is unrealistic to assume that one person can be proficient not only in early childhood education, child development, *and* the content disciplines, but *also* as a change agent in the public schools. Teacher preparation programs, therefore, need to recognize early childhood education as a multifaceted profession and support greater differentiation and specialization in their teacher educators.

Universities also expect scholarly activity from their faculty, an expectation that appears to be increasing at regional public universities such as my own (Goodlad, 1990). After personally experiencing the intensity of undergraduate teacher education, Katz (1988) questioned whether teacher education could be implemented at colleges and universities whose mission was primarily expressed through research and publication, rather than teaching. Katz's conclusion can be extended to in-service teacher education.

This tension, of course, is not limited to early childhood teacher educators. Goodlad (1990) has identified it as a major issue of concern in his study of teacher education. Lieberman (1990) argues that "the university must change its view of scholarship so that it recognizes and rewards active participation in schools . . . as valuable—and time-consuming—scholarly activity" (p. 533). Importantly, she emphasizes this as a change needing serious attention so that universities can increase their impact upon educational policies and practices, that is, join with public schools as change agents.

The advocacy efforts of early childhood teacher educators, however, should extend beyond advancing appropriate early childhood programs to include nurturing the activism of practicing teachers. This conclusion is informed by the Turner teachers' apparent passive acceptance of a host of practices that they themselves considered inappropriate, a finding that also has been noted by others (Hatch & Freeman, 1988; Smith, 1987). Teachers seemed unaware that they might have some control over change. Their comments revealed feelings of helplessness. Yet none complained that, as professionals, they resented their lack of influence.

Too often, responses to suggested changes emphasized all the reasons nothing could change versus how teachers might impact the circumstances being questioned. After this attitude became apparent, discussion of teachers' responsibilities as change agents on behalf of appropriate early childhood practices were integrated into our interactions. Eventually, *one* kindergarten teacher acknowledged that, "In public education, the dominoe starts here. We need to start talking about what that dominoe looks like."

Early childhood teacher educators will need to be sensitive to the unique context of public schools, however, and the ways in which this context influences the provision of early childhood education, if our advocacy efforts are to be successful. It will also be necessary to expand beyond a focus on teacher autonomy as primarily an intellectual activity (for example, Kamii, 1985).

The Turner Project highlighted the restrictive impact of class sizes too large, inadequate materials, unsupportive building principals, and inappropriate expectations dictated by individuals who sign one's paycheck—circumstances beyond the individual control of even the most intellectually autonomous teachers. The fatal flaw in failing to recognize the emotional security, courage, and strategic knowledge required to advocate for appropriate early childhood practices can be found in the experience of an early childhood teacher who attempted to impact the early childhood practices of her private school. At the end of the school year, when she was informed her contract would not be renewed, her principal mocked, "You early childhood teachers think you're so autonomous of me."

Early childhood teacher educators will also need to be more successful than I was in expanding their interactions to include first-grade teachers and building principals. Despite the successes associated with the Turner Project, first-grade teachers and principals were not significantly impacted. This goal, similar to the goals of linking with the early childhood and parent community, suffered from inadequate conceptualization and insufficient time. Although the impact of individual teacher change should not be underestimated, teachers' changes have occurred, for the most part, in isolation from the system in which they practice, despite the support of the central administration.

Becoming Proactive:
Preparing Early Childhood Teachers for the Public Schools

The success of advocacy efforts on behalf of appropriate early childhood programs is dependent upon the knowledge base of advocates. The Turner Project primarily supported practicing teachers in reconceptualizing early childhood education and teachers' roles within transformed classrooms. Public schools and teacher educators, however, will want to move as quickly as possible from this reactive stance to one that is proactive.

This step could be greatly enhanced by the establishment of specialized early childhood certification standards in every state, developed exclusively for teachers working with children from birth to age eight, distinctive and independent of existing elementary and secondary certifications. A similar position has been advanced by the Commission on Early Childhood Teacher Education, established by the Association of Teacher Educators, and jointly endorsed by the Association of Teacher Educators and the National Association for the Education of Young Children (1991).

The existence of such standards should help to clearly define the boundaries of early childhood education and help assure that public schools can hire teaches to work with children up through third grade who understand the developmental characteristics, and ways of learning, characteristic of young learners. Unfortunately, such uninamity is sorely lacking. According to McCarthy's (1988) survey of early childhood certification standards across the 50 states:

> The certification process which states use to prepare teachers of young children can best be summed up with one word: variety. Patterns vary from actual certification in early childhood education to add-on endorsements to programs in elementary education with additional combinations in between. (p. 2)

Critically, certification in early childhood education, when existing, is frequently juxtaposed with elementary certification, exacerbating the perceptions of prefirst-grade programs as apendages to the primary grades.

State Departments of Education exert critical leadership in setting standards for teacher preparation programs. The consistent recognition of early childhood education as continuing through third grade would minimize school-university collaborations concentrating on the content and practices in appropriate early childhood education, permitting collaborations to focus on its successful implementation.

In conclusion, early childhood teacher educators are in a position, given adequate support, to assume a larger role in facilitating the advancement of appropriate early childhood programs in the public schools. Securing this position, however, will require that, as teacher educators, we expand our responsibilities beyond campus classrooms and traditional activities of field supervision, and seek to become better informed about the complexities of individual and institutional change. We are being presented an important opportunity to advocate in a new arena, on behalf of appropriate early childhood programs.

REFERENCES

Association of Teacher Educators and the National Association for the Education of Young Children. (1991). Early childhood teacher certification. A position statement of the Association of Teacher Educators and the National Association for the Education of Young Children. *Young Children, 47*(1), 16–21.

Almy, M. (1985). New challenges for teacher education: Facing political and economic realities. *Young Children, 40*(6), 10–11.

Bredekamp, S. (1987). *Developmentally appropriate practice in early childhood programs serving children from birth through age 8* (expanded ed.). Washington, DC: National Association for the Education of Young Children.

Darling-Hammond, L. (1985). Valuing teachers: The making of a profession. *Teachers College Record, 87,* 205–218.

Elliott, J. (1989). Educational theory and the professional learning of teachers: An overview. *Cambridge Journal of Education, 19*(1), 81–101.

Goffin, S. G. (1990). *Public schools and developmentally appropriate practice: Securing the relationship.* Paper commissioned by the National Association of State Boards of Education, Alexandria, VA.

Goffin, S. G. (1991). Supporting change in a school district's early childhood programs: A story of growth. *Early Child Development and Care, 70,* 5–16.

Goodlad, J. I. (1990). *Teachers for our nation's schools.* San Francisco: Jossey-Bass.

Green, T. F. (1973). *The activities of teaching.* New York: McGraw-Hill.

Hatch, J. A., & Freeman, E. B. (1988). Kindergarten philosophies and practices: Perspectives of teachers, principals, and supervisors. *Early Childhood Research Quarterly, 3,* 151–166.

Kamii, C. (1985, November). *Turning out autonomous teachers in a heteronomous world.* Keynote address at the annual conference of the National Association of Early Childhood Teacher Educators, New Orleans, LA.

Katz, L. G. (1988). Memo to the Department Chair: Or confessions of a teacher educator. *Newsletter of the the National Association of Early Childhood Teacher Educators, 93*(30), 2–7.

Katz, L. G., & Goffin, S. G. (1990). Issues in the preparation of teachers of young children. In B. Spodek & O. N. Saracho (Eds.), *Yearbook of early childhood education* (Vol. 1, pp. 192–208). New York: Teachers College Press.

Lieberman, A. (1990). Navigating the four C's: Building a bridge over troubled waters. *Phi Delta Kappan, 71*(7), 531–533.

McCarthy, J. (1988). *State certification of early childhood teachers: An analysis of the 50 states and the District of Columbia.* Washington, DC: National Association for the Education of Young Children.

National Association of Early Childhood Specialists in State Departments of Education. (1987). *Unacceptable trends in kindergarten entry and placement.* Alexandria, VA: Author.

National Association of Elementary School Principals. (1990). *Early childhood education and the elementary school principal.* Alexandria, VA: Author.

National Association of State Boards of Education (NASBE). (1988). *Right from the start.* Alexandria, VA: Author.

Sarason, S. B. (1987). Policy, implementation, and the problem of change. In S. L. Kagan & E. F. Zigler (Eds.), *Early schooling: The national debate* (pp. 226–126). New Haven, CT: Yale University Press.

Schorr, E, with Schorr, D. (1988). *Within our reach: Breaking the cycle of disadvantage.* New York: Anchor Press.

Smith, D. (1987). *California kindergarten practices 1986.* Fresno: California State University, School of Education and Human Development.

Smith, F. (1989). Overselling literacy. *Phi Delta Kappan, 70*(5), 353–359.

Staton, J. (1990, April). *Teacher beliefs and dialogue journal use as indicators of responsive teaching potential.* Presentation at the annual meeting of the American Education Research Association, Boston, MA.

Wood, T., Cobb, P., & Yackel, E. (1990). The contextual nature of teaching: Mathematics and reading instruction in one second-grade classroom. *The Elementary School Journal, 90,* 497–513.

Chapter 11
Federal Initiatives for Exceptional Children: The Ecology of Special Education

Karen S. Gallagher
R. J. Pat Gallagher
University of Cincinnati, Teachers College

Most of you, indeed, cannot but have been part and parcel of one of those huge, mechanical, educational machines, or mills, as they might more properly be called. They are, I believe, peculiar to our own time and country, and are so organized as to combine as nearly as possible the principal characteristics of the cotton mill and the railroad with those of the model state's prison. (Charles Francis Adams, addressing the National Education Association, 1880)

It is the business of the school to help the child to acquire such an attitude toward the inequalities of life, whether in accomplishment or in reward, that he may adjust himself to its conditions with the least possible friction. (Frank Freeman, "Sorting the Students," *Educational Review*, 1924)

Every gun that is made, every warship launched, every rocket fired signifies . . . a theft from those who hunger and are not fed, those who are cold and are not clothed. This world in arms is not spending money alone. It is spending the sweat of its laborers, the genius of its scientists, the hope of its children. (Dwight David Eisenhower, presidential address, 1953)

Defining public policy as it relates to exceptional children is like the parable of the blind men in the cave who encounter an elephant. As each man touched some distinct part of the elephant—the tail, the trunk, the ears—he believed he knew what he had found. For example, the one who felt the tail thought he could describe the whole as something like a rope. Trying to describe educational policy or any public policy is like being one of those blind men. The description comes from the orientation of the beholder.

The topic of this chapter is public policy vis-á-vis exceptional children, specifically the relationship between special education policy at the federal government level and the system of public schools in the United States. Before discussing this relationship, a statement of our understanding of the concept of policy is necessary. Many formal definitions of policy have been proffered. They all rest on the assumption that policy is the outcome of rational calculation to achieve specific goals by a unitary governmental actor (Dunn, 1981; Estler, 1988; Seekins & Fawcett, 1986). With such an assumption in place, these definitions have serious limitations for describing many public policies and the implementation of specific policies such as those relating to special education. Just as each blind man was unable to understand the whole elephant from feeling a part of it, formal definitions concentrating solely on individual rationality and intentionality miss the irrationality and fortuity of life in schools for all children but most definitely for those labeled "disabled" or "handicapped" or "special education."

Long's (1958) discussion of the local community as an "ecology of games" and Weick's (1976) description of schools as "loosely coupled systems" are examples of theories that illustrate the inconsistency of collective action at the individual level. Firestone (1989) built upon both notions in developing his metaphor that educational policy is an ecology of games. He points out that while individuals act in patterned ways in communities, there is rarely a single, guiding intelligence to coordinate the activities of diverse community members. The ecology of games metaphor is an effort to reconcile the unified, goal-driven system with individual rationality and goal maximization. A community or socially organized system like a school district provides space for many games: one for state government, one for the board of education, one for local businesses, and so on. (See Figure 11.1 for a visual representation of this relationship.) Individuals compete in one or a few of the available games. Each game has a structured competition with its own rules, its own winners and losers, and its own scoring system.

The use of the ecological metaphor allows for an understanding of the relationships among individuals and the complex social systems in

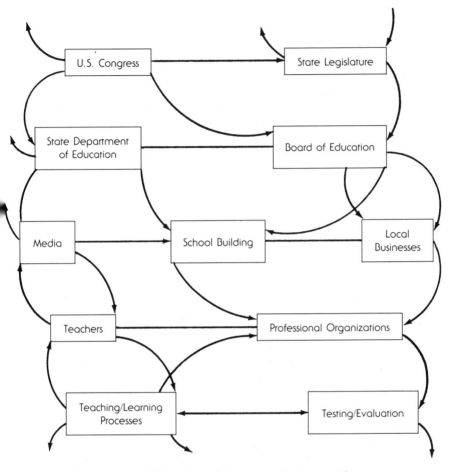

Figure 11.1.   Educational Policy as an Ecology of Games

which they interact. Ecology is the study of the interrelationships of species in their environment and, as such, it recognizes that relationships evolve based on environmental context and individual needs. For example, competition occurs among species vying for the same space. Such competition can lead to specialization and the development of separate functions, as in redwood trees and ferns in the forest, gorillas and primates in the jungle, and principals who have authority over classrooms and teachers who have authority over pupils within their classrooms in schools. Mutual noninvolvement can replace competition just as readily as cooperation can result. Although other relationships can occur, the important insight of this metaphor is the lack of a single, rational, coordinating presence in education or any other arena of public interest.

Specific federal policy directed to practices in public schools is a relatively recent phenomenon. Policies relating to special education and early intervention have an even shorter history. This chapter discusses the evolution of public policies related to traditional school-age children with disabilities and public policies related to early intervention programs for handicapped and at-risk preschool children. It reviews past practices and current policies like Public Law 94-142 and Public Law 99-457 that provide programs and services for young handicapped children and their families. Finally it closes with a discussion of the evolving patterns of relationships linking the various policy "games" to one another.

PUBLIC ATTITUDES AND VALUES
ABOUT SOCIAL PROBLEMS

A long history of political and social policies in America has effected the emergence of formal systems of public education. By the latter part of the 19th century, the organization, scope, and role of schooling as we know it in the 1990s had been transformed. No longer casual adjuncts to the home or the workplace, schools had become formal institutions designed to play a critical role in the socialization of the young, the maintenance of social order, and the promotion of economic development.

The origins of our current public educational systems coincided with several important developments that reshaped American society during the first three quarters of the nineteenth century: industrialization, urbanization, and immigration; the state's assumption of direct responsibility for some aspects of social welfare, the invention of institutions as means for solving social problems, and the redefinition of the family. Each of these developments continues to affect current public policies and practices.

In the first half of the 19th century, urbanization, industrialization, and immigration reshaped the economy and society in the United States. One consequence was the formation of a working class. Although the development varied by region, a close connection existed between social development and the creation of public educational systems. Systems of educational governance did not constitute the sole thrust of governments into the area of social welfare during this era. State governments began to exchange their haphazard and minimal concern with social problems for a systematic approach to questions of welfare. At the turn of the 19th century, problems of poverty, public health, crime, insanity, disease, and the condition of labor remained more or less untended, subject to legislation, custom, and public and private charity. By the 1870s, each had become subject of public debate, legislative activity, and the supervision of newly created state administrative bodies with full-time, expert staffs (Polanyi, 1957). However, the state did not extend its role in public welfare without serious opposition. Its activity began at a time when a clear distinction between public and private had not emerged. Typically, voluntary activity preceded state action. Philanthropic associations, composed primarily of women, first undertook the alleviation of such social distresses as orphans, widows, the elderly, and paupers as well as people labeled idiotic, insane, crippled, and epileptic. In part, their efforts reflected the inadequacy of the public apparatus for coping with the increased misery in the growing cities of the United States; in part it reflected the belief that social distress represented a temporary, if recurring, problem that charitable activity could alleviate. The activities of voluntary associations, however, usually convinced their members that problems were far more widespread and intractable than they believed, and this often led charities to turn to the public for assistance. At first, this assistance was in the form of grants, later it became the assumption of formal and permanent responsibility by city and state governments (Boyer, 1978).

Few models for action existed 130 years ago and people concerned with social policy debated not only the legitimacy of public activity but also its organizational form. On the issue of education, their disagreements over the nature of public organizations reflected fundamental value conflicts and alternative visions of social development. The shape eventually represented in 20th-century American public schools, the bureaucratic model, was debated with great intensity even after it appeared as a general institutional reality.

In part, the victory of bureaucracy reflected a new faith in the power of formal institutions to alleviate social and individual distress, which was a radical departure from previous social policy. Before the Civil War, institutions played a far smaller and much less significant social role: The mentally ill generally lived with other members of the community or in an undifferentiated poorhouse; criminals remained for relatively brief periods in jails awaiting trial and punishment; and children younger than 11 or 12 years averaged no more than two to three months of formal schooling in total (Campbell, Cunningham, Nystrand, & Usdan, 1990). After the Civil War, much changed. In place of a few, undifferentiated almshouses, jails, and schools there existed in most cities and states a series of new inventions: mental hospitals, penitentiaries, reformatories, and public schools. Shapers of public policy had embodied in concrete form the notions that rehabilitation, therapy, medical treatment, and education should take place within large, formal and often residential institutions. In the process, they created the institutional state that governs and regulates our lives today.

The last social development centered on the family. In the late 19th century, both critics and supporters of institutions shared the widespread sense that families were in trouble, though they were vague about the exact nature of the difficulty. However, there is evidence that families were simply changing, not deteriorating. Important shifts in domestic relations and structure occurred. The most dramatic family change during the period of industrialization was the separation of home and workplace. This separation formed one part of the process through which the boundaries between families and communities became more sharply drawn. In the urbanized industrial society, one's social role, both job and social worth, was dependent upon the value of one's work in the competitive labor market. In the late 19th-century marketplace, the elderly, the young, and the disabled could not compete on equal footing.

THE PAST: PUBLIC EDUCATION POLICIES

From the perspective of early proponents of compulsory education like Horace Mann, the schools were to provide a way to socialize the young and train them to be better, more productive workers. Katz (1987) and others have argued that schools were designed not only to teach students the skills necessary to function in the workplace, but also to inculcate the values and beliefs necessary for the maintenance of an urban working class. Many argue that schools went beyond this initial mission, teaching students and parents alike to blame themselves for failure.

The spread of compulsory education meant that schools had to begin to deal with students with disabilities. Prior to the latter part of the 19th century, the typical places at which mentally retarded, blind, or deaf children could receive an education were in institutions. From 1890 on, the public schools were confronted with large numbers of "backward" students, the children of millions of European immigrants. Many educators were upset by the disruptive influence of children who were inattentive, slow in learning, or otherwise disabled. As the superintendent of Baltimore Public Schools stated in 1908, "School authorities must greatly reduce this number, employ more teachers . . . or else they must withdraw into small classes these unfortunates who impede the regular progress of normal children" (Sarason & Doris, 1979, p. 263).

As these remarks reflect, public school systems began to segregate disabled and otherwise "deviant" students who were forced on them through compulsory education. Separate schools and special classes were soon established throughout the country. Boston established the first public day school for the deaf in 1869; by 1900, many large cities had started special education classes for the mentally retarded: Chicago in 1898, Philadelphia in 1899, and New York City in 1899 (Scheerenberger, 1983).

Many of the first special education classrooms served as dumping grounds for a broad range of students who did not fit into typical school classes. Students with such labels as "slow learners, the mentally subnormal, epileptics, learning disabilities, chronic truants, behavior problem children, physically handicapped or immigrant children suffering from language or cultural handicaps" (Sarason & Doris, 1979, p. 267) could be found in one classroom.

Throughout the 20th century, special education programs grew. In 1922, 133 cities in 23 states enrolled approximately 25,000 pupils in special education. New Jersey passed a law mandating special education for the mentally retarded in 1911. But despite the gradual expansion of special education programs, students with severe disabilities were largely excluded from public education until the late 1970s. School administrators in the 1920s, based on the principles of scientific management, advocated the exclusion of "imperfect material" or "low grade" students from public school programs. A national survey of schools in 1940 showed no "trainable mentally retarded" students in public schools. Not until the 1950s did special education programs serve more mentally retarded pupils than public institutions.

School-based programs of special education increased sporadically during the period from 1920 to the mid-1950s, however, there was little public debate about common perceptions of who the disabled were or how they were to be treated. At the federal level, a few public policy initiatives directed at individuals with disabilities were passed, legislation like providing benefits to disabled veterans of both world wars and establishing the basic income maintenance program for people with disabilities in the Social Security Act of 1935. However, the main thrust in public schools during this period was maintenance of the status quo (Knoblock, 1987).

The 1950s and 1960s marked a change in the history of societal treatment of people with disabilities. Tentatively at first and then with increased conviction, professionals, parents, and people with disabilities began to question the legitimacy of school policies and practices that excluded or segregated any child for any condition. Pleas for modest reforms gave way to parent and professional leaders and disability advocates demanding fundamental changes in educational and social service systems. It became obvious that federal legislation was needed, both to equalize educational opportunities across the country and to bring qualified people into special education. The legislation was not easy to pass. It violated strong traditions, first argued 100 years earlier, that education was a state and local responsibility. But organized parent groups with the support of other civil rights advocates convinced Congress to help. In 1963, Public Law 88-164 authorized funds for training professional personnel and for research and demonstration. The law represented a strong initiative by President Kennedy, whose interest was heightened by his sister's mental retardation. Those first efforts were followed by many others, as shown in Table 11.1. These federal provisions served notice that a strong coalition of forces within the federal government had accepted the responsibility for providing support resources for children with handicaps and for encouraging states to carry out their basic responsibilities.

By 1973, the number of special education programs had increased dramatically across the country. States began putting a much greater share of their educational dollars into educating children with handicaps, increasing their contributions almost 300 percent over the previous decade (Gallagher, 1984). Still, programs and resources were not consistent from state to state. To deal with the inconsistency and to help states handle the costs of court-mandated programs, Congress passed Public Law 94-142, the Education for All Handicapped Act. The law, which took effect in 1977, required that all handicapped children have available to them special education and related services designed to meet their unique needs.

Parallel to the development of public policies and support for special education, the 1960s also spawned federally initiated policy milestones for early intervention programs and preschool children. Figure 11.2 shows the evolution of early intervention federal policy. Federal developments initially focused on intervening early in order to promote optimal development. Two federally legislated enactments included Public Law 88-156, which expanded maternal and child health care services to expectant mothers from low-income areas in an effort to prevent mental retardation, and Public Law 89-313, which provided federal education money to state-operated schools and institutions for handicapped individuals. This latter piece of legislation has often been used by states to start experimental early intervention services (Allen, 1984).

Table 11.1.   Highlights of Federal Education Policy for Handicapped Children

Title	Purpose
P.L. 85-926 (1958)	Provided grants for teaching in the education of handicapped children, related to education of children who are mentally retarded.
P.L. 88-164 (1963)	Authorized funds for research and demonstration projects in the education of the handicapped.
P.L. 89-10 (1965)	Elementary and Secondary Education Act. Title III authorized assistance to handicapped children in state-operated and state-supported private day and residential schools.
P.L. 89-313	Amendments to P.L. 89-10. Provided grants to state education agencies for the education of handicapped children in state-supported institutions.
P.L. 90-170 (1967)	Amendments to P.L. 88-164. Provided funds for personnel training to care for individuals who are mentally retarded, and the inclusion of individuals with neurologic conditions related to mental retardation.
P.L. 90-247 (1968)	Amendments to P.L. 89-10. Provided regional resource centers for the improvement of education of children with handicaps.
P.L. 90-538 (1968)	Handicapped Children's Early Education Assistance Act. Provided grants for development and implementation of experimental programs in early education for children with handicaps, birth to age 6.
P.L. 91-230 (1969)	Amendments to P.L. 89-10. Title VI consolidated into one act—Education of the Handicapped—the previous enactments relating to handicapped children.
P.L. 92-424 (1972)	Economic Opportunity Amendments. Required that not less than 10 percent of Head Start enrollment opportunities be available to children with handicaps.
P.L. 93-380 (1974)	Amended and expanded Education of the Handicapped Act in response to right-to-education mandates. Required states to establish goal of providing full educational opportunity for all children with handicaps, from birth to 21.
P.L. 94-142 (1975)	Education for All Handicapped Children Act. Required states to provide a free appropriate education for all handicapped children between the ages of 3 and 18 by September 1, 1977.
P.L. 94-142, Section 619	Amendment to P.L. 94-142. Expanded services to preschool handicapped children (ages 3 to 5) through provision of preschool incentive grants.

SOURCE: Behr, S., & Gallagher, J. (1981). Alternative administrative strategies for young handicapped children. *Journal of the Division of Early Childhood, 2,* 113–122. Reprinted with permission.

Figure 11.2.   The Evolution of Early Intervention Public Policy.

Date	Policy
1963	Maternal and Child Health expanded.
1965	Project Head Start created;
	Education assistance to state-operated schools for handicapped created.
1967	Early and Periodic Screening, Diagnosis and Treatment (EPDST) created.
1968	Handicapped Children's Early Education Programs (HCEEP) created.
1972	Head Start required to enroll 10 percent handicapped children.
1975	Preschool Incentive Grants Created.
	Expansion of State Policies
1985	HCEEP state planning grants created.
1986	P.L. 99-457, Preschool and Infant/Toddler Programs created.

Project Head Start was the first nationwide attempt to intervene directly with the young child with the goal of improving the child's development through a variety of services—educational, medical, nutritional, and parent training. Project Head Start was launched in 1965 as part of the War on Poverty. It was designed to help economically disadvantaged preschool-aged children achieve their full potential by attempting to remedy the damaging effects of poverty on their development through early intervention. (See Chapters 2, 3, 4, and 5 in this volume for a more extended discussion of Project Head Start.)

In the late 1960s, Congress passed two federal policy initiatives that have become the foundation of current early intervention programs and services. In 1967, Public Law 90-248 established the Early and Periodic Screening, Diagnosis and Treatment (EPSDT) program. EPSDT, a component of Medicaid, focused on early identification and treatment as a method of preventing developmental and medical problems. In 1968, Public Law 90-538, the Handicapped Children's Early Education Assistance Act, was passed. This legislation established the landmark Handicapped Children's Early Education Program (HCEEP), which has provided federal support for 20 years for the development of model programs, methods, and state policies in early intervention and preschool services for handicapped children.

In 1968 few services for the handicapped preschool child existed, and the importance of early intervention was just emerging as a social policy. That year Congress passed Public Law 90-538 with the legislative intent of expanding the knowledge base about the potential impact of early intervention. Since 1968, HCEEP has funded over 500 projects that have demonstrated early intervention model practices, developed curricula and assessment instruments, and provided training to thousands of programs and educators throughout the U.S. In addition to the development of effective models and practices, HCEEP has also provided support for research in early intervention, delivered technical assistance to projects, and encouraged state-level planning of universal services to young handicapped children (Garland, Black, & Jesien, 1986).

In the early 1970s early intervention for handicapped children took a leap forward with the establishment of a new requirement that Head Start set aside 10 percent of its enrollment opportunities for handicapped children. Public Law 92-924 and Public Law 93-644 stipulated that 10 percent of the Head Start enrollment should be handicapped children and that these children should be provided services to meet their special needs within Head Start (Allen, 1984). Consequently, Project Head Start has been the largest provider of "mainstreamed" services for preschool-aged handicapped children in the nation. In 1985, over 98 percent of Head Start programs enrolled at least one handicapped child. Over 60,000 handicapped children are currently enrolled in Head Start programs (U.S. Department of Health and Human Services, 1986).

The passage of Public Law 94-142 was as important for preschool-aged handicapped children as it was for all handicapped individuals. While it fell short of mandating services for children below traditional school age, it did establish the Preschool Incentive Grant to encourage states to serve 3- to 5-year-old handicapped children. The Preschool Incentive Grant was voluntary; however, once a state received the funding it was required to assure all rights and services of Public Law 94-142 to the preschool child.

Concurrent with these federal initiatives in the 1970s and the early 1980s, the number of state policies mandating early services increased. By 1984, over one-half of the states required early services to some portion of the 3- through 5-year-old population and over 10 states began services at birth to some portion of the population. To encourage further expansion of state policy, Congress passed Public Law 98-199 in 1984. This legislation established a new state planning component within HCEEP, providing federal funds to states for the purpose of planning, developing, and implementing comprehensive services for handicapped and at-risk children from birth through five years of age.

Then in 1986, Congress passed Public Law 99-457, The Education of the Handicapped Act Amendments, capping 20 years of evolution in early intervention policy. Prior to the passage of this legislation, federal policy was focused primarily on supporting effective models and technology, providing training for professionals, and encouraging the generation of new knowledge through research and development activities. However, with Public Laws 94-142 and 99-457, Congress took one step closer to a national policy of access to services for all handicapped and at-risk children, birth through 21 years of age, and their families.

THE PRESENT: P.L. 94-142 AND P.L. 99-457

Two public laws dominate the current policy arena with regard to early childhood special education. While trends in federal education funding for school-aged handicapped children and for early intervention for infants, toddlers, and preschoolers with disabilities include programs like the Handicapped Children's Early Education Programs, Public Laws 94-142 and 99-457 have received the most attention. An overview of each piece of landmark legislation is given.

Public Law 94-142, the Education for All Handicapped Children Act, is based on six principles: (a) zero reject, (b) nondiscriminatory testing, (c) individualized educational plan (IEP), (d) least restrictive environment, (e) due process, and (f) parent participation. The implementation of this law was, and remains in many areas, a difficult task, mainly because its provisions contain much more than a commitment of federal resources. Anything that requires fundamental changes in the work patterns of professionals can be counted on to cause some difficulty.

Zero reject. All children with handicaps are to be provided a free and appropriate public education. This means local school systems do not have an option to decide whether to provide needed services. As Turnbull and Turnbull (1978) noted, the zero reject concept is intended to prevent (a) exclusion of some or all handicapped children from schools, (b) exclusion of some handicapped children while others with the same handicap are given schooling, and (c) exclusion of all persons with certain handicaps while persons with a different handicap are served.

Nondiscriminatory testing. Each student must receive a full individual examination before being placed in a special education program, with tests appropriate to the child's cultural and linguistic background. A reevaluation is required every three years. This concept tackles the problem of how to devise tests that are fair and at the same time related to academic outcomes. The most common barriers to the successful implementation of this principle include: tests used are biased and inappropriate; test administration is often performed incompletely; special education programs are inadequate; and placement in special education classes is stigmatizing (Kirk & Gallagher, 1986).

Individualized Education Program (IEP). An IEP must be provided for every handicapped child receiving special education programming. This requirement ensures that education will be tailored to a child's individual needs and that the accountability of those responsible for the education of the child rests with the school. Each IEP must include the following elements:

1. A documentation of the student's current level of educational performance.
2. Annual goals or the attainments expected by the end of the school year.
3. Short-term objectives, stated in instructional terms, which are intermediate steps leading to the mastery of annual goals.
4. Documentation of the particular special education and related services which will be provided to the child.
5. An indication of the extent of time a child will participate in the regular education progam.
6. Projected dates for initiating services and the anticipated duration of services.
7. Evaluation procedures and schedules for determining mastery of short-term objectives at least on an annual basis.

Least restrictive environment. As much as possible, children who are handicapped must be educated with children who are not handicapped. The philosophy is to move as close to the normal setting (regular classroom) as feasible for each child. It is important to realize that the LRE clause does not mean that all children will attend regular classes for an entire school day, although the legal preference is for regular classroom placement. The more severely retarded and those who have multiple problems may require services such as speech therapy and vocational education. In order for the staff to coordinate these services and implement the educational plan (IEP) fully, the child may have to spend part of the day in a more restrictive setting.

Due process. Due process is a set of procedures to ensure the fairness of educational decisions and the accountability of both professionals and parents in making those decisions. These procedures allow parents to call a hearing when they do not agree with the school's plans for the child, to obtain an individual evaluation from a qualified examiner outside the school system, or to take other actions to ensure that both family and child have channels through which to voice their interests and concerns.

Parental participation. A major goal of Public Law 94-142 is to ensure that the parents of handicapped children participate in decisions about the education of their children. This provision guarantees certain rights to parents, including the right to inspect school records, the right to request an explanation or interpretation of the records, and the right to request the records be amended if information is incomplete or inaccurate. Parents are to be involved in the planning for their child as well in the development of the individualized education plan.

Although the original intent of Public Law 94-142 was to include all handicapped children age 3 to 21, in practice the traditional school-aged child was the recipient of the majority of services and funding under this law. Planning for a delivery system started with the established public school system and even if parents wished to deviate from this established practice, at least they knew where the starting point began.

Public Law 99-457, the Education of the Handicapped Act Amendments of 1986, extends the specific provisions of Public Law 94-142 to 3- and 4-year-olds and contains other provisions relating to handicapped children of all ages. Specifically, Public Law 99-457 extends the six principles previously discussed to all children ages three years and up by the 1990–91 school year, and significantly increases funding for this age group. However, the law also provides many far-reaching initiatives for children in the birth to 5-year age group. Programs are provided for two age-grouped categories, birth through 2-year-olds and 3- through 5-year-olds. Provisions for the birth through 2-year-old category will be discussed in greater detail.

Congressional intent is elusive, particularly so with legislation as comprehensive as Public Law 99-457. However, a few of the concrete outcomes that Congress expects from the enactment of this legislation include reduced institutionalization and increased family participation, comprehensive and coordinated state service delivery systems, and the availability of appropriate technologies, personnel, and funds to ensure effective implementation of this early intervention initiative. In the four years since enactment of this law, some tentative steps toward these goals have been made, but like its earlier companion legislation, Public Law 99-457 requires major changes for professionals who have not always worked in teams or with handicapped or at-risk infants and toddlers.

Within Public Law 99-457 is the Handicapped Infants and Toddlers Program, Part H of the Education of the Handicapped Act. This section creates a new federal program for handicapped infants and toddlers and provides financial assistance to states to develop and implement a statewide, comprehensive, coordinated, multidisciplinary, interagency program of early intervention services. It facilitates the coordination of early intervention resources from federal, state, local, and private sources including private insurers. Last, it enhances the states' capacities to provide high-quality early intervention services. The Infant/ Toddler Program is voluntary for states. If a state does choose to participate, it must meet all requirements of the law. In addition, by the fifth year of a state's participation, all eligible children must be served.

Eligible children are defined as those from birth to their third birthday who need early intervention because:

1. they are experiencing developmental delays in one or more of these areas: cognitive, physical, language and speech, psychosocial, or self-help skills
2. they have a physical or mental condition that has a high probability of resulting in delay, that is, Down syndrome
3. they are at risk medically or environmentally for substantial development delays if early intervention is not provided.

Under this program, the infant or toddler's family may receive services that are needed to facilitate their capacity to assist in the development of their child.

If a state applies for funds under this program, it must meet the following requirements. For the first two years of funding, the governor must establish an Interagency Coordinating Council made up of parents, state agency representatives, personnel trainers, and state legislative representatives. The governor must also designate a lead agency which may be the Interagency Coordinating Council. The state ensures that the funds will be used to plan, develop, and implement statewide services. As of 1987, all 50 states have entered the program and have designated a lead agency. In 19 states, the department of education or public instruction has been designated at the lead agency for this categorical program.

In the third and fourth year of state participation in this Infant/ Toddler Program, a state must write and adopt a comprehensive policy with 13 required components including a definition of the term "developmentally delayed," timetables for ensuring services for all eligible children by the fifth year of participation; provision of a written individualized family service plan (IFSP); a central directory containing state resources, services, experts and research and demonstration projects; a comprehensive system of personnel development; and a system for compiling data on the early intervention programs. The fifth and succeeding years, the state must ensure that the system is in effect and full services are available to all eligible children.

All early intervention services must be provided at no cost to parents, except where federal or state law provides for a system of payments by parents, including provision for a schedule of sliding fees.

At this time, four obvious policy challenges lie ahead for early childhood special education policy makers, educators, parents and advocates. First, will there be full participation in Public Law 99-457 by all states? Second, how effective will implementation of the intent of Public Law 99-457 be at the state and local levels? Third, what kind of evaluation of the effects of Public Law 99-457 and other state and local policies on young children and their families will be designed and completed? Fourth, how will Public Law 99-457 be revised based on the evaluation data?

THE FUTURE: EDUCATIONAL POLICY IN THE TWENTY-FIRST CENTURY

Describing educational policy with the ecology-of-games metaphor provides some direction to policy makers in meeting the challenges outlined in the previous section. This metaphor weans one away from the image of a single, all-powerful policy maker. It counters the vision that "out there somewhere" is someone or some body that can make things better if only he, she, or they would listen. Instead the metaphor emphasizes the imbroglio nature of policy making and the variety of games played by different people for different reasons as part of the policy implementation process. Educational policy as a chain of decisions from the legislature to the classroom is a by-product of all those games and relationships. No one is responsible for the whole thing.

This very brief review of special education policies since the late 1800s reveals several recurring themes, highlighting the ecology-of-games metaphor. First, the social policy debate over the distinction between public and private interests is ongoing. This policy game involves politicians and citizens in such issues as determining the boundaries between family and governmental responsibility for infants and young children who are disabled, retarded, or abandoned because of poverty, disease, or indifference. The debate over individual and societal responsibilities centers most frequently on public funding and public control of programs and institutions designed to alleviate individual distresses and disabilities. One hundred years ago, the educational policy debate focused on the legitimacy of using taxes to fund schools. In the last 10 years of the 20th century, the question is *who* will control tax-supported schools.

The second theme centers on the relationship between the federal government and the 50 state governments. In the century since the general acceptance of governmental responsibility for some aspects of social welfare, the burden of the special education policy game has shifted back and forth between state governments and federal government. However, especially in the case of special education policy, neither state nor federal policy mandates have ensured that schooling will be widespread or accessible for most exceptional populations, nor has it guaranteed attendance even where programs are in place.

The third theme involves the bureaucratic hierarchy of public schools. Topdown policy initiatives, whether from state legislatures, state departments of education, local boards of education, or district administration have had little effect on individual classrooms. Despite such principles as "zero reject," "least restrictive environment," and "due process" embodied in Public Law 94-142, special education classes in 1990 are still segregated, isolated, dumping grounds for the majority of youngsters labeled "special education," just as they were in the 1890s. Nationwide, statewide, and systemwide directives almost always fail to achieve their goals. This does not mean, however, that children with disabilities are not served. When programs are effective, it is in the individual school where a coalition of parents, teachers, and students work with the building principal to create the needed programs and services.

The fourth theme centers on the current images of the American family. Statistical indicators show that poverty has increasingly become a youthful condition; that the nature and degree of parental engagement with their children has been altered through divorce, dual-income families, and erosion of financial conditions; that there is a widening gap between the economic, social, and political well-being of children and the aged; and that more and more families who fit the idealized images of the nuclear family have uncertain economic and educational futures, a condition that nontraditional families have experienced consistently in the past.

IMPLICATIONS

To some policy makers, parents, and educators, the recurrence of these themes throughout the last century of educational policy may seem to indicate that nothing works. And indeed, if educational policy is viewed as the rational, goal-driven tool used to force compliance, it has not worked as national and state policy makers had hoped. On the other hand, the ecology of games metaphor reinforces an understanding that suggests that if policy makers tried to take advantage of the messiness of the educational policy system instead of trying to organize it, creative and constructive programs for all children might be developed locally.

For parents, the implications of viewing early childhood–special education policies as an ecology of games are numerous. Parents of handicapped children have the interests of their children at heart. Thus, the "game" they play with school personnel is focused on getting the most appropriate services for their individual child. On the other hand, school personnel play a "game" of decision making based on balancing the interests of many groups who need services and the requirements of complex legislation with often conflicting goals. Legislation like Public Law 99-457 occurred because enough lawmakers voted to pass it, not because they all agreed on the purpose or outcomes. Implementation will vary from state to state and from individual program to individual program. Parents need to articulate their desires clearly and often to ensure that their child receives what they believe are the appropriate services. No common, rational vision existed among lawmakers and advocates at the passage of this legislation nor does it exist as implementation begins.

REFERENCES

Allen, K. E. (1984). Federal legislation and young handicapped children. *Topics in Early Childhood Special Education, 4,* 9–18.

Boyer, P. (1978). *Urban masses and moral order in America, 1820–1920.* Cambridge, MA: Harvard University Press.

Campbell, R. F., Cunningham, L. L., Nystrand, R. O., & Usdan, M. D. (1990). *The organization and control of American schools.* Columbus, OH: Merrill Publishing Company.

Dunn, W. N. (1981). *Public policy analysis: An introduction.* Englewood Cliffs, NJ: Prentice-Hall.

Estler, S. E. (1988). Decision making. In N. Boyan (Ed.), *Handbook of research on educational administration* (pp. 305–320). New York: Longman.

Firestone, W. A. (1989). Educational policy as an ecology of games. *Educational Researcher, 18,* 18–24.

Gallagher, J. J. (1984). Policy analysis and program implementation (P.L. 94-142). *Topics in Early Childhood Special Education, 4,* 43–53.

Garland, C., Black, T., & Jesien, G. (1986). *The future of outreach: A DEC position paper.* Unpublished manuscript. Arlington, VA: Council of Exceptional Children, The Division of Early Childhood.

Katz, M. B. (1987). *Reconstructing American education.* Cambridge, MA: Harvard University Press.

Kirk, S. A., & Gallagher, J. J. (1986). *Educating exceptional children.* Boston: Houghton Mifflin Company.

Knoblock, P. (1987). *Understanding exceptional children and youth.* Boston: Little, Brown and Company.

Long, N. E. (1958). The local community as an ecology of games. *American Journal of Sociology, 50,* 251–261.

Polanyi, K. (1957). *The great transformation: The political and economic origins of our time.* Boston: Beacon Press.

Sarason, S. B., & Doris, J. (1979). *Educational handicap, public policy and social history.* New York: Free Press.

Scheerenberger, R. C. (1983). *A history of mental retardation.* Baltimore: Paul H. Brookes.

Seekins, T., & Fawcett, S. (1986). Public policy making and research information. *The Behavior Analyst, 9,* 35–45.

Turnbull, H. R., & Turnbull, A. P. (1978). *Free appropriate public education: Law and implementation.* Denver: Love Publishing.

U.S. Department of Health and Human Services. (1986). *The status of handicapped children in Head Start programs.* Washington, DC: U.S. Government Printing Office.

Weick, K. E. (1976). Educational organizations as loosely coupled systems. *Administrative Science Quarterly, 21,* 1–19.

Chapter 12
Emerging Policy Issues: Summary and Synthesis

Dolores A. Stegelin
Peggy M. Elgas

INTRODUCTION

This chapter provides an overview of the salient issues discussed by the authors and a synthesis of key recommendations toward policy development. While each author brings his or her own unique perspective to early childhood policy, the forging of new policy for young children must reflect a synthesis and a merger of the key and current needs of the early childhood population. This chapter is designed then to facilitate policy making decisions by identifying the most critical variables in early childhood policy and by summarizing collectively the recommendations of these noted policy makers, researchers, and early childhood advocates. The chapter includes summaries and a synthesis of each of the three sections of the book.

EARLY CHILDHOOD POLICY DEVELOPMENT
AT THE STATE AND NATIONAL LEVELS

Governor Clinton

Governor Clinton's chapter on state policy related to disadvantaged and at-risk preschoolers presents a compelling argument for the active involvement of state government in the development of sound early childhood policy. Clinton addresses the historical difficulties of attempting to discuss family issues in public arenas. Identifying family needs, especially related to poverty and social welfare, brings to bear our own pain that we experienced as children. Hence, early childhood policy has evolved slowly and within the context of an ever-increasing trend toward a more liberal perspective of the family unit.

Perhaps the most poignant aspect of Governor Clinton's contribution to this text on policy is the account of his own childhood in Arkansas, documented with anecdotes and examples of his own early experiences which were characterized by working females, intimate extended family relationships, and a deep and abiding commitment toward preservation of the family unit Clinton's concern for the lack of family connectedness in today's society and the need to reconnect the generations seems to form the foundation philosophy for his own interest and commitment to issues related to young children and their families. The genuineness of Clinton's narrative is perhaps its greatest strength. He provides us with a very believable rationale of how and why an energetic and exceptionally bright young governor can address early childhood issues and be continually successful at reaching those goals.

Clinton identifies three great challenges for American policy makers in the area of early childhood education: (a) poverty of today's young children, (b) work patterns and parent support needs, and (c) structure of the family unit itself.

Poverty

In Arkansas, as in most of the 50 states, child poverty has risen dramatically. Today, one in four children under the age of five lives below the poverty line. Ironically, states Clinton, this condition exists in the face of America's longest peacetime economic expansion. The risks to these young children include low birth weight, failure in school, failure as citizens, welfare dependency, illness, incarceration, and other social ills. According to Clinton, America is paying at the back end for young children (remediation) rather than at the front end (prevention).

Work

By 1995, two-thirds of all preschoolers will have mothers in the work force. Today, two thirds of all married women in the work force have husbands with incomes under $15,000. Simply stated, women need to work, says Clinton. However, the work patterns common to our society discourage child bearing among those parents who would be the strongest and best parents because restrictions are put on women, directly and indirectly, as to their ability to meet the needs of their young children. Clinton's wife, Hilary, an attorney, has studied women's work patterns and discovered that parental leave practices of our larger employers discourage working women from having and nurturing children. Clinton implores policy makers to help resolve this conflict: Life's most important job is still parenthood.

Family Structure

Clinton's examples of the changing dynamics and structure of the American family are convincing. With high divorce rates and increasing numbers of single-headed households, Clinton addresses the need for early childhood policy to focus on this fragmentation of the family unit. He states that women are typically 42 percent worse off in terms of their income levels within three years of a divorce. States are experiencing the inability to enforce existent child support laws which compounds the financial situation for most single mothers. Thus, Clinton weaves the three great challenges—poverty, work, and the family structure—into a strong and integrated call for increased and enhanced policy effort on behalf of young children.

WHAT IS THE ROLE OF GOVERNMENT?

Government is not a savior, says Clinton, and we should not expect it to be. Neither should government be a spectator. Instead, Clinton encourages us to conceptualize the role of government in developing child-related policy as one of a catalyst and partner. He sets out to identify the appropriate goals of government in early childhood policy.

Parent Support

Clinton's first goal for government is to help parents succeed and, when they fail, to save as many young children as we can. Specifically, Clinton believes that we should commit ourselves to bringing healthy babies into the world and then strive to keep them healthy. Policy should reflect these goals. According to Clinton, this is the most cost-effective thing we can do for children and their families. Prevention is much more fiscally sound than remediation and rehabilitation. He cites successful efforts in Arkansas that address these parent support issues. He also cites free immunizations and the initiation, albeit controversial, of 13 clinics in schools with expanded health services. Clinton repeatedly emphasizes the value of preventive measures.

Child Care

We are the last advanced economy in the world to have an adequate system of child care, according to Clinton. He suggests that state funds can be added to decreasing federal funds for child care to close the gap in state-supported child care services. He also cites the need to increase the state standards for child care, to require child care training, to explore tax credit options for working parents, and to begin to address the emotional concerns of working parents who constantly worry about the quality of their children's care.

Corporate Involvement

Clinton's final recommendation toward early childhood policy is that of increasing incentives for corporate involvement in child care and parent support practices. He encourages developing greater partnerships with businesses and assisting smaller businesses in establishing child care options. The old adage of putting mother back in the home is "pie in the sky," according to Clinton. Instead, policy should reflect the forward-looking trends in today's families. Maternal employment is here to stay, is desirable and necessary, and is in need of greater policy support. The lack of a parental leave policy critically strikes at the heart of today's family. Clinton describes the expression on the face of the child whose parent is unable to attend an important school function as being like a "body blow." Indeed, says Clinton, those companies who have been responsive to child care needs have reaped many benefits, including improved employee morale, improved productivity, and increased profits. Nobody is losing money by doing the right thing, according to Clinton.

Putting the Family First

Clinton summarizes his chapter with an earnest plea for a realignment of policy priorities. The most successful family polices are those that enable parents to succeed. If sound family policy is given high priority, then the need for remedial services will be reduced. Finally, for those families who have not succeeded, the responsibility of government must be to support and enable their growth toward change and success. Clinton states that we all must work to make sure parents can impart their dreams to their children.

Kagan

In an exquisitely written chapter on birthing collaborations in early care and education, Dr. Sharon Lynn Kagan of Yale University describes the polemic of pain and promise in the complex and interrelated ecosystem of early childhood education. She begins with quotes from 1972 policy recommendations by a panel on the assessment of community coordinated child care programs which cite the great need for collaboration among providers and reflect the growing concern about the fragmentation and discontinuity of early care and education. This chapter explores the rationale for and the history of collaboration and then assesses its utility in early childhood education.

Today's Buzzword

According to Kagan, collaboration is the buzzword in early childhood circles today. The concept of collaboration has captured the attention of education, health, psychology, mental health, social work, business, industry, and the arts. These linkages or partnerships know no geographic or disciplinary boundaries, says Kagan. The history of collaboration began over 25 years ago when changes in organizations were predicted, due to value changes, demographic shifts, and dissatisfaction with existing bureaucratic systems.

Changing Organizations

While preindustrial and industrial organizational order was characterized by stability and lack of change, today's systems are, in contrast, more turbulent, complex and uncertain. According to Kagan, the increasingly unstable economy of the 1970s compounded by stricter environmental policies, deregulation, and a rise in foreign competition, required new approaches to business organization. "Team workers" became more desired and the rights of workers were expanded, due to the civil rights movement, a new sense of fairness and equity, and a concern for the disenfranchised in our society. Workers became more educated and more active.

Along with changing organizational systems, theoretical frameworks were evolving that fostered the notion of collaboration. Kagan cites the ecological perspective of Bronfenbrenner as being central to this changing theoretical paradigm. Taking a holistic orientation, the ecological approach became a more desired way to view the needs of individuals. This theory greatly influenced the human services systems. The systems perspective evolved for addressing service delivery problems, with an eye toward diminishing fragmentation, duplication, and inequity of services. Clearly a more integrative approach was needed.

Changing Dimensions of Social Problems

With increasing technological sophistication, urbanization, and the women's movement, Americans became more transient, according to Kagan. In turn, family patterns began to change dramatically, including escalating divorce rates, numbers of single parent families, and the poverty rates of females. With these structural changes in the family came family stress, as reflected in child and spouse abuse, a sense of crisis, and new reflections of poverty. Within this framework, collaboration came to be seen as an antidote, says Kagan.

THE IMPETUS TO COLLABORATE IN EARLY CARE AND EDUCATION

According to Kagan, early care and education was at the forefront of the press for collaboration. The impetus for collaboration in early childhood was more intense for several reasons, including deeply fragmented services and competition for financial resources in the 1980s. However, Kagan notes the emerging collective pedagogy of early care and education that has created less mistrust and has somehow begun to soften the competitive and distrustful interactions of earlier child care and education services. Also, new mandates are being legislated that require states and communities to work together for the benefit of young children in order to obtain new funds for these evolving programs.

Legacy of Fragmentation

According to Kagan, fragmentation resulted from social policy that lacked a cohesive mission or undergirding plan. Programs emerged at different times with different purposes and inconsistent variables arose, including funding, regulation, and accountability. As a result, these differences have resulted in inequitable services for children, families, and programs in the area of staffing, regulation, and access. In addition, program expansion in the mid- to late 1980s dramatically intensified competition and acrimony, says Kagan.

Growing Community

In the 1990s, according to Kagan, there will be a growing sense that no single entity will be able to solve the challenges of early care and education independently. Pedagogically, early care and education is coming together and is finally reaching a consensus of what constitutes program quality. Such terms as developmentally appropriate practice are permeating the field, says Kagan, and these indicators bode well for future collaboration.

Examples of collaboration in early care and education, according to Kagan, include community councils, advisory groups, task forces, commissions, and resource and referral centers. Typically, the goals of these collaborative groups cited by Kagan are to increase the quantity and quality of available services, ensure more equitable distribution of services, minimize expenses and duplication, and build public support and advocacy for early care and education.

The Next Step

Kagan implores policy makers, advocates, and practitioners in the field of early care and education to move onward to the next step: amplifying knowledge about collaboration, developing a consensus of definition, and developing a true policy commitment to collaboration. Collaboration has evolved over nearly three decades and now has reached a stage of refinement that can carry early care and education to new heights in program delivery, continuity, and concern for the young child and his or her family. Dr. Sharon Lynn Kagan makes a very convincing statement that collaboration is here to stay and policy must continually reflect that commitment.

Cervantes

Robert Cervantes, associate superintendent of the California State Department of Education, presents public policy issues in child care and child development from the state administrator's perspective. As director of all early childhood programs in the California Department of Education, he colorfully paints the rich historical picture of California's child development programs, beginning in 1929 with the Parent Participation Preschool Program and then the WWII programs that resulted from the Lanham Act of 1943. Cervantes cites the 1972 Child Development Act and the 1981 state legislative initiatives that placed California in a leadership position among the states in the administration of child care and development programs.

California's programs resulted from progressive legislative action spanning some 60 years, says Cervantes. He cites two critical points to consider: (a) program quality, which consists of trained committed staff, appropriate developmental and sequential instruction, appropriate adult/child ratios, safe and nurturing environments, health and nutrition components, parental support services, and strong management and fiscal accountability; and (b) an early social investment in young children in addition to the educational dividends of quality early childhood programs.

California's State Preschool Program

California's State Preschool Program is a half-day educational program, primarily for 4-year-olds and is quite similar to Head Start. He contrasts custodial and formal day care and identifies the key criteria for all programs. The current imperatives for child care include bipolar groups of children: advantaged and disadvantaged. The juxtaposition, says Cervantes, is individual needs versus government involvement: Should the government provide programs and in what manner and form?

The differences between the social-welfare and the educational-developmental perspectives are addressed by Cervantes. He states that an investment in child development will provide a return on that investment that is most certainly worth doing right with quality standards even at the risk of having smaller programs. The bifurcation of California's state subsidized child care and child development programs under education and the private-profit programs under the department of social services is historical, says Cervantes, and has presented philosophical and management issues for the state.

Cervantes concludes his chapter with a call for high-quality programs, affordable and accessible programs, and the training and employment of professionally trained early childhood staff. The public expects a lot, says Cervantes, but does not wish to pay for it. Cervantes delivers this message to policy makers:

What states elect to do in the form of child care and or child development must be done well and without compromise or apology regarding program quality, even if it means limited programs. Program quality is everything. Anything less would be a failure to reap full benefits of establishing child care and development programs.

Schweinhart and Weikart

The historic Perry Preschool study is reviewed in this chapter by Schweinhart and Weikart. They state that a critical role in the national debate on early childhood policy is played by the research that shows the relationships between quality early childhood programs and the long-term benefits to society and the individual. They cite the misunderstanding of research, quoted repeatedly in the halls of Congress, but without the context that is often needed. Early childhood programs have been described by policy makers, on the one hand, as a panacea to all social ills and, on the other hand, as unworthy due to only short-term effects. The purpose of this chapter is to contribute to the national debate by relating the salient findings of the Perry Study, and similar studies, to policy making decisions in the United States.

Schweinhart and Weikart describe the Perry Preschool Study succinctly as one that identified young children living in poverty, randomly assigned them to preschool and no-preschool groups, operated a high-quality child development program, and collected data on both groups of children throughout their childhood and adolescence. The original study had 128 subjects; the follow-up longitudinal study had 123. They state that the strength of the internal validity of the study was due to the random assignment of the children to groups: Neither parents nor teachers had a choice about which children did and did not attend the preschool program.

The two groups were controlled on many variables: mean Stanford-Binet intelligence test scores, mean socioeconomic status, parental unemployment rates, percentage of fathers absent, mean school years completed by mothers and fathers, girl/boy ratio, mean family size, or mean birth order of the participating child. The subjects were all African-American and the teaching staff and administrators represented a racial/ethnic mix.

Sources of data were multiple: parent interviews when children were 3 and 15; annual intelligence and language tests from ages 3 to 10 and at age 14; annual achievement tests from ages 7 to 11 and at ages 14 and 19; annual teacher ratings from ages 6 to 9; participant interviews at ages 15 and 19 and now at age 28; school record information collected at ages 11, 15, and 19; and police and social services records information collected at age 19 and now at age 28. Age 28 data are now being collected and have not yet been analyzed.

The results, reported in this article only, are those whose probability of chance occurrence is less than .05, based on the directional (one-tail) hypothesis that the preschool group did better than the no-preschool group. (Previous reports have been based on the less appropriate but more conservative nondirectional two-tailed tests of statistical significance.) The results are well known and are summarized as follows:

> The preschool group surpassed the no-preschool group in intellectual performance from ages 4 to 7. Probably because of this boost, state Schweinhart and Weikart, the children achieved greater school success; higher school achievement and literacy; better placement in school; stronger commitment to schooling; and more years of school completed. Also, this boost contributed to greater teenage socioeconomic success, social responsibility, higher rates of employment and self-support, lower welfare rates, fewer acts of serious misconduct, and a lower arrest rate.

Implications

From this study, Schweinhart and Weikart cite the substantial return on dollars invested in quality early childhood programs. In the Perry Preschool Program $3.00 was returned for every dollar invested in the 60-week (two-year) program at age 3 and 4 and $5.95 for every dollar invested in the 30-week (one-year) program at age 4. They cite the Head Start Synthesis Project meta-analysis and eight other long-term studies as further documentation of the value of quality early childhood education as a long-term investment.

The implications for U.S. policy making, according to Schweinhart and Weikart, are these:

1. Good early childhood programs contribute to the development of young children who live in poverty and young children whose mothers are in the labor force; poor early childhood programs do not contribute and many even have negative effects on development.
2. Poor 3- and 4-year-olds need quality early childhood programs, full-time if mothers are employed and part-time if mothers are unemployed.
3. Public funding is needed to subsidize good programs for nonpoor young children whose mothers are in the labor force.
4. Quality issues are paramount: The U.S. must be willing to invest more for quality programs. (Total public and private cost to pro-

vide needed good early childhood programs in the U.S. is 31.5 billion; the nation now invests 14.9 billion).

5. Additional investment in good early childhood programs for poor children must come from public sources and private sources acting in the public's interest; additional investments in good early childhood programs for nonpoor children will come from public, corporate, and family sources.

Finally, Schweinhart and Weikart state that government can leverage additional funding by creating incentives for corporations and families to spend more. Distinctions in family circumstances (poor and nonpoor and employed and nonemployed) do not require distinct programs. They state that society is better served if children from diverse family circumstances enroll together in the same programs. They cite the need for more unified and better coordinated federal-, state-, and local-level services and the placement of an office of early childhood education in either human services or the state education departments. "The costs of good early childhood programs for the nation are great. The eventual costs of not providing them, in money and in decreased quality of life, are greater" (see Chapter 5, this volume).

Major Policy Issues

A synthesis of these five authors—Clinton, Kagan, Cervantes, Schweinhart and Weikart—results in several key early childhood policy issues being identified (see Table 12.1). All five authors address three issues: (a) work patterns and parent support needs, (b) changing family structures, and (c) service fragmentation and program quality variables. Three authors, Clinton, Schweinhart, and Weikart, discuss child poverty as a critical issue also. As one surveys these four topics, we discover that they are broad-based and inclusionary in nature. Indeed, they all seem to be interrelated. For example, work patterns and parent support needs are directly related to changing family structures and service fragmentation and program quality concerns. Certainly the escalation in need for quality early childhood programs is connected to the work force patterns of females in the United States and the changing family structures, particularly single-headed households. The child poverty issue relates to an increase in female-headed households, thus contributing to the 25 percent poverty rates of the preschool population in the United States. The feminization of poverty seems to be reflected in the single-headed households which are lead by females, either divorced, teenage, or never-married.

Table 12.1.   A Synthesis of State and National Policy Issues and
Recommendations of Clinton, Kagan, Cervantes, Schweinhart and Weikart

Major Policy Issues Identified	
Major Policy Issues Identified	Addressed by Whom
(1) Child Poverty	Governor Clinton
	Schweinhart & Weikart
(2) Work patterns and parent support needs	Governor Clinton
	Schweinhart & Weikart
	Cervantes
	Kagan
(3) Changing family structures	Clinton
	Cervantes
	Schweinhart & Weikart
	Kagan
(4) Service fragmentation and program quality variables	Kagan
	Schweinhart & Weikart
	Cervantes
	Clinton

Ten Major Policy Recommendations	
(1) Parental support for poor and nonpoor parents (leave policies and child care supplements)	Clinton
	Cervantes
	Schweinhart & Weikart
(2) Infant mortality and early intervention	Clinton
(3) Health care for children	Clinton
	Cervantes
(4) Child care regulations and information/referral	Clinton
	Cervantes
(5) Partnership with corporations and small businesses	Clinton
	Schweinhart & Weikart
(6) Realignment of policy priorities toward families	Clinton
	Schweinhart & Weikart
	Cervantes
	Kagan
(7) Collaboration/continuity of services & programs	Kagan
	Cervantes
	Schweinhart & Weikart
	Clinton
(8) Regulations/DAP/training requirements	Kagan
	Cervantes
	Schweinhart & Weikart
	Clinton
(9) Focus on child development and educational orientation	Cervantes
	Schweinhart & Weikart
	Clinton
(10) Establishment of state office of early childhood/ child development	Schweinhart & Weikart
	Clinton
	Cervantes

Major Policy Recommendations

Again, the specific policy recommendations of these four national and state policy leaders would suggest a high degree of interrelatedness and interdependency among variables. All five authors address three recommendations: (a) realignment needs of policy priorities with a new focus on families, (b) collaborative and continuity needs for services and programs, and (c) regulations, developmentally appropriate practice and professional training requirements.

Three authors address (a) the need for a child development and educational orientation to service provision (versus a social-welfare orientation), (b) the establishment of a state level office of child development/early childhood education, and (c) policy needs related to parental support for poor and nonpoor parents who are employed.

Other policy recommendations include (a) infant mortality and early intervention, (b) health issues for young children, (c) child care regulations and information/referral, and (d) corporate partnerships. These national and state leaders call for policy measures to be developed in the above areas, with a priority as listed above. Again, these recommendations seem to be broad-based and interrelated to the four major policy issues discussed above.

POLICY ISSUES RELATED TO CHILD CARE

Galinsky

The numerous roles that corporations can adopt in promoting child care and family support are outlined in Ellen Galinsky's chapter. Galinsky identifies four major areas: (a) providing information and financial resources, (b) providing direct service, (c) increasing supply and improving the quality of child care, and (d) advocating through the legislative process.

In the first option, corporations can provide financial assistance through flexible spending accounts and salary reduction. They can disseminate information through providing parent seminars in the workplace and a resource and referral system where parents are counseled in finding and evaluating child care. While programs such as these do exist, Galinsky identifies the problem of equity. These existing programs seem to be concentrated in geographical areas where care is of higher quality and incomes are prosperous.

The second option is probably the best known: providing direct service. Galinsky states that approximately 200 corporations throughout the country have created child care centers. Various types of centers exist, ranging from company-owned to employee-owned and operated. The effects of these corporate child care centers have been questioned. While some argue that better salaries and better quality care available in corporate centers will "trickle down" into the community, others argue the opposite. They fear that these centers will draw the best local teachers and the community centers will thus have less qualified teachers. The only way this could be alleviated is to open the enrollment to nonemployees.

In the third option, increasing supply and improving quality of child care, Galinsky describes various roles for corporations. Corporations can become involved in recruiting and training by providing corporate child care resource and referral programs and/or establishing training institutes for an accreditation model. Corporations can also become involved through participation in task forces investigating available child care and thus impacting change.

The fourth and final option identified is advocating through the legislative process. Galinsky cites mixed results for this approach. On the one hand, corporate child care has inadvertently reduced quality in some cases through a press to reduce standards for corporate child care. On the other hand, in several states CEOs of companies have supported increased funding for government child care and national standards for child care.

In summary, Galinsky describes the major impact of corporate involvement as strengthening child care by increasing its supply and improving its quality. She concludes by raising several important concerns and questions still unanswered. The concerns include: family support, quality child care programs, depletion of community resources, and lower standards. The direction and effect of these programs have yet been determined.

Szanton

In Eleanor Szanton's chapter on infant care, she addresses three views of infant care. These include: (a) work and family issues, (b) efforts to reduce the number of families on welfare, and (c) concerns about educable labor force for the economy of the 21st century.

The first issue centers around the increase of women entering the workforce and the subsequent need for infants and toddlers to be care for in out-of-home settings by nonfamily members. This is a twofold problem for families. Parents are made anxious by these arrangements and infants, because of their total dependency, are more vulnerable to mistreatment than any other age group.

The second issue centers around the requiring of teenage mothers on AFDC to continue schooling after their infant's first birthday. Along with this requirement is a reimbursement for child care. However, reimbursements are insufficient to cover the cost of quality care.

The third and last view is what Szanton terms "the right start" (programs available for low income-families). While the majority of funds and the existing movement is toward prekindergarten or Head Start programs, some do include family resource programs.

After discussing these views, Szanton then describes the state of crisis of infant care in this country. Infant day care suffers from a smaller supply, less trained staff, and greater staff turnover. The most salient problem is that acceptable quality is not affordable to most families. Szanton points out that the infant child care crisis is complicated by the controversy within the field of early childhood education. While many questions are left unanswered and experts in the field have differing and opposing views on the effects of day care, recent research suggests that if parents are able to secure quality care, both the child and the family can benefit. Szanton hopes that collaborative research of the present and future will highlight the potentially positive effects of day care.

The remaining part of the chapter is devoted to the special characteristics of infant toddler care. Szanton discusses important issues such as the rapid development in infancy, their total dependency on adults and their vulnerability, thus making caregiver training imperative for high-quality care. Szanton further outlines areas for caregiver training, identifying important caregiver behaviors, including developing a safe and responsive environment, facilitating a language-rich environment and identifying and meeting individual needs.

Szanton summarizes by acknowledging the controversy surrounding infant care in this country. However, she concludes with a strong statement regarding the necessity of training for infant caregivers to ensure quality care.

Blank

Helen Blank's chapter is a comprehensive overview of the present state of American child care. She begins with a description of the "child care crisis," outlining the rapidly growing demand for child care and the change in the family system. She describes the plight of low-income families: their inability to locate and then finance quality care. She introduces staggering statistics of families from all socioeconomic groups in search of child care solutions.

Blank describes the characteristics of quality care including small group size, small adult/child ratio, and trained caregivers. In contrast to this, she describes child care in one low-quality center. She presents the costs of child care and the inability of many families to afford this care, thus forcing them to settle for questionable child care placements like the one described.

Next, she outlines the gaps in America's child care system. She calls for involvement by the federal government including legislation and increased financial support for programs such as Head Start and Title XX. Blank then presents a detailed "action agenda" outlining various ways the federal government can increase their involvement. She concludes by outlining State government involvement, thus, endorsing a collaborative effort.

A Synthesis of Child Care Issues

The focus of the individual chapters in this section range from a broad overview of child care to more specific topics such as corporate care and infant care. While each author certainly addresses some issues that are important/inherent to her particular focus, several themes and issues run throughout this section.

Child Care Status

The first issue addressed, and possibly the most significant, is the status of child care in this country. All authors agree that child care has become a reality in the United States, regardless of whether or not our social and cultural views support this idea. Due to the economic state of this country, it is difficult for most women to be full-time caregivers.

Galinsky and Blank provide staggering statistics of women entering the workforce, thus increasing the need for child care in this country. Coupled with low income and poverty status of many dual- and single-parent families and the lack of a support system for these families, the state of child care is seen as an impending crisis. However, the positive tone of these chapters is the concerted effort to turn the crisis into a positive move forward. Each chapter includes a call for involvement, a call for an examination of options, and a call for provision of quality services. All of the authors agree that this involvement is long over-due. Each of the chapters includes a description of current practices and recommendations for involvement, change, and future hopes.

Quality Care Needs

One of the most important changes advocated by the authors is the need for quality care. All recognize the shortage of high-quality centers available. While there are many questions still unanswered concerning effects of child care, results of the research suggest that day care may be a positive element for families, if care is of high quality.

Recent research identifies certain variables in determining quality care. These include low child-teacher ratios, low staff turnover, and trained/educated staff. While these variables have been identified, providing a quality service (one that incorporates these variables) is difficult for many reasons.

These staff issues are many and varied. Galinsky insightfully identified the problem of professionalism for the child care field. A pervasive attitude still exists that child care is basically a babysitting service; that child care workers will instinctively know what to do for children. This attitude complicates the necessity for sound educational training in child development. As with any other profession, these skills do not come naturally. Caregivers must understand human development and be certain the formative, early years are filled with optimal, developmentally appropriate experiences. This is only achieved through education and training.

Caregivers must understand child development in order to deal with the different issues that arise for the child and to structure the environment and the interactions in the environment to support and meet the individual needs of the child within each stage of development. For example, infants require a stimulating, yet regulated environment. They are the most vulnerable age group, unable to protect themselves or complain about an inappropriate environment, and yet this group is often cared for by untrained staff. The authors suggest this is due to the pervasive attitude that babies' needs can be met by untrained, uneducated caregivers.

Toddlers, moving into the walking and talking stage, need a safe environment to establish autonomy through exploration, and preschoolers continue in this need for autonomy and exploration. and develop a need for experimentation and interaction with materials and caregivers. Healthy development is dependent on fulfilling those needs and, consequently, dependent on a caregiver being sensitive to those needs.

While each stage requires special consideration, all children share the same need for quality child care. They need a safe, nurturing environment and quality interaction with a trained caregiver.

Table 12.2. Major Child Care Issues Identified*

Issue	Addressed by Whom
Quality of Child Care Programs	Galinsky
	Blank
	Szanton
Status of Child Care in the United States	Galinsky
	Blank
	Szanton
Professionalism for the Child Care Field	Galinsky
	Blank
	Szanton
Increased Emphasis on Infant/Toddler Child Care	Galinsky
Need for Policy Change	Galinsky
	Blank
	Szanton

*Identified by Galinsky, Blank, and Szanton as the foremost policy recommendations: Increased federal funds for Head Start and Title XX; tax deductions for child care; and increased use of corporate monies.

Policy Recommendations

The last issue addressed in each of the chapters is the need for change or future recommendations. In order for quality care to be available for all families, including low-income families, there is a call for government (both Federal and State) and corporations to form an active partnership. The need for quality care is a nationwide problem and, thus, the need for support from all agencies on all levels is imperative. The authors promote several options, including: increased federal funding for Head Start and Title XX programs, tax deductions and the use of corporate monies. Whatever the option chosen, the need is for involvement now.

These chapters outline the problems of child care in the 1980s and 1990s and subsequently propose a supportive model for change. The child care issue is an important one, and one we all share. As early childhood educators we realize the importance of the early years for healthy development. These children are the future leaders of society and their future rests in our hands, but, just as important, these are the families of the present and their present and future rests with us also (see Table 12.2).

POLICY ISSUES RELATED TO PUBLIC SCHOOL EARLY CHILDHOOD PROGRAMS

Schultz

In a convincing chapter related to public school early childhood programs, Thomas Schultz, Ph.D., National Association of State Boards of

Education, presents an overview of salient policy issues related to developmentally appropriate practice and the challenge of public school reform. He begins his chapter by citing how the worlds of early childhood education and the public school system are intertwined by expectations of students and the competition for staff, facilities, and children themselves. He cites three different roles for early childhood educators as (a) the need to be responsive to public schools, (b) the need to view their competitiveness in a positive but realistic light, and (c) the need to serve as change agents or advocates in the move toward public school early childhood practice reform.

In the latter role, promoting constructive change in public school policy and practice in the 1990s, Schultz declares the need for early childhood advocates to establish clearly the significance of Developmentally Appropriate Practice within the present policy context for public education, to realize the degree of difficulty in doing so, and then advance a set of possible strategies for promoting the agenda of developmentally appropriate practice in the public school sector.

Converging Agendas

In a most articulate way, Schultz describes how converging agendas are surfacing which impact the policy challenges for both early childhood education and public schools. Two major converging educational issues cited by Schultz include (a) the need to reduce the gap between low income/minority students and more advantaged counterparts, and (b) improving the overall abilities of students to apply knowledge and skills, solve problems, and communicate effectively. Policy makers at all levels seem focused on these two concerns, therefore, they are valid and intertwining issues for early childhood and public school policy making.

Some of the misgivings being experienced by the early childhood community regarding public school involvement, according to Schultz, include concern about part-day programs being unresponsive to working parents, the quality of early childhood programs not being safeguarded, the competition between public schools and community-based programs for the enrollment of young children, funding patterns and criteria that frequently segregate children by income and race, and the basic question of efficacy of preschool programs. However, Schultz contends that developmentally appropriate practice offers substantial promise to *all* young children, not just low-income children. He cites the "intellectual performance" crisis as a sound reason to advocate for public school programs that serve integrated and diverse preschool populations, rather than at-risk or other targeted populations, which has been an early childhood policy of the past.

Schultz presents facts to support the notion of developmentally appropriate practice as being a valid issue for policy consideration. He cites the comprehensive prescription of DAP that includes elements of instruction, materials, assessment, and social organization across all areas of curriculum content and the need for increased problem-solving ability of all children, not just preschoolers. Thus he makes a convincing statement on the need for DAP at all educational levels and postures that DAP serves as a means to provide enhanced continuity between curriculum and pedagogy as children move from preschool programs into the public schools.

Challenges in Promoting DAP

On the plus side, says Schultz, is the fact that the term "developmentally appropriate practice" is now nearly universally adopted as a phrase by policy makers and educators, thus providing some consistency and integration in communication circles, both educational and policy-related. Such organizations as the National Association for the Education of Young Children, the California State Department of Education, and the National Association of State Boards of Education have emerged recently with policy and position statements that share a common theme: developmentally appropriate practice. Still out for determination is the assessment of whether rhetorical endorsement is leading to major and substantive policy change.

Perceived Barriers to DAP

According to Schultz, the major barriers to teacher change, educational reform, and the implementation of DAP include the size and complexity of the public education system, the complexity of decision making in public education arenas, the scope and tone of developmentally appropriate practice recommendations, the accountability theme in current educational policy, and the constant voices of educational reform that make it hard for any single agenda to be taken too seriously. The paradox, so convincingly described by Schultz, is that if schools are always being urged to change, they are unlikely to change in any substantial fashion.

Lessons from the Past

One of the real strengths of Schultz's chapter is the realistic way in which he gleans lessons from educational policy reform in the past. Citing Fullen, Cuban, and Cohen, he describes reviews of educational policy research that indicate that in order for educational change to occur, three components must be in place (a) a need for change, (b) clarity of recommended change, and (c) support for the necessary personal costs and benefits (to both the student and the teacher). It is indeed sobering to realize that under the best of scenarios, educational reform usually results in real change in only 25 percent of classrooms and that many of these do not sustain themselves.

Cohen's concept of "adventurous" teaching may be noteworthy within the context of early childhood educational reform. Innovations in classrooms and for teachers usually entail considerable personal cost in both time and energy and this is a major barrier to teacher change and educational reform. The lesson to be learned, says Schultz, is that developmentally appropriate practice cannot really happen without major efforts to support teachers through the change. The complexity of classroom life is a reality that must be faced by those who so glibly advocate for developmentally appropriate practice in kindergarten and early primary grades.

Support Indicators for DAP

In reviewing the history of educational reform over the past century, Schultz also finds reason for hope. Other proposals for curriculum reform are compatible with DAP, as are the research-based recommendations by cognitive psychologists and content area learning specialists in math and science. There appears to be a converging recommendation that children need hands-on learning experiences that build individual child resourcefulness and encourage the child toward self-initiated learning and discovery. These coinciding recommendations are reassuring to both practitioners and policy makers. Also, Schultz cites the plans to reform educational assessment as a plus in the movement toward developmentally appropriate practice. Lastly, Schultz applauds the teachers who are currently in the classrooms as being invaluable resources in the move toward DAP.

Conclusions

In concluding his chapter, Schultz identifies four areas of promising strategies for early childhood policy makers. First, he states the need for presenting a rationale and content of DAP that is clear and convincing and that can be tailored to varying presentational strategies. Secondly, Schultz cites the need to generate and convey the evidence of positive outcomes of DAP on student learning. Third, there is a need to advocate for the reasonable implementation of these practices. Finally, he urges early childhood advocates to continue to refine and debate the content of Developmentally Appropriate Practice.

Goffin

Stacie Goffin's unique chapter on creating change with the public schools lends the reader a first-hand perspective of the early childhood teacher educator in action. Goffin's own energy and vitality shine through in her account of her personal experiences as a university-based early childhood expert and advocate who weaves new relationships with public school administrators, teachers, parents, and young children in the public school early childhood sector.

Goffin's detailed summary of the year-long Turner Project in Kansas City portrays the complexity of the interactions of the college professor who wishes to make a contribution to developmentally appropriate classroom practice. She vividly depicts her attempts to connect with kindergarten and primary teachers, the building administrators, and others who wish to begin the journey of knowing about developmentally appropriate practice. This chapter also sheds light on the demanding role of current early childhood teacher educators in this country who also wish to extend their expertise into the community, as well as manage the usual responsibilities of college teaching, supervision of students, and conducting and publishing research.

Operating from a succinct list of project goals and operating assumptions, Goffin provides an overview of the journey she took from organizational meetings to the conclusion of the project, a journey of 18 months. Goffin's chapter is helpful in its contribution to the growing need for interaction between universities and public schools and the policy implications for the placement of young children in developmentally appropriate classrooms in these schools. The final section includes policy implications in three major areas: (a) the role of the public schools as catalysts for expanding the quantity and quality of appropriate early childhood programs, (b) the needed changes in university expectations, in general, and teacher preparation programs, in particular, in promoting school-university collaborations on behalf of appropriate early childhood education, and (c) The need for increased numbers of state certifications targeted to early childhood education, birth through age 8.

Stacie Goffin's contribution to this book on early childhood policy issues is significant, as the need to train early childhood/child development specialists reaches unprecedented levels. Her thoughtful reflection of the difficult and challenging process of changing how teachers view young children's learning is immensely helpful for those early childhood specialists anticipating weaving new relationships with the public schools.

Gallagher & Gallagher

In their chapter entitled "Federal Initiatives for Exceptional Children: The Ecology of Special Education," Karen and R. J. Gallagher trace the complex history of educational policy as it relates to special education and exceptional children. They utilize an effective parable by defining the history of educational policy making as an "ecology of games." Their chapter addresses public policy vis-á-vis exceptional children, specifically the relationship between special education policy at the federal level and the system of public schools in the United States.

Lack of Unity

Gallaghers cite the lack of a single, rational and coordinating presence in education or other arenas of public interests in the area of special education. The history of educational policy in this area is described in a parallel fashion with the industrialization, urbanization, and immigration eras of the United States in the first half of the 19th century. Only with serious opposition did the state extend its role in public welfare and few models existed for action 130 years ago.

With the victory of bureaucratic involvement with social welfare was reflected a new faith in the power of formal institutions to alleviate social and individual distress, which was a radical departure from previous social policy. The Gallaghers state that the last social development centered on the family and the separation of home and workplace.

Public Education Policy in the Past

According to Horace Mann, schools were to provide a way to socialize the young and train them to be better, more productive workers. The compulsory education movement required the schools to deal with disabilities and, from 1890 onward, public schools began to be confronted with large numbers of "backward" students, many of them the children of European immigrants. This led to a segregation of disabled students into separate classes. In fact, separate public day schools were established in Boston, Chicago, Philadelphia, and New York City. In 1922, according to the Gallaghers, 133 cities in 23 states enrolled approximately 25,000 pupils in special education. But not until the 1950s did special education programs serve more mentally retarded pupils than did public institutions.

The 1950s and 1960s brought change in the societal treatment of people with disabilities. With increased conviction, professionals, parents, and people with disabilities began to questions the legitimacy of school policies and practices that excluded or segregated any child for any condition. Federal legislation became a necessity to equalize educational opportunity. This legislation was difficult to pass because it countered the century-old belief that education was a state and local responsibility.

Recent Policy Movement

In a descriptive table, the Gallaghers present the recent history of legislation in support of early intervention and programs for special needs young children. They cite the initiatives of John F. Kennedy, which he took in part because of his own sister's mental retardation, as a significant point in the development of this policy. By 1973, the number of special education programs had increased dramatically across the country. States increased their contributions to children with handicaps by almost 300 percent over the previous decade. In 1977, with the passage of Public Law 94-142 to deal with inconsistencies in programs, schools became responsible to provide special education services. The initiatives of the Great Society in the 1960s, including Project Head Start, propelled the special education movement.

Present Status

With the passage of PL 94-142 and PL 99-457, new emphases have been placed on services for young children with special needs. Such terms as zero reject, nondiscriminatory testing, IEP, Least Restrictive Environment, due process, and parent participation have become commonplace. Four policy challenges to early childhood special education policy makers, educators, parents, and advocates include addressing these four questions: (a) Will there be full participation in PL 99-457? (b) How effective will implementation be? (c) How will PL 99-457 be evaluated? and (d) What will be revisions based on this evaluation?

The Future

The ecology of games metaphor, according to the Gallaghers, is an accurate one because history has taught us that there is no omnipotent

Table 12.3.   Major Public School Early Childhood Issues

Issue	Addressed by Whom
Developmentally appropriate practice: Defined and Implemented	Schultz Goffin
Integration of child populations	Gallagher & Gallagher Schultz
Increased funding and program support	Gallagher & Gallagher Schultz Goffin
Collaborative alliances between the schools, communities and families	Goffin Gallagher & Gallagher Schultz
Administrative knowledge and involvement in early childhood public school programs	Goffin Schultz Gallagher & Gallagher

policy source for young children with special needs. Instead, policy trends in this area include a continuing social policy debate over the distinction between public and private interests and the relationship between the federal government and the 50 state governments. The bureaucratic hierarchy of public schools, which creates a top-down policy, has had little effect on individual classrooms. Finally, the current images of the American family as being characterized by poverty, having reduced parental engagement with children, reflecting a widening economic gap between children and the aged, and experiencing uncertain futures (including the nuclear, traditional family) leave us with food for thought. If policy making for special needs young children is indeed an ecology of games, then much must be done at the local and state levels to reduce the confusion and to create more continuity of services. Parents must continue to be strong voices for advocacy for this population. In this case, history has taught us a great deal.

This chapter provides a summary and synthesis of emerging early childhood policy issues in three areas (a) national and state policy making for children and families, (b) child care policy, and (c) public school early childhood policy development (see Table 12.3). The decade of the 1990s promises to be a significant one as policy for young children and their families evolves and matures. It is the author's hope and expectation that the issues identified in this text will contribute to the policy process and that specific recommendations made by the authors will help shape the future for young children.

AUTHOR INDEX

SUBJECT INDEX

A

Accreditation efforts, 127, 128–129
Arkansas
  Child Care Resource Center, 27
  Child Facilities Guarantee Loan Fund,
    26–27
At-risk youth, 5, 139

C

California child care and development
  programs, 52–56
California Child Care Initiative Project
  (CCCIP), 128
Caregivers, infant, 95–100
  non-intuitive behaviors and knowledge
    group health and safety, 96
    individual differences, 98–99
    receptive language, 96
    responsive environment, 96–97
    training of, 95–96, 99, 100
    and self-awareness, 99
CCR&R (Child Care Resource and
  Referral), 121, 122, 129
  training and recruiting, 126–127
Center Accreditation Project (CAP),
  39–40
Chambers of commerce, 130
Child care; see also Delivery system
  issues; Infant care
  access to, 38, 61
  characteristics of effective programs,
    78
  corporate involvement in, see
    Corporate involvement in
    child care
  curriculum for, 13, 63
  demand for, 105–108
  government involvement in, 26–28,
    59–60, 110–111, 113–115

history of, 3–4, 5–6
as policy issue, 11–12, 79ff
and public education, 13, 83; see also
  Head Start; Public education
quality of, 109–110
regulations, 38
types of, see Children's services
Child care workers
  infant caregivers, 95–100
  in Perry Preschool Program, 69–70
  ratios of, 62–63
  requirements of, 62
  training, 6, 37–38
  wages for, 10, 12, 37–38, 80–81
Child Development Associate Program, 6
Children's services, 54–56
Cincinnati Youth Collaborative, 7
Collaborations, 31ff
  developmental stages of, 41–42
  future of, 44–46
  impetus to, 36–40
  mediating variables in, 43–44
  rationales for, 32–36
Corporate involvement in child care
  analysis of employee needs, 119–120
  direct service, 123–126
    company-owned and operated,
      123–124
    company-owned, contracted, 124
    employee-owned and operated,
      124–126
  donating products and expertise, 119
  impact of, 131–133
  information and financial resource
    child care resource and referral, 121
    flexible spending account (FSA),
      121–123
    parent seminars at the workplace,
      123

225